WINSTON CHURCHILL
A BIOGRAPHY

WINSTON CHURCHILL

A BIOGRAPHY

by

PIERS BRENDON

1817

HARPER & ROW, PUBLISHERS, New York
Cambridge, Philadelphia, San Francisco, London
Mexico City, São Paulo, Singapore, Sydney

FIRST U.S. EDITION

Library of Congress Cataloging in Publication Data

Brendon, Piers.
  Winston Churchill.

  Bibliography: p.
  Includes index.
    1. Churchill, Winston, Sir, 1874–1965.   2. Great Britain—Politics and government—20th century.   3. Great Britain—Foreign relations—1936–1945.   4. Prime ministers—Great Britain—Biography.   I. Title.
DA566.9.C5B674   1984   941.082'092'4 [B]   83–48784
ISBN 0–06–015286–9

---

84 85 86 87 88 10 9 8 7 6 5 4 3 2 1

CONTENTS

ACKNOWLEDGEMENTS

I WOULD LIKE to express my warmest thanks to all who have helped me with this book. I have received considerable assistance from the staff at the British Library, the Cambridge University Library and the Churchill College Library. I have also benefited enormously from the criticisms of those who have read the book in manuscript and made helpful suggestions, especially Alison Samuel, Jane Wood and Tom Rosenthal. Tom and Nancy Sharpe gave me generous aid and comfort. Andrew Best worked extremely hard on my behalf and made invaluable comments. I am particularly grateful to him and to Nick Furbank who, as only a master of his craft could, assisted me out of countless verbal traps and semantic pitfalls. My wife not only scrutinized my words; she encouraged and sustained me throughout, as did my children.

Extracts from *The World Crisis, My Early Life* and *Great Contemporaries*, by Winston S. Churchill and originally published by Odhams Press Limited, have been reproduced by kind permission of the Hamlyn Publishing Group Limited. Churchill's own words from *Winston S. Churchill: A Biography* edited by Martin Gilbert, have been quoted by kind permission of William Heinemann Limited.

LIST OF ILLUSTRATIONS

These photographs will be found following pages 76 and 140.

Acknowledgements

The photographs in this book are reproduced by kind permission of the following: Associated Press Limited, 26; BBC Hulton Picture Library, 1, 2, 5, 6, 7, 8, 10, 11, 12, 14, 15, 18, 19, 20, 21, 24, 27, 28, 29, 46, 47, 48, 49; British Film Institute, 30; Broadwater Collection, 13; Central Press Photos Limited, 16, 22, 31, 44, 50, 51; Churchill College, Cambridge, 43; Colorific Photo Library Limited, 45; Frost Picture Library, 42; Imperial War Museum, 4, 9, 33, 34, 36, 37, 38, 39, 40; Keystone Press Agency Limited, 3, 32, 35, 41, 52; National Portrait Gallery, 23, 25; The Press Association Limited, 17.

KEY DATES IN
CHURCHILL'S CAREER

1874   30 November, Born at Blenheim Palace
1886   August to December, His father, Lord Randolph Churchill, Chancellor of the Exchequer
1888   April, Winston to Harrow
1893   September, Entered Sandhurst
1895   24 January, Lord Randolph died
1895   February, Winston commissioned and joined Fourth Hussars
1897   October, To Cuba, where he saw first shots fired in anger
1898   2 September, Took part in charge of 21st Lancers at battle of Omdurman
1899   October, To South Africa as *Morning Post*'s war correspondent
1899   November, Captured by the Boers
1899   December, Escaped
1900   October, Elected Unionist MP for Oldham
1904   May, Joined Liberal party on Free Trade issue
1905   December, Parliamentary Under-Secretary for the Colonies
1906   January, MP for North West Manchester
1908   April, President of Board of Trade and MP for Dundee
1908   12 September, Married Clementine Hozier
1910   February, Home Secretary

1911	3 January, 'The Battle of Sidney Street'
1911	October, First Lord of the Admiralty
1914	October, Directed defence of Antwerp
1915	February, Naval attack on the Dardanelles
1915	May, Removed from Admiralty and made Chancellor of Duchy of Lancaster in coalition government
1915	November, Resigned and went to western front
1916	January to May, Colonel 6th Battalion Scots Fusiliers
1917	July, Minister of Munitions
1919	January, Secretary of State for War (and Air)
1921	February, Colonial Secretary
1922	September, Bought Chartwell Manor
1922	November, Defeated at Dundee after fall of Lloyd George's coalition
1924	February, Defeated as Constitutionalist candidate for Abbey Division of Westminster
1924	October, Elected for Epping and appointed Chancellor of the Exchequer
1925	April, Returned Britain to the gold standard
1929	May, Baldwin's government defeated at polls
1931	January, Churchill left shadow cabinet over Indian question
1935	June, Joined Air Defence Research sub-committee on understanding that he would not necessarily abate his campaign for rearmament
1936	December, Supported King Edward VIII during abdication crisis
1939	September, 'Winston is back' as First Lord of the Admiralty on outbreak of war with Hitler
1940	10 May, Succeeded Chamberlain as Prime Minister
1941	June, Welcomed Russia as an ally
1941	August, Placentia Bay meeting with Roosevelt: Atlantic Charter
1941	December, Declared war on Japan after Pearl Harbor. Addressed Congress in Washington. First (minor) stroke
1942	February, Made governmental changes after loss of Singapore.
1942	June, To America: gained more support from Roosevelt after fall of Tobruk

1942 **August,** To Cairo and Moscow
1942 **November,** Ordered church bells to be rung after victory at El Alamein
1943 **January,** Casablanca Conference
1943 **August,** First Quebec Conference
1943 **November,** Teheran Conference
1943 **December,** Illness in north Africa
1944 **June,** Visited France after D-Day
1944 **September,** Second Quebec Conference
1944 **December,** To Athens: secured Regency for Greece
1945 **February,** Yalta Conference
1945 **8 May,** VE Day
1945 **23 May,** Formed 'Caretaker government'
1945 **July,** Potsdam Conference
1945 **26 July,** Defeated by Labour in general election
1946 **March,** 'Iron curtain' speech at Fulton, Missouri
1949 **August,** Attended first session of Council of Europe at Strasbourg. Suffered second stroke.
1950 **23 February,** Defeated in general election
1951 **26 October,** Won general election and formed government
1953 **23 June,** Third stroke
1953 **October,** Awarded Nobel Prize for Literature
1955 **5 April,** Resigned as Prime Minister
1964 **July,** Left House of Commons
1965 **24 January,** Died in London
1965 **30 January,** State funeral. Buried in Bladon churchyard, near Blenheim
1977 **12 December,** Clementine Churchill died

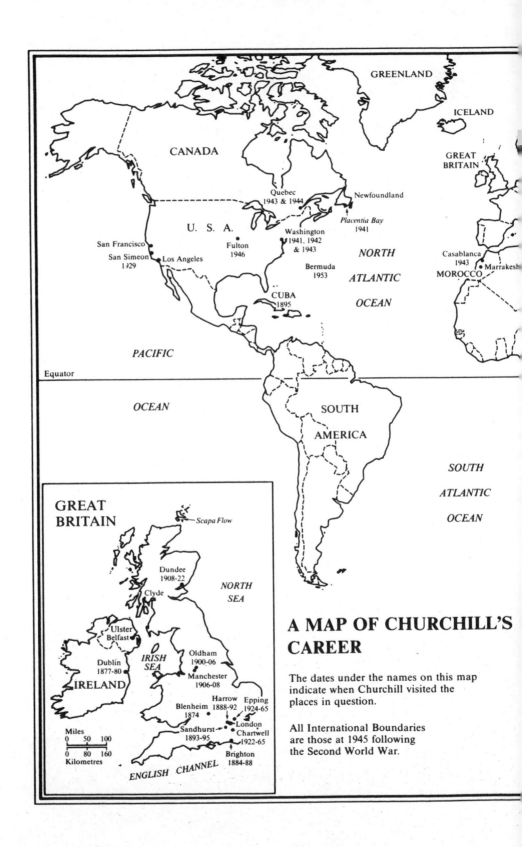

A MAP OF CHURCHILL'S CAREER

The dates under the names on this map indicate when Churchill visited the places in question.

All International Boundaries are those at 1945 following the Second World War.

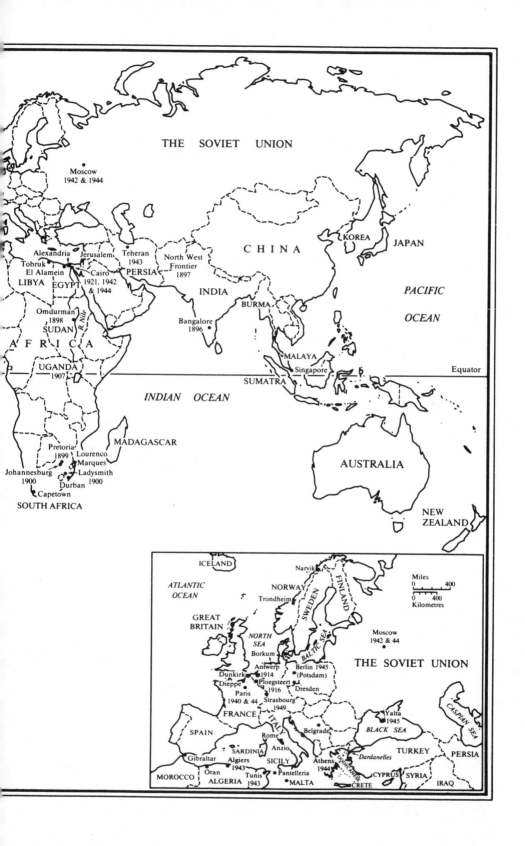

INTRODUCTION

IT MAY seem odd to write such a short biography of someone who enjoyed such a long life. Winston Churchill
reached the age of ninety and his political career was a
marathon even by Gladstonian standards. However, Churchill
is in danger of being buried under the weight of words devoted
to him. He began the process himself, compiling enormous
multi-volume autobiographies disguised, to quote Balfour's
jest, as histories of the universe. Later authors, taking their cue
from him, have written about Churchill at intimidating length.
Yet one of his favourite quotations might serve as a warning:
'L'art d'être ennuyeux c'est de tout dire' – bores say everything.
This book, which takes these words as its motto and its justification, aspires to be as interesting as it is succinct.

Of course it is easy to understand why Churchill should be
interred in a vast literary mausoleum. A potent cross between
English aristocracy and American plutocracy, he was famous as
a soldier and war correspondent before the end of Queen
Victoria's reign, when he would sometimes inform – and convince – complete strangers that he was fated to be Prime Minister. He was a successful cabinet minister in his thirties and
played an important part in laying the Edwardian foundations
of the modern welfare state. At that time he could justly reckon
that he was the youngest man in England who really *counted* and
remark that although we are all worms he really believed himself to be a glow-worm. Churchill held the vital office of First

1

Lord of the Admiralty during the Great War. Despite his fall, caused by the Dardanelles disaster for which Churchill was held responsible, Lloyd George brought him back into the government. Later he was Chancellor of the Exchequer, towering, as Asquith put it, 'like a Chimborazo or Everest among the sandhills of the Baldwin cabinet'. During the 1930s he was a voice crying in the wilderness that Britain should re-arm. He saved his country and, having forged a successful alliance with Stalin and Roosevelt, led it to victory in the Second World War. And he resigned as Queen Elizabeth's first premier in 1955, full of years and honour, to become 'an ancient monument during his own life-time'.

If the scale of Churchill's achievement was gargantuan, his character also seemed far larger than life. This was not just a matter of grandiose oratory, superlative acting ability or a massive projection of those familiar symbols – cigars, 'V' signs, siren suits, eccentric hats. Churchill's personality was formed on heroic lines. It was a monstrous compound of courage, energy, imagination, tenacity, humour, compassion; and of ambition, impatience, volatility, obsessiveness, egotism, brutality. Churchill could behave like a cheeky urchin making mud-pies on the beach, like a picturesque swashbuckler in some tale of romance, or like an exotic bird of paradise preening its brilliant plumage on the dingy benches of Westminster. But he always saw himself through the basilisk eye of history, as a man of destiny bestriding his narrow age like a colossus. And so powerful was his personality, so compelling his eloquence, that he managed to make others share this glittering vision – not just devoted admirers like General Ismay who thought him 'a superman', but critical colleagues like Lord Alanbrooke who considered him a 'superhuman genius'.

Such verdicts on such a character, such a career and such exploits, explain why Winston Churchill has been the victim of biographical excess. But the vast accumulation of knowledge about Churchill is in some ways an obstacle to understanding him. Comprehensiveness impedes comprehension. More availability means worse accessibility. Even scholars find it hard to assimilate the outpouring of facts about Churchill without getting intellectual indigestion. In an era when the explosion of information blurs the shape of past existences, a

INTRODUCTION

writer's skill may best be measured by what he omits. Paradoxically, a brief life can capture a long life and an epitome may say more than a tome. For when everything is known nothing is known. The biographer's art consists in chiselling away the inessentials until a clear outline of his subject appears. This is not to say that details are redundant, quite the reverse. The seemingly trivial and the apparently peripheral often prove to be crucial. Incidental vignettes can often reveal more than reams of pedantry – Churchill's telling Stalin that he was very fond of goldfish, for example, and the dictator hospitably suggesting that he should have some for breakfast. Still, it is the purpose of this book to select the most important and evocative features of its subject. It aims to present the general reader with what is amazingly not otherwise obtainable – a vivid, balanced, complete but miniature portrait of Winston Churchill set against the background of his career.

CHAPTER I

FATHER AND SON

WINSTON Churchill was born, two months prematurely, on 30 November 1874 at Blenheim Palace. Horace Walpole had snobbishly described Blenheim as 'the palace of an auctioneer who has been chosen King of Portugal'. But it was, of course, the reward given by a grateful nation to Winston's illustrious ancestor, the Duke of Marlborough. Built of gold-coloured stone by Vanbrugh and set in country-side sculpted by Capability Brown, the vast edifice com-memorated the first of Marlborough's famous victories. Winston's father, Lord Randolph Churchill, was a younger son so Winston did not inherit the dukedom. But, as Lloyd George later remarked, he always had a soft spot for dukes, especially dukes of Marlborough. Although his cousin 'Sunny', the ninth Duke, was an aristocratic boor, Winston was devoted to him. In fact family piety – Churchills against the world – was to be one of his strongest traits. So was impatience. In later years Winston liked to say that he had chosen to arrive early in order to make his entry into life at Blenheim.

For his parents to whom he was also devoted lived in London where, although relatively poor, they were notable ornaments of high society. His beautiful mother was the daughter of Leonard Jerome, an American freebooter who was known as 'the King of Wall Street'. By bold financial speculation Leonard had made and lost millions of dollars. He named his second child Jennie after the Swedish singer Jenny Lind, the current love of his lubricious life. Jennie Jerome, who had some Red Indian blood on her mother's side, was as self-willed and as self-indulgent as her father. She became an international belle, spoilt and caressed in the gilded salons of Europe and moving with a panther's grace through 'a whirl of gaieties and excitement'. Aged only twenty, she caught the gooseberry eye of Lord Randolph Churchill. He proposed to her almost at once.

There followed much family haggling about whether the Jeromes were respectable enough for the Churchills, and rich enough, for Leonard had just lost a small fortune. But in April 1874 Lord Randolph and Jennie were married. Seven months later the birth was announced of Winston Leonard Spencer-Churchill – the hyphen was generally dropped in deference to Lord Randolph's contempt for pretentious double-barrelled names. Jennie took her son's unexpected arrival in her stride. The baby was consigned to a nurse and his parents continued to engage in what Winston himself later called 'the frivolous and expensive pursuits of the silly world of fashion'. They rode to hounds, raced at Ascot and Goodwood, went deer-stalking in Scotland and yachting at Cowes, attended the best dinners, balls and parties of the season, and entertained the Prince of Wales (with the help of their skilled French cook). When Jennie noticed Winston at all it was usually to scold him for being a nuisance. But he seldom saw his mother. To quote his classic summary (from *My Early Life*): 'She shone for me like the Evening Star. I loved her dearly – but at a distance.'

Winston not only adored his mother, he idolised his father. Yet whereas Jennie merely neglected her first-born, Lord Randolph treated him harshly. Winston sometimes became the victim of savage paternal rages. In appearance Lord Randolph was a swaggering dandy. Known as 'the Champagne Charlie of politics', he sported a jaunty moustache, violet waistcoats, tan shoes and an amber cigarette-holder embossed with a large diamond. Superficially he seemed to be a typical member of the fast set, an arrogant, untutored patrician mainly interested in pursuing women and foxes, not necessarily in that order. But uncontrollable passions seethed within Lord Randolph's breast. The fierce pride he felt in his ducal origins sometimes exploded into violence.

At Eton he had managed to accumulate fifteen personal fags

and he bullied the smaller fry. At Oxford he enjoyed collisions with 'cads'. Once when drunk he smashed up a hotel and assaulted a policeman. As a young member of parliament (for the family pocket borough of Woodstock) he was barely able to restrain his furious impulses:

> I heard one of the lower orders, who were there in crowds, say 'there is a rum specimen', evidently alluding to me. I was so angry and should have liked to have been an Ashantee King for the moment and executed him summarily.

Worse still, Lord Randolph was prone to fits of inexplicable rudeness on polite occasions. Disraeli could not understand why at one dinner party Lord Randolph was 'quite uncivil' and glared at him 'like one possessed of the Devil'. From an early age Winston himself was the occasional object of this demonic aggression, often for trivial offences.

Lord Randolph's lack of self-control was well displayed in his celebrated quarrel with Edward Prince of Wales in 1876. It was provoked by his rakish brother, the Marquis of Blandford, who was engaged in an adulterous affair with the Prince's former mistress, Lady Aylesford. If the aggrieved Lord Aylesford instituted divorce proceedings, as the Prince urged him to do, Blandford might become the lone scapegoat for what were also royal misdemeanours. So Lord Randolph determined to salvage the family honour by the novel expedient of blackmailing the heir to the throne. Asserting boldly, 'I have the Crown of England in my pocket', he threatened to publish Edward's love letters, which he had obtained from Lady Aylesford, unless the Prince used his influence to prevent the divorce. Edward was outraged and challenged Lord Randolph to a duel. The subject declined to fight his future sovereign (though he was willing to oblige a substitute) and the scandal was hushed up. Lord Randolph was eventually induced to apologise, which did not stop the Prince declaring that he would ostracise anyone who received the Churchills. This led to their exile for nearly four years and to their exclusion from high society until 1884, when a reconciliation was effected.

Thus Winston's first memories were of Dublin. For Disraeli tactfully appointed the Duke of Marlborough Viceroy of Ireland so that Lord Randolph could go over and serve his father as political secretary. Perhaps Winston's near-regal status contributed to the magnificent self-assurance which was so noticeable from his infancy upwards. Maybe his constant naughtiness as a child was designed merely to attract his parents' attention. Perhaps his pugnacity was a reflection of Lord Randolph's behaviour. Or was it a reaction against these outbursts? Who can plumb the depths of a personality? Certainly Churchill himself was in later life ribald at the expense of those who attempted to do so by scientific means. Perhaps this ribaldry was itself a defence mechanism, for introspection might bring on depression, the 'Black Dog' which prowled at Churchill's heels all his life. What can be said with assurance is that in his early childhood Winston was anything but crushed or demoralised by the callous and perfunctory treatment he received at the hands of his parents.

In fact, he did know the warmth of spontaneous love. It was provided in abundance by his nanny Mrs Everest. He in turn doted on her, calling her 'Womany' or 'Woom' (womb? – surely the psychologists could make something of that). Mrs Everest was typical of her kind, full of nursery maxims about the need to 'keep regular', the efficacy of Eno's Fruit Salt and the importance of knowing your place. None of this had the slightest effect on Winston who, even as a small boy, was wilful to the point of violence. No one could control him. His dancing teacher thought him the the naughtiest boy in the world. The servants found him aggressive and overbearing, determined in his parents' absence to make the household revolve round himself. His behaviour shocked the governess whom he shared with his five-year-old contemporary Rupert Guinness (later Lord Iveagh). Rupert had been given a toy harness and coachman's whip and Winston had no doubts about who should be the driver and who the horse. Handing Rupert the harness and grabbing the whip himself Winston lashed his play-mate across the forehead, leaving a permanent scar. Neither had forgotten the incident when in 1960 they met again at an investiture of Knights of the Garter.

Victorian small boys of all classes were rougher, and were treated more roughly, than is the case today. Aged seven Winston was sent away to a fashionable preparatory school, St George's Ascot, where he was bullied by the boys and beaten

7

by the headmaster, a sadist called Sneyd-Kynnersley who liked to flog his pupils until their blood spattered his study. Nothing could break Winston's rebellious spirit. He remained stubbornly unamenable to discipline and was always getting into scrapes. Though far from being the hopeless dunce suggested by his autobiography, he refused to exert himself at those studies which did not interest him. He read precociously – *Treasure Island* was a favourite – but remained bottom of his class. And when his fellows threw cricket balls at him frightening him so much that he hid among some trees, he resolved to give as good as he got. Although he was small his belligerence became a by-word. His Jerome grandmother called him 'a naughty, sandy-haired little bulldog'. Having been moved from St George's, on account of its brutality, to a school at Brighton, Winston entered Harrow where he met Richard Meinertzhagen. Attempting, as was the custom, to dispute the pavement with Churchill, Meinertzhagen found himself bounced into the gutter and subjected to a glance from Churchill's cold, blue, deep-set eyes which he never forgot. As his biographer recorded:

> It was neither victorious nor amused, merely a warning to keep off but of a menacing intensity that Richard recognised later in the eyes of a wild boar about to charge him.

Yet it would be a mistake to regard Winston as a mere aristocratic thug in the making. Indeed, his ardour for combat was part of a boyishness which neither he nor his father ever really lost. It is this quality which helps to explain Winston's undiscouraged devotion to Lord Randolph, a devotion which he was to express by copying his father's dress and mannerisms, learning his speeches, pursuing his policies and writing his biography. Lord Randolph's own tastes were juvenile ones. He enjoyed the antics of jugglers, conjurors, ventriloquists, fire-eaters, acrobats, freaks and performing animals. He even took Winston to Barnum's Circus, though he refused to let him see 'The Boneless Wonder', judging that 'the spectacle would be too revolting and demoralizing for my youthful eyes'. Fifty years later Churchill recalled the incident in a famous jibe directed at Ramsay MacDonald, 'The Boneless Wonder sitting on the Treasury Bench'.

Morose and fitful as an adolescent, Lord Randolph also

possessed what Winston called 'a personal attractiveness and a wonderful manner'. This was well displayed on the public platform. With his youthful looks, rolling eye and expressive moustache, with his racy style, flailing arms and outrageous indiscretions, Lord Randolph transfixed his audiences. He spoke, it was said, with 'the infallibility of a Pope and the readiness of a cheapjack'. Known variously as 'Yahoo Churchill', 'Cheeky Randy' and 'The Music Hall Cad', he was one of the first politicians to stump the country on speaking tours. He thus established himself as a popular orator second only to Mr Gladstone, the tree-felling Prime Minister being the butt of his sharpest barbs – 'the forest laments that Mr Gladstone should perspire'. In private, as Lord Rosebery observed, Lord Randolph's 'demeanour, his unexpectedness, his fits of caressing humility, his tinge of violent eccentricity, his apparent daredevilry, made him a fascinating companion'. He was, when he wanted to be, a model of courtesy, elegance, polish. His manners were perfect, except to servants. His charm, when the mood took him, was exhilarating. Indeed, contrasting the father with the son, Asquith was to remark: 'Randolph was irresistible. He had incomparably more charm, more wit. But – Winston is by far the better fellow.'

Like any schoolboy Randolph loved to shock. He bicycled round the terrace of the House of Commons. As Chancellor of the Exchequer he professed inability to make out the meaning of 'those damned dots' – decimal points. He informed his sister-in-law: 'I don't like ladies at all – I like rough women who dance and sing and drink – the rougher the better!' Lord Randolph fizzed with irreverent humour: when in India he discovered that: 'any Hindoo whose ashes are thrown into the Ganges, goes right bang up to heaven without stopping no matter how great a rascal he was', which gave him the idea that Mr Gladstone should embrace that religion. Cackling with weird 'jay-like' laughter, agog with some audacious enterprise, delighted with a pungent new phrase, Lord Randolph invested life with a febrile excitement which Winston, already a connoisseur of adventure, could not but relish.

Politics in particular gave zest to Lord Randolph's life. As he said:

I have tried all forms of excitement from tip-cat to tiger-shooting;

all degrees of gambling from beggar-my-neighbour to Monte Carlo; but have found no gambling like politics and no excitement like a big division.

However, parliament was not the breath of life to the father as it later became to the son. The motives behind Lord Randolph's rise to political prominence after the Conservative defeat in 1880 were mixed. In part he intended to flout and to end the social boycott – the Prince of Wales worshipped success and much approved of Lord Randolph's assaults on the republican Bradlaugh. In part he wanted to have fun, to turn Westminster into a circus with himself as ring-master, cracking the whip to put the 'old man in a hurry' (Mr Gladstone) through his paces. He also enjoyed drawing the 'badger' (Joseph Chamberlain), goring 'the Goat' (Sir Stafford Northcote), skewering the 'rodent' (Lord Derby) and twisting the tail of the 'boa-constrictor' (Lord Hartington). In part Lord Randolph aspired to restore Tory fortunes, creating his own ginger group to do so.

Known as the Fourth Party (Parnell's Irish Nationalists were the third), it consisted of a quartet of Tory dissidents. They had no binding commitment to one another (the ambiguous Arthur Balfour was, in Chamberlain's phrase, 'the fourth part of the Fourth Party'). Their only coherent purpose was to make life difficult for the Grand Old Man (Mr Gladstone) and impossible for the Grand Old Woman (as Lord Randolph otherwise nicknamed Northcote, leader of the Conservatives in the Commons). The Fourth Party wanted a strong Tory chief and Northcote suffered, literally and metaphorically, from weak knees. Lord Randolph's politics were thus a mixture of wrecking, rhetoric and opportunism. Yet by means of scintillating speeches and unscrupulous manoeuvres he became within five years a commanding parliamentary and public figure or, as Winston put it, 'a great elemental force in British politics'. In the process he deeply alienated many members of his own party. The fifteenth Earl of Derby's verdict, written in his diary of 1885, was typical: 'Churchill, with all his remarkable cleverness, is thoroughly untrustworthy; scarcely a gentleman, and probably more or less mad.' Winston was to inherit Lord Randolph's mantle. In 1916 the sixteenth Earl of Derby, unwittingly echoing his father's words, told Lloyd George that

Winston had 'a very attractive personality but he is absolutely untrustworthy as was his father before him'.

This inveterate suspicion stemmed largely from the Churchills' political chopping and changing. But whereas Winston's vagaries were attributed to a flaw of character (he was supposed to have genius without judgement) Lord Randolph's seemed to derive from a moral fault (he was thought to be lacking in principle). There is much to be said for the first opinion and more, despite Winston's loyal attempts to ascribe political high-mindedness and consistency to his father, to be said for the second. Lord Randolph's supreme skill was as an opposition tactician and he had few, if any, positive strategic goals. He shifted his ground on almost every issue, so much so that Gladstone likened him to a flea. Lord Randolph moved from Fair Trade (or Protection) to Free Trade. He paraded through India as a liberal but behaved at home as an imperialist, insulting 'baboo' visitors and ordering the annexation of Upper Burma. He toyed with a Conservative version of Home Rule for Ireland and flirted with Parnell and the Nationalists; but when it suited him he uttered that notorious rallying cry, 'Ulster will fight and Ulster will be right.' Even where his own interests were concerned Lord Randolph had a reckless disregard for consistency. In opposition he favoured heavy expenditure on the army and navy. But within five months of having become Chancellor of the Exchequer in Lord Salisbury's government, in December 1886, he resigned because he was not allowed sufficiently to cut the military estimates. This impulsive abdication on a trivial issue thoroughly discredited Lord Randolph and he never regained power. He had been a tumultuous colleague and his departure caused Hosannas to ring out at Lord Salisbury's residence, Hatfield House. Having rid himself of one boil on the back of the neck, to employ the Prime Minister's own image, Salisbury did not intend to get another.

Lord Randolph's course had been meteoric. He went from obscurity to oblivion with hardly a pause. Yet his career had been a brilliant one and Winston was the most fascinated beholder of his father's brief interlude of political glory. Moreover, Winston was to recapitulate many of Lord Randolph's policies and contradictions, several times, for example, changing his attitude towards military spending.

11

Winston was also to perform quite seriously variations on a theme that his father had rehearsed as something of a comedy – Tory Democracy. Like Disraeli, Lord Randolph had perceived the Conservative working man – an angel released from his block of marble – and visualised his alliance with the country's natural rulers. As he put it in a characteristic flash of candour: 'The aristocracy and the working class are united in the indissoluble bonds of a common immorality.' Actually Tory Democracy was real Toryism and sham democracy. It was, as Lord Randolph cynically remarked, 'democracy which supports the Tories'. Lord Randolph had little interest in improving the lot of the masses and much hatred for middle-class Liberals. They were the suburban 'Lords of pineries and vineries', the pseudo-gentry whose pretensions were mocked in Lord Randolph's favourite (almost his only) reading, Jorrocks. Winston, who was to feel a similar aversion for bourgeois socialists and 'adjectival grocers', converted this specious mish-mash into a policy of radical social reform during the Edwardian era. And as a politician he conducted a life-long search for a middle party which would be supported by the populace and dedicated to their welfare.

This is to anticipate. As a schoolboy Winston was exalted and inspired by his father's career even though by the time he went to Harrow in 1887, aged thirteen and a half, that career was virtually finished. Lord Randolph doggedly refused to acknowledge this. Winston's own failure at public school was also a product of obstinacy. It was not that he was stupid or even lazy. He displayed great energy when anything caught his fancy. He enjoyed the cadet corps, became a champion fencer, recited 1200 lines of Macaulay's *Lays of Ancient Rome* off by heart and learnt how to write an English sentence – 'a noble thing'. But when it came to subjects like Latin and French he refused to invest an iota of his extraordinary powers of concentration. Indeed he wrote English essays for other boys in exchange for their doing his Latin prose. When, as a young member of Asquith's cabinet, he larded his speech with occasional Latin tags, a look of surprise and pain would flit across the features of the scholarly Prime Minister. Nor did Winston's French progress much beyond the schoolboy stage. It remained an astounding mixture of high-flown Gallic words and English expressions pronounced with superb self-confidence in a John Bull accent. Only Frenchmen with a colloquial knowledge of English could understand it.

Winston regarded Harrow as a hell, a boring and irrelevant obstacle course impeding his entry into the great adventure of life. His behaviour reflected this attitude. It was a standing affront to the headmaster, Dr Welldon. Winston was unpunctual, careless, forgetful, spendthrift, opinionated and deliberately troublesome. Welldon acutely recognised that his refractory charge had 'some great gifts' and obtusely sought to evoke them with a rod. He birched Winston more frequently than any other boy. Winston was unmoved and even had the impertinence to tell the headmaster how to carry out his duties. Winston invariably tried to teach his instructors and was always convinced that he knew better than the experts. He once told a specialist who had examined his throat, 'I entirely disagree with your diagnosis.'

Nevertheless, though he remained in the Lower School, Winston did learn some important lessons at Harrow. Or rather Harrow corroborated what he already knew. It endorsed his strong belief in the necessity for self-reliance and the importance of tribal loyalty. It strengthened his conviction – part romanticism, part Darwinism, part egotism – that destiny helps those who help themselves and that only the fittest, and the bravest, survive. It also confirmed his instinctive trust in the supreme virtue of allegiance to his star, to his family, to his class, to his country and its monarch, to the British Empire and, more nebulously, to the English-speaking peoples. With pardonable exaggeration H. G. Wells later accused Winston's '*beastly* public school' of having 'be-Kiplinged' him. 'Empire and Anglo-Saxon and boy-scout and sleuth are the stuff in your mind.' Despite having loathed Harrow Winston eventually became a devoted Old Harrovian. From the war years almost to the end of his life he would return to sing the school songs. Indeed he seemed to think that this was what education was all about. Music gave a first-class fillip to esprit de corps and love of country. He liked to descant on the noble beauty of 'Rule Britannia' and to exhort troops to sing martial and patriotic songs.

Harrow also taught Winston its gentlemanly code of honour,

though he was to be selective in the parts of it which he adopted. Thus in financial matters he was unusually scrupulous: tradesmen could wait for their money, of course, but he insisted on paying, as Prime Minister, for the cost of private journeys made in official cars. Insofar as he acknowledged their existence Winston tended to idealise women. His excitement chiefly stimulated by physical danger and his drive mainly directed towards political power, he meticulously observed the sexual proprieties. He was always chivalrous towards the defeated and would never 'kick a man when he was down'. He even had a touching faith in the moral efficacy of sport, at any rate in the worth of aristocratic sports which he himself took up; polo, pig-sticking, fox-hunting. On the other hand he had no respect for hierarchies – they were for others to rise in but for himself to vault over. Similarly rules and conventions were for the timid to obey and the bold to flout. Harrovian religion made no impression on Winston's mind; instead he calculated that he could live indefinitely off the large capital of church-going which he had amassed there. Finally, Winston was ebullient, ambitious, immodest and self-serving. He could not help it. Yet 'putting on side' was by public school standards the worst possible 'form'. It is therefore not surprising that many contemporaries thought him, as did his embittered former friend Desmond Morton, 'a howling cad'.

Winston's parents might have been disposed to agree on the infrequent occasions when they focussed their attention upon the growing boy. Thick-set, carrot-topped, freckle-faced, watery-eyed, accident-prone, Winston was an unprepossessing youth. Though affectionate, he was no less obstreperous at home than at school. At nearly seventeen he was, Jennie told Lord Randolph, at a particularly unattractive stage, troublesome, sloppy, needing a man's control. Or perhaps a French governess would do, provided she were ugly. Winston's resistance to working in the holidays was an epic of obstinacy. Tutors were simply overborne by his will-power. It is true that by now he read eagerly and wrote well. He was already a connoisseur of language and enjoyed the sensation of rolling piquant phrases round his tongue. But he seemed to have no serious interests apart perhaps from military ones. He built an outdoor castle complete with moat and drawbridge and made a large catapult (chiefly used to shoot green apples at a cow). He liked to drill his cousins and his brother Jack, a somewhat dull and docile boy four years his junior (and probably not sired by Lord Randolph), on whom Winston doted. He also revelled in the thrill of mock warfare as commander of his armies of toy soldiers. This fascination with martial manoeuvres was life-long. At the height of the Battle of Britain, in September 1940, Churchill spent an afternoon crawling round the library floor at Blenheim Palace re-enacting Marlborough's victory with tin soldiers, imitating the bangs of the cannons and providing the smoke with puffs from his cigar.

Winston's fate was determined by his toy soldiers. Inspecting them one day, and considering his son too stupid for any other profession (except perhaps the Church, which had been briefly considered and wisely rejected), Lord Randolph suggested a military career. Winston adopted the idea with alacrity. In 1893 he managed, at his third attempt and with the help of a London crammer, to qualify for a cadetship at Sandhurst. But he only got into the cavalry, which required less intellectual ability and more private means from its recruits than the infantry. Lord Randolph was furious. He subjected Winston to a withering rebuke for his 'slovenly, happy go lucky, harum scarum style of work' and his 'idle, useless, unprofitable life'. Unless he reformed, Lord Randolph continued, Winston would degenerate into 'a mere social wastrel', leading 'a shabby, unhappy and futile existence'. Winston dutifully apologised and promised to improve. But this setdown was a shattering conclusion to what had been the most miserable years of his life.

Actually the vehemence of the reproof reveals more about the father than the son. Lord Randolph had bouts of manic activity which alternated with his moods of depression and lassitude. These moods grew blacker after his fall from power and he would sometimes sit for hours buried in silent gloom. Yet he could still rise to dazzling heights and there was a hectic brilliance about his conversation as he defended daring paradoxes, indulged in 'piercing personalities' or denounced 'the senile drivellings of Mr Gladstone'. Unsoothed by cigarettes, which he smoked as constantly as Winston later smoked cigars, Lord Randolph had always been rash, mercurial and capricious.

He was unable to bear any restraints, even those of logic. Queen Victoria herself had commented on his instability, finding him 'so mad and odd'. But by the 1890s he was definitely ill, in the grip of general paralysis of the insane. Probably this was the result of syphilis, which he contracted – according to the most credible story – from a Blenheim housemaid soon after Winston's birth. At any rate, all Lord Randolph's natural characteristics were now exaggerated to the point of dementia. Bearded, haggard, prematurely aged, he made spasmodic efforts to continue his political career. His halting, incoherent speeches were a terrible travesty of the spirited performance of earlier days. Exposed to the popular gaze, his tragic decline was a source of sad embarrassment to friends. Lord Rosebery summed up the last period of his life: 'He was the chief mourner at his own protracted funeral, a public pageant of gloomy years.'

At Sandhurst Winston was the object of further flurries of paternal anger, often over trifles such as using a typewriter or losing his watch. He spared no pains to mollify his father. Winston was especially eager to please because, in acknowledgement of his new status, Lord Randolph began to introduce him into the overlapping social circles in which he moved, political, aristocratic and bohemian. On a few occasions Winston even achieved a degree of intimacy with his father, who made at least one winning appeal for sympathy. But although he could display entrancing personal warmth Lord Randolph usually froze Winston off. He discouraged the exchange of confidences, perhaps fearful of what they might reveal. Still, despite his son's persistent extravagance and unpunctuality, Lord Randolph was quite pleased with his progress at Sandhurst. Subjected as he was to strict military discipline, even Winston could not fail to improve in general conduct.

Splendid in his scarlet and gold uniform he enjoyed the military life. There were compensations for the Spartan physical conditions. Winston learnt to ride well (but drill badly), sometimes spending as many as eight hours a day in the saddle. He also took a great interest in finding out about the art of war. The instruction, to be sure, hardly entailed much intellectual exertion. For, as one colonel remarked, the sole duties of the cavalry were to 'look smart in time of peace and get killed in war'. Indeed the *arme blanche*, that part of the battle array said by *Punch* to give tone to what would otherwise be a vulgar brawl, was already obsolescent. But Winston, though no respecter of military mystique, never forgot the lessons of fighting on horseback – the supreme need for 'pluck', 'dash' and 'offensive spirit'. In many ways he remained all his life a subaltern of hussars and he later tended to regard tanks, aeroplanes, even ships, as squadrons of cavalry.

Much of Winston's energy at Sandhurst was devoted to the strenuous task of enjoying himself, though he frequently complained that the leave was ungenerous. Most of his recreation involved riding and he was once observed taking part in a donkey race dressed as a pierrot. But he also learnt to drink champagne and he acquired expensive tastes in food, clothes and entertainment. As Winston liked to say, he was always quite willing to be satisfied with the best. At this stage, however, he sometimes needed the help of a pawnbroker to pay for it. He also became fond of music halls and so retentive was his memory that he could sing the popular songs of the naughty nineties well into his own eighties. It was actually the theatre which provided the opportunity for his earliest political enterprise and his maiden public speech, both hilariously chronicled (though slightly bowdlerised) in *My Early Life*.

Briefly what happened was that a progressive purity campaigner called Mrs Ormiston Chant tried to clean up a notorious rendezvous for toffs and tarts at London's Empire Theatre in the Haymarket. Winston was outraged by this prudish intolerance and agitated against it. With a mob of his fellows he tore down the canvas screens erected by Mrs Chant to separate promenading courtesans from drinking theatre-goers. Then, amid the ruins of the barricades, Winston harangued the crowd, urging all right-minded citizens to vote against Mrs Chant at the next local elections. At the time he was lucky to escape a reprimand from the Sandhurst authorities. The charge was subsequently made that the Military College was itself a hotbed of vice. Winston always denied it. Himself accused by a newspaper of having participated in 'acts of gross immorality of the Oscar Wilde type' while at Sandhurst, he successfully sued for damages. No doubt Winston was innocent, but he could not have been ignorant, of the dissipations of his contemporaries. It was almost obligatory for cadets to have 'a fling', the results of which could not be concealed. The highlight of Sandhurst's term was an inspection by the old Duke of Cambridge, Commander-in-Chief of the army, who once gave the assembled company a stern warning against venereal disease: 'I hear you boys have been putting your private parts where I wouldn't put this umbrella.'

In his attack on the prudes, shortly before discovering the true nature of his father's illness during the autumn of 1894, Winston had said that nature's law meted out greater and more terrible punishments to 'the *roué* and libertine' than man's law could do. Lord Randolph's end horridly confirmed such ideas of poetic, or melodramatic, justice. In a vain search for health he had travelled round the world, a tour made more ghastly for Jennie by her husband's erratic and violent behaviour. On their return Lord Randolph declined quickly and what relations called his 'softening of the brain' became clearly apparent. He experienced swiftly changing moods of dejection and euphoria, delusions of grandeur and spasms of berserk fury during which he had to be restrained. Finally he sank into a state of torpor and idiocy. On 24 January 1895, aged only forty-five, he died, seventy years to the day before Winston himself. The Churchills were understandably secretive about Lord Randolph's final symptoms and the cause of his death, though rumours abounded. At about the same time as Winston passed out of Sandhurst (twentieth out of 130) and was gazetted into the Fourth Hussars, he also became head of the (relatively impoverished) family. Harshly though he had been treated, no son ever did more to honour his father's reputation.

Filial loyalty apart, Winston was bound to promote Lord Randolph's reputation because he himself traded on it so unashamedly. He used it, for example, to gain entry to the great houses, there to cultivate the leaders of the day. For already his political designs were crystallising and he burned to emulate, perhaps even to outdo, his father. Sir Charles Dilke considered Lord Rosebery the most ambitious man he had ever met – until he encountered Winston Churchill. But as a panoply with which to enter the political lists Lord Randolph's reputation, though splendid, was distinctly flawed. Winston's career reflected the ambiguities of his legacy. He inherited a certain fame but also a certain notoriety. He quickly branded himself with that dire stigma: 'Brilliant but unsound'. He succeeded to a few vague causes such as Tory Democracy, but they did him as much harm as good. He saw what could be won by energy but not what might be lost by impetuosity (though in his entire career he only resigned once). Above all, Winston's ambition was fed and whetted by the vision of an extremely hazardous but intensely exciting political style.

The retrospect and the prospect dazzled him. Unspoilt by education and undeveloped in intellect, Winston was nevertheless in some ways extraordinarily sophisticated. In particular he knew what he wanted and he had a precocious understanding of how to get it. He was also ruthlessly determined to trample down any obstacle to his plans. These plans were simple. After a stimulating preliminary draught of adventure on active service, duly rewarded with medals and fame, Winston proposed 'to beat my sword into an iron dispatch box'. He would take Westminster by storm and attain in due course glittering offices and political glory. As he embarked on adult life his usual optimism was joyfully in the ascendant, eclipsing its glum counterpart depression. He later remarked that the world opened for him like Aladdin's cave. Winston had only to enter and possess himself of its treasure. He might have said with Nelson, one of his heroes, 'In my mind's eye I ever saw a radiant orb suspended which beckoned me onwards to renown.'

CHAPTER II

THE CHAMPAGNE YEARS

A FINAL link with Winston's childhood was broken with the death of his beloved nurse 'Womany' in the summer of 1895. Mrs Everest had been treated badly by his parents but Winston had exerted himself to make her last years happy and secure. He sat at her deathbed and mourned at her grave. Doubtless Mrs Everest's demise reminded Winston of how little time he had left. For he was spurred by the conviction that his life, like his father's, would be short. Her death also seemed to harden his character, even to give it a grim and cynical twist. Fond as he was of his mother, he used her quite cold-bloodedly as a resource. To further his own ends he exploited her social and even her sexual contacts. The latter were plentiful. According to George Moore she had over two hundred lovers, not to mention a further brace of embarrassingly unsuitable husbands; but if Winston disapproved he was uncensorious. One of Jennie's lovers was an American politician called Bourke Cockran, whose gift of the gab excited Winston's interest in what he himself could accomplish by way of oratory. Winston stayed with Cockran, and was introduced into New York society by him, *en route* to his first military adventure in Cuba.

Rather than spend the autumn leave of 1895 fox-hunting, Winston and a subaltern friend Reginald Barnes had decided to see action of a headier sort. It was available only in Spain's rebellious colony of Cuba, the 'Pearl of the Antilles' as

Winston liked to call it. Pulling all possible strings he obtained letters of introduction to the general in charge of hunting the insurgents. He procured a commission from the *Daily Graphic* to write about the conflict at five guineas a letter. He also got War Office approval to supply information about a new Spanish bullet. This was a coup. It was the first, but not the last, occasion on which Winston managed to transform a private journey into an official mission. From the start he had the self-confidence – others called it effrontery – to deal only with men at the top and not to be fobbed off with minions. He behaved as though he were important and he was usually treated as such.

On arriving in Havana the two British officers attached themselves to a column which was scouring the interior for rebels. To Winston's delight he came under fire for the first time on 30 November 1895, his twenty-first birthday. Churchill, as he must now be called, was unscathed in this skirmish and the few that followed. Indeed, he took away from Cuba very little in the way of experience apart from a taste for the local cigars and the habit of having a *siesta* – which enabled him to cram one and a half days' work into each twenty-four hours during the Second World War. Later Churchill was to reflect on the absurdity of travelling three thousand miles at considerable expense and venturing into the jungle with strangers all for the purpose of risking death. Yet he could do no other. He revealed as much in his only novel *Savrola*, written a couple of years later, which was more autobiography than fantasy.

> 'Vehement, high, and daring' was the cast of his mind. The life he lived was the only one he could ever live; he must go on to the end. The end comes often early to such men, whose spirits are so wrought that they know rest only in action, contentment only in danger, and in confusion find their only peace.

No sooner had Churchill returned than he was agitating to be off again to one or other of the world's trouble spots, Crete or Matabeleland. He badgered his mother incessantly to make her influential friends 'do something for me', but without success. A peaceful life was nonsense for a soldier, he thought, and military routine was gall and wormwood. Only in warfare could Churchill gain the distinction, the advantage, the exhilaration which he craved. There was surely no need to be modest about such ambitions for he was prepared to stake his life on their outcome. Churchill's irritation, when the Fourth Hussars were posted to India for garrison duties in 1896, knew no bounds. He even contemplated entering politics at once and marrying money to finance the enterprise. In the event Churchill endured Bangalore, though he found the life 'intolerable' and chafed bitterly at the lack of 'nice' or 'interesting' people. He tried to assuage his frustration by taking vigorous physical and mental exercise. He played polo energetically and well, despite having injured his right shoulder on jumping ashore at Bombay – for the rest of his life it was liable to be dislocated by any sudden movement. Moreover, conscious of the inadequacy of his education as well as the dangers of intellectual stagnation in a community which regarded 'brainy' officers with suspicion, Churchill embarked on a strenuous course of study during the long hot afternoons.

He was not interested in acquiring a literary culture: he was to assume that Blake's poems were written by the Admiral until told otherwise by Violet Asquith, and he did not read *Hamlet* for the first time until the 1950s. Nor did Churchill want knowledge for its own sake. He was too intelligent to belong to the intelligentsia, too creative to value information as anything more than a stimulus to his own thought. Indeed, he resented the fact that his own freshly minted notions had often been anticipated. The Greeks and Romans, for example, had stolen a march on him by the unfair expedient of being born first. No, Churchill's intention was to equip himself with intellectual weapons in order to win political victories. Thus he read copies of the *Annual Register* and tested his own opinions against those expressed in parliamentary debates. He quickly discovered that facts depend for their significance on interpretation and that by skilful argument he could arrange them into almost any pattern he chose. Similarly, ideas rather than events were the building-blocks of historiography. Churchill's own vision of imperial glory and progress was distilled from Gibbon and Macaulay. He gulped down their works with awed delight and so steeped himself in their heady language that he remained word-intoxicated ever afterwards. Each historian made an indelible mark on his style, that sonorous vehicle which carried his career to the heights.

If Gibbon and Macaulay were archaic influences a more modern creed, secular and materialist, was provided by Winwood Reade. His *Martyrdom of Man*, an important book in its time, imbued Churchill with a strange mixture of scientific optimism and evolutionary fatalism. In other words, he believed in the advance of his own race via 'the combined influence of Rationalism and machine-guns'. But although science and war might bring tremendous short-term gains, individuals faced annihilation at death and the universe was doomed to final extinction. Immortality could be won only in the here and now.

Churchill's reading included many other works, some about Napoleon, a life-long interest, as well as that rich source of spurious erudition, Bartlett's *Familiar Quotations*. These books transformed him intellectually from boy to man. He developed late but maturity, when it came, arrived at a gallop. This is not to say that Churchill's opinions were notably refined. As a young man he spouted the usual contemporary clap-trap about the absurdity of women's suffrage and the danger of universal education. Nevertheless Churchill had trained his mind and evolved a world-view, which made him confident that he could eventually dominate Westminster. His bumptiousness grew accordingly. Even his fellow subalterns, whose reading seldom strayed beyond Ruff's *Guide to the Turf*, were offended. One evening they tried to suppress him by force, placing a large sofa on top of his struggling form. He emerged from the scrimmage, bedraggled but triumphant, exclaiming: 'You can't keep me down like that.'

Nor could they. It is true that his attempt to report the Graeco-Turkish war was foiled, for it ended too quickly. Instead he spent his leave in England where he made his first proper political speech, finding, to his relief, that his lisp was no real impediment. Then, in April 1897, he heard while at Goodwood that General Sir Bindon Blood was organising what became known as the Malakand Field Force to punish the unruly Pathans, Afghan mountain people who were struggling to assert their independence while being squeezed between the hostile empires of Britain and Russia. Churchill raced to the North West frontier of India. Places were hard to come by on what Blood called his 'pheasant shoot'. But Churchill had met the General socially and he secured permission to act as a war correspondent and later as a serving officer. The expedition aimed to quell the tribesmen by burning their villages and crops. This procedure, although 'cruel and barbarous, as everything is in war', Churchill defended because it was effective. So was the dum-dum bullet, 'from the technical point of view a beautiful machine'. All his life Churchill was to have double standards about using this weapon: as late as 1940 he reckoned that it was 'the best way of killing Huns'. Because of the ghastly wounds it caused the soft-nosed bullet was outlawed internationally in 1899. But although Churchill would condemn the Boers for using it he equipped himself with dum-dums during the South African war and certainly approved of their employment against the Pathans. For they were 'pernicious vermin', savage, immoral and fanatical, 'as degraded a race as any on the fringe of humanity'.

Still, the Pathans gave Churchill the most vivid and valuable experience of his life to that date. For their instincts were warlike and their courage was unflinching. Several times they drove back ill-commanded British columns, a fact which Churchill skated over in his drum-beating reports for the *Daily Telegraph*. It was axiomatic that 'intrinsic merit is the only title of a dominant race to its possessions' and he was reluctant to call the superiority of the British in question. Churchill himself was a match for any Pathan when it came to bravery and he rejoiced to display the fact during the few small fights in which he engaged. During a dangerous action in the Mamund Valley, for example, he became the rearguard of the rearguard and the tribesmen actually came close enough to throw stones at him. Several times he rode his grey pony along the skirmish lines when everyone else was lying down. 'Foolish perhaps,' he told his mother, 'but I play for high stakes and given an audience there is no act too daring and too noble.' Churchill hungered for decorations to set the seal on his reputation. He greeted the news that Blood had mentioned him in despatches with ecstasy.

These despatches he printed in full in his first book *The Story of the Malakand Field Force* (1898). To his intense mortification ('I scream with disappointment') the book was marred by many typographical errors, the fault of a literary uncle to whom he had entrusted the proofs in his haste for publication. Another cause of offence was that Churchill had made various criticisms of official policies, commenting adversely, for example, on the state's neglect of wounded soldiers. Today his remarks appear mild, even circumspect, but at the time they seemed grossly presumptuous. Here was a 'pushy' young medal-hunter lecturing his superiors in public: what 'cheek'! No matter that many of the most ambitious officers, including Lord Wolseley himself, had risen by judicious resort to press and print. Gentlemen were gentlemen, and journalists were (to use Kitchener's expressive word) 'swabs'. Churchill's writing was particularly infuriating because it was so cocksure and so magisterial. Yet his book received excellent notices. It earned him the equivalent of two years' pay. It also attracted the favourable attention of many who mattered from the Prince of Wales and Lord Salisbury downwards. Churchill seldom basked in approval; he converted its rays into power to drive forward his schemes. When Lord Salisbury politely asked if he could be of any service Churchill, once more home on leave, begged to be included in Kitchener's expedition to reconquer the Sudan.

However the army was closing ranks against this self-advertising subaltern. Churchill had already been frustrated in his efforts to fight in the Tirah campaign on the North West frontier in March 1898, compensating for this disappointment by making himself the statesman-hero of his Ruritanian romance *Savrola* – his only novel, a juvenile work which he later (understandably) tried to forget. Now Kitchener seemed bent on thwarting him, even though it meant opposing the Prime Minister. Churchill persisted. He would not take no for an answer and he was quite unabashed at thrusting himself forward. He simply had to play a part in avenging the death of General Gordon, killed at Khartoum in 1885 during the Holy War by which the Mahdi (or Messiah) had won independence for the Sudan. Finally, exploiting his family's friendship with Lady Jeune, a leading society hostess, Churchill managed to get himself appointed by the War Office, which resented Kitchener's dictatorial assumptions, as a supernumerary officer in the 21st Lancers. He also secured a commission to send letters to the *Morning Post*. In this highly suspect dual capacity he travelled up the Nile.

Churchill killed two horses in his impatience to reach the front. He also managed to lose himself in the desert. After a lonely, cheerless night he found the river, then a village and sustenance. A meal of dates and milk, he reported in a clanking Gibbonian antithesis, 'if it will not gratify the palate of the epicure, will yet sustain the stomach of a traveller'. Finally he reached the outskirts of Omdurman. His squadron was patrolling ahead and from a knoll above the mud city he was thrilled to observe the Dervish horde. There was a black swarm of movement, banners waved and the sun glinted 'on perhaps forty thousand hostile spear points'. It was an awe-inspiring spectacle, he wrote, the vision of a life-time. Eagerly he galloped back to report the enemy's advance to Kitchener who was riding up at the head of the main Anglo-Egyptian army, itself a picturesque array including 'chocolate-coloured men on cream-coloured camels'. Churchill anticipated some show of resentment at his unwelcome presence. But the moustached Commander-in-Chief, barely acknowledging the lieutenant who reined in at his side, was his usual aloof, ungracious, matter-of-fact self. Kitchener might be a general, Churchill later reflected, but he was never a gentleman.

At dawn the next day, 2 September 1898, Churchill was again on his knoll sending off reports of the Dervish progress until the last moment. He then took up his post with the 21st Lancers on the left of the defensive arc, backing onto the Nile, in which Kitchener had organised his forces. The Dervishes might have attacked at night or harried Kitchener's long line of communication. Instead they charged *en masse* across open ground in daylight, straight at the muzzles of Lee-Enfield rifles and Maxim guns (which, as Hilaire Belloc said, 'we had got and they had not'). They were mown down in their thousands. It was not a battle but a massacre. Yet, as if impatient to rival the Dervish Khalifa in military incompetence, Kitchener ordered a premature advance on Omdurman. This involved the unnecessary mauling of his right flank as it debouched into an exposed position. It also led to one of the last cavalry charges in British history. Churchill was delighted to add this to his military repertoire and ever afterwards cheered up when the opportunity arose to re-engage the enemy at the dinner table, with the assistance of cutlery, sugar-lumps and cigar butts.

The 21st Lancers were ordered to advance and harass the enemy's right wing. Encountering what seemed to be a small detachment of sharpshooters they trotted forward to brush it aside. Suddenly the Lancers came under heavy fire and it was evident that they were facing two or three thousand Dervishes concealed in a dry water-course. The bugle sounded, the khaki-clad cavalry wheeled into line and within seconds they were riding full-tilt into the dense blue-jibbahed ranks of the foe. Churchill probably owed his life to two circumstances. First, because of his wrenched shoulder he fought with an automatic Mauser pistol instead of a sword. It served him well in the crush and he killed several of his assailants. Secondly, his troop was on the extreme right, which just overlapped the main Dervish mass and thus broke through more easily. At the solid centre the stabbing, hacking, shooting Dervishes wreaked terrible havoc among the Lancers, killing or wounding five officers, sixty men and 120 horses – a quarter of their strength. The remainder formed up within moments of the bloody collision. But they did not attempt another charge, as Churchill himself wanted in order to incur a properly 'historic' number of casualties. Instead they sensibly drove the enemy back from long range with their carbines.

There is no doubt that this charge was, as the *Daily Mail*'s correspondent George Steevens wrote, 'a gross blunder'. In attacking unbroken infantry of untested strength over unknown ground, the Lancers displayed 'indisputable heroism' and 'equally indisputable folly'. Churchill himself later acknowledged that it had been a 'futile' episode in which only thirty or forty Dervishes were killed. In his reports at the time he put the figure at sixty. And he extolled the charge, which won the Lancers three Victoria Crosses, as glorious proof of the martial spirit of the imperial race. In a bold rhetorical passage he even claimed that this made it as valuable as the victory of Omdurman itself. Here was a striking early instance of Churchill's alchemical power with words. By means of fiery eloquence he could transmute the dross of disaster into the gold of triumph.

Before long Kitchener himself was to experience the lash of Churchill's language. In his published account of *The River War* (1899) Churchill denounced as a 'wicked act' the General's inhuman treatment of the Dervish wounded after the battle of Omdurman. He condemned as a 'foul deed' Kitchener's destruction of the Mahdi's tomb and the desecration of his body.

The latter particularly offended people at home. For although he was 'Gordon's murderer', the Mahdi had also been a religious leader. Yet the Commander-in-Chief had toyed with the idea of using his large and shapely skull as an inkstand or a drinking-bowl. Kitchener later claimed that he had returned the Mahdi's skull to the Sudan in a kerosene tin but Churchill did not believe him. As he remarked sardonically, the tin might have contained anything, perhaps ham sandwiches.

Soon, however, Churchill became less critical of Kitchener. He toned down the hostile remarks in his first draft of *The River War* and omitted them altogether from the second edition. Churchill was attempting a political not a literary balancing act – speaking out without being outspoken, attracting attention without causing offence. For he had now determined to leave the army though only, like some *Boy's Own* hero, after winning the Meerut Inter-Regimental polo tournament. Having duly accomplished this, scoring three out of the four goals in the final, he resigned his commission in March 1899. Westminster beckoned. True, Churchill found time to write, to go out in society, even to fall in love with Pamela Plowden, the first of several young ladies who attracted his romantic attentions before he married in 1908. But everything was subordinate to his insatiable ambition. Churchill was quite candid about the craving. He told his mother that it would break his heart if it did not come off, for he had only ambition to cling to. He revealed in *Savrola* that ambition was his sole motive force, a force which he was powerless to resist. J. B. Atkins, a fellow war correspondent, wrote of Churchill at about this time:

> When the prospects of a career like that of his father, Lord Randolph, excited him, then such a gleam shot from him that he was almost transfigured. I had not before encountered this sort of ambition, unabashed, frankly egotistical, communicating its excitement, and extorting sympathy.

So when the opportunity arose for Churchill to contest a by-election at Oldham in the summer of 1899 he grasped it eagerly. Standing in the name of Tory Democracy, he fought a brisk campaign but was narrowly defeated.

Churchill had no time to lament. For as one avenue closed another, equally enticing, opened. It led to South Africa and to the deeds of derring-do which made him famous. When hostilities with the Boers became imminent, in October 1899, Churchill at once arranged to report the war for the *Morning Post* at an initial salary of £250 a month plus expenses. These were generous terms but Churchill deserved them and so earned the paper's gratitude that he was later permitted to revise its reports of his speeches in proof – he once surprised the editor by deleting '(Cheers)', and surprised him again by inserting '(Loud and prolonged applause)'. From the Colonial Secretary, his father's friend Joseph Chamberlain, Churchill procured letters of introduction to everyone of importance. Equipped with the journalist's vital impedimenta – several cases of wines and spirits – he boarded the *Dunottar Castle*, which was also taking the British Commander-in-Chief Sir Redvers Buller to the Cape. Unlike the stately Buller (whose own well-stocked baggage train fatally impeded his progress) Churchill passed the voyage in a frenzy of impatience.

Once in Cape Town he hastily interviewed the war's true author, High Commissioner Sir Alfred Milner, of whom he approved at this time. Then he raced Buller to the Natal front, just south of Ladysmith, now besieged by the Boers. Their advance towards Durban seemed imminent and every day the British sent out reconnaissance sorties. At the invitation of its commander, his friend from India Captain Aylmer Haldane, Churchill accompanied one patrol. It was transported by armoured train. In a characteristic piece of magniloquence Churchill described this as 'a locomotive disguised as a knight-errant; the agent of civilisation in the habiliments of chivalry'. The prosaic Boers were less impressed by the spectacle than by the train's vulnerability and on its return journey they sprang an ambush.

The Boers shot at the train causing it to pick up speed round a bend and crash into an obstacle which they had placed in its path. The front three coaches were derailed but the engine, in the middle of the train, and the rear trucks containing two companies of troops, remained on the track. While Haldane's soldiers held off the Boers, who were pouring deadly fire onto the train, Churchill undertook to clear the line ahead. Unfortunately the leading coaches were jammed together in an awkward fashion and the locomotive had to engage in much shunting to move them. Churchill induced the wounded driver to return to his cab while he himself directed operations from the ground. So exhilarated was Churchill by the struggle that he scarcely noticed the hail of bullets and shrapnel. After about an hour the engine butted its way through the wreckage but it could not return to fetch the troop waggons. The tender was therefore crammed with wounded and the infantry began to retreat on foot, using the engine as a shield. Soon its pace grew too fast for the soldiers. They fell behind, becoming easy meat for the Boers to whom they shortly surrendered. Churchill stopped the locomotive and ran back up the line by himself to hurry on the troops. Instead he encountered a couple of Boers who shot at him. Caught in a narrow cutting, he scrambled up an embankment onto the open veldt and almost at once found himself looking down the wrong end of a Dutchman's rifle. Churchill reached for his Mauser pistol and then remembered that he had left it on the engine. So, with the illest of graces, he allowed himself to be taken prisoner.

More than most Churchill smarted under confinement. It was not that he was badly treated, though being fed initially on roasted strips of newly slaughtered ox made him feel like a cannibal. But he feared that inactivity would breed depression. Also Churchill's pride was hurt by his sudden change of status to convict and thus honorary proletarian. It was his vivid appreciation of the loss of dignity involved in the loss of liberty which later made prison reform one of his priorities as Home Secretary. This explains his immediate determination to get free. Incarcerated in the State Model Schools, a temporary prisoner-of-war camp in Pretoria, Churchill fired off appeals in all directions claiming, somewhat disingenuously, that he was a non-combatant. The Boers were unconvinced though perhaps inclined to treat the son of a lord with clemency. But the release was slow to come. Churchill spent his twenty-fifth birthday 'in durance vile', fretting over the terrible voracity of time. He made plans to escape with Haldane and another officer, plans which he nearly gave away such was his fevered state of excitement.

Behind an outside lavatory they had discovered a small section of the perimeter wall that was invisible to the guards. Churchill was first over it. He hid outside in the darkness waiting for his friends, but something had alerted the sentries.

After an hour or so a voice from the lavatory informed Churchill that it was 'all up'. He resolved to proceed alone. He had no map, no compass and no Afrikaans. But he did have a few bars of chocolate, seventy-five pounds sterling and all the audacity in the world.

Sauntering down the middle of the road, this squat, scrubby, unshaven figure made his way out of Pretoria in an easterly direction. He jumped on board a slow goods train, disembarked before dawn and spent the next day hiding in a grove of trees. His only companion, later to feature in a number of cartoons, was 'a gigantic vulture, who manifested an extravagant interest in my condition, and made hideous and ominous gurglings from time to time'. The next night, in the absence of another train, he trekked onwards becoming increasingly tired and demoralised. Finally in desperation he knocked at the door of a house. To his intense relief the inmate, a colliery manager, turned out to be of British extraction. He fed Churchill and hid him down a rat-infested mine until the hue and cry, stimulated by a twenty-five pound 'Alive or Dead' reward, had abated. With the help of a few English-born miners this brave man then organised the long last lap of the fugitive's journey. Churchill made it concealed in a goods waggon full of wool. Having safely crossed the border into Portuguese East Africa he danced with elation and fired his new pistol into the air. At Lourenço Marques Churchill obtained fresh clothes from the British Consul, telegraphed the news of his escape and took ship for Durban, arriving on 23 December 1899. He was hailed as a hero by the crowd, delighted to have something to cheer after the disasters of Black Week, and he delivered a carefully prepared impromptu speech in front of the Town Hall. Churchill had been in Boer hands for less than a month.

The interval was just enough to make the adventure into a single sensational story. It had all the right ingredients: heroism with aristocratic overtones; controversy, especially over whether Churchill was journalist or soldier; suspense; success. Once again Churchill did not rest on his laurels: he used them as a springboard. He persuaded Buller, quite against new regulations drawn up by the army with Churchill himself in mind, to give him a commission while he continued to act as war correspondent. Sporting, appropriately enough, a

31

cockyolibird feather in his hat, Churchill became a lieutenant in the South African Light Horse. He thus attained his heart's desire, being not only a witness but also a participant in some of the sharpest engagements in the war. Churchill sustained his anomalous role by muting his criticisms of the 'bone-headed' (Botha's word) British generalship. But the Boer War confirmed his view that military intelligence was a contradiction in terms. Churchill was at Spion Kop, for example, where the Omdurman butchery was repeated in reverse – concealed Boers shot down massed British troops like sitting Dervishes. Quite unbidden, Churchill acted as liaison officer between the monocled General Warren and his exhausted front-line subordinate Colonel Thorneycroft. Apparently, however, the brash young lieutenant did not try to persuade Thorneycroft to hold the hill, though victory was just a matter of staying put. Churchill took part in a number of other skirmishes during Buller's lumbering attempts to break the strong Boer position on the Tugela River. And his cavalry squadron was among the first to enter Ladysmith, though Churchill arrived later than he suggested in his bogus eye-witness account of the relief.

The decisive theatre of operations now shifted to the Orange Free State where Lord Roberts was advancing on such a broad front that the Boers were constantly outflanked. Churchill obtained leave from the South African Light Horse and applied for permission to accompany this march. Once again the generals, resenting even the mild criticisms of this military-literary upstart, were obstructive. Churchill was kept dangling at Cape Town where he spent his time hunting jackal with Sir Alfred Milner's pack of hounds under the shadow of Table Mountain. Only after much wire-pulling did Churchill obtain his pass and it was made clear that he owed it entirely to Lord Roberts's former friendship with Lord Randolph. Churchill joined the column of General Sir Ian Hamilton whom he liked and admired as a nonconformist. Trusting his star, sustained by a waggon-load of tinned delicacies and hard liquor, revelling in the landscape, the climate, the companionship and the danger, Churchill had the time of his life. South Africa was a fairyland full of dragons to slay and pots of gold to be won.

Churchill took part in several skirmishes and had a number of hair's-breadth escapes. On one occasion his cavalry unit lost its race with a Boer patrol to occupy a ridge, his horse bolted and he was left alone in the middle of the open veldt with bullets whizzing round him. He would certainly have been killed or wounded but for the courage of a trooper who reined in, gave him a stirrup and galloped off with him. As the Boers were evacuating Johannesburg a mufti-clad Churchill bicycled through the city with dispatches from Hamilton to Roberts, a feat which restored him to favour with the Commander-in-Chief. Churchill was also one of the first into Pretoria. He and his cousin 'Sunny' Marlborough cantered to the prisoner-of-war camp and induced the Boer sentries to throw down their arms. Amid the cheers of his former comrades Churchill tore down the Vierkleur from the flagstaff and replaced it with the Union Jack. It was, as he said, just like the climax to an Adelphi melodrama. After a concluding act of heroism in which he captured a crucial Boer position at the battle of Diamond Hill, Churchill duly took his bow. By the summer of 1900 the war seemed to be over, though as Churchill said, anticipating Mao Tse-tung, the Boer guerrillas had now become fish swimming in the sea of the population – Kitchener could not catch them so he tried to drain the sea. Anyway the 'Khaki Election' was imminent, and Churchill yearned to make his debut on the parliamentary stage.

His reception in England was a triumph. Everywhere he was fêted. He behaved like a lion and was treated as such. Like the young Oscar Wilde sending his sonnets to Mr Gladstone, Churchill invited himself to call on Lord Salisbury. The enthusiasm of the electors of Oldham knew no bounds, especially when they discovered at one meeting that the wife of a miner who had helped Churchill to escape was sitting in the gallery. Joseph Chamberlain (to whom Churchill had earlier expressed his complete confidence in Lord Roberts) came to speak for him and he was duly elected. Capitalising on his success, he in turn addressed meetings for other Conservatives. After his party's victory, in October 1900, he set off on a strenuous paid lecture tour. In Britain and North America (where he met President McKinley and Theodore Roosevelt) he enthralled audiences with the tale of his adventures. Churchill thus amassed £10,000. It was a great sum though not much for an unpaid member of parliament with grand ideas and a pronounced love of luxury. What is more his mother had recently married a dim, handsome, impecunious young Guards officer named George Cornwallis-West (one paper, Churchill told her in a flash of anger, likened it to Chief Lobengula's wedding a white woman) and she was making further inroads into the depleted family fortune. But Churchill never allowed lack of money to cramp his style. He was confident that with those pliant instruments, the pen and the tongue, he could pay his way in the bright new political career which had dawned with the century.

The twentieth century, as George Steevens wrote in the *Daily Mail*, was in Churchill's marrow. He had the demagogic skill and self-advertising flair which would infallibly bring success in the new age. Steevens's sharp assessment pointed towards what Churchill himself had already spotted as his 'mental flaw'. In a letter to his mother he admitted to caring less for the principles he professed than for the impression his words created and the reputation they brought him. In short – and here Churchill anticipated the charge which was so often to be levelled against him – he adapted his facts to his phrases. This was a perceptive, and a rare, piece of self-analysis. But Churchill went on to modify it in a way that many future critics would have found unacceptable. A great cause or a burning issue, he claimed, would purge him of insincere verbal posturing. For 'I believe that *au fond* I am genuine.' Here he was surely right. His guilelessness was well displayed over the Boer War. He supported it at first. Later he deplored its brutality. Finally he advocated a generous peace and implemented a conciliatory settlement. Churchill was also honest about war in general. It was, he knew, a barbarous and squalid business. But unlike many humanitarians whose instincts were revolted by the carnage, Churchill acknowledged that war also brought out the noblest qualities in its heroes. It was both savage and sublime. Moreover, he could not and would not disguise his own horrified addiction to this delectable experience. War was at once a glorious calling, a gentleman's game and the most romantic of all adventures. Certainly he always looked back with radiant happiness to his active service as soldier and war correspondent. These were his champagne years, when the proximity of death made him fizz and sparkle with life.

CHAPTER III

HOOLIGAN TO MINISTER

CHURCHILL delivered his maiden speech to the House of Commons only four days after taking his seat, in February 1901. It was 'a terrible, thrilling, yet delicious experience'. He concluded by thanking the House for its attention which he owed not to his own merits but to 'a certain splendid memory' cherished by many members. This graceful tribute was an announcement that Churchill was his father's political heir and proposed to come into his kingdom. Without delay Churchill took up the cause over which Lord Randolph had submitted his fatal resignation, military expenditure. In a couple of months Churchill had distanced himself from the Conservatives by joining a small group of Tory dissidents, in their way successors to Lord Randolph's Fourth Party. This radical band, led by Lord Hugh Cecil, was known as the 'Hughligans' or 'Hooligans'. Churchill also espoused Tory Democracy, that capacious portmanteau which enabled him to carry off the most attractive policies from each party. His initial choice, with its emphasis on social progress, seemed to be more democratic than Tory. But in private he was already canvassing the formation of a middle party which would avoid the extremes of capitalism and socialism. Churchill never had a blind loyalty to either of the major parties he joined. They were simply vehicles for his own advancement.

This is not to suggest that he was unprincipled. On the contrary, Churchill saw himself from the first as a national not a party politician. Like his ancestor the first Duke of Marlborough, he was primarily a servant of the crown. Like the great Whig aristocrats, of whom he was in a sense the last, Churchill regarded himself as a natural ruler. And he knew that only from a place of power could he promote the country's interests. The need was urgent. For the Boer War had tarnished the gilt of Empire, revealed that Britain's isolation was more dangerous than splendid and exposed her inefficiency in a dozen different ways. Churchill, like many others, determined to make his nation and his race fitter, if not fittest, to survive. He began to preach the gospel of social reform. He advocated old age pensions, a graduated income tax, universal suffrage, payment of MPs, state intervention to relieve poverty, health and educational advance. These were certainly principles, but they seemed more Liberal than Tory. The Conservative government, now led by Lord Salisbury's nephew Arthur Balfour, looked askance at its noisy young recruit. Even the Hooligans, fond of political mischief as they were, came to regard Churchill as something of a juvenile delinquent.

This was due as much to the way he spoke as to what he said. Like his father he was frequently rude and sometimes brutal, qualities made more offensive by the fact that all his speeches were carefully honed and polished in advance. Churchill was a superb orator but an indifferent debater. He expressed his ideas in vivid words but he could be nonplussed if the stream of his eloquence was interrupted. So in public speaking he relied on memory rather than on spontaneous inspiration. He could repeat a column of print accurately after having read it only four times and his practice was to write out his speeches in advance and learn them by heart. In 1904 he lost the thread of his argument while holding forth to the House of Commons and broke down. Members wondered whether this was an early sign that he would go the way of his father, but Churchill guarded against a recurrence of the disaster by always thereafter clutching full notes of his memorised speeches.

Rhetoric was the most powerful weapon in his armoury and he took immense trouble with it. He thundered out his perorations in the bath. At his mother's country mansion he had an 'aerial summerhouse' built in the branches of an old lime tree where he rehearsed his harangues. He also practised them on his friends who complained that he confused dialogue with soliloquy. The society hostess Ettie Grenfell told Arthur Balfour: 'Winston leads general conversation on the hearth rug addressing himself in the looking glass – a sympathetic and admiring audience.' Like Walpole complaining about the unruliness of that 'terrible cornet of horse' William Pitt, Balfour was to protest that with all this preparation Churchill ought to be less violent and more considered in his speeches.

The trouble was that words were Churchill's toys and he could not resist playing with them. He was mesmerised and enslaved by glittering phrases. They put him off his stroke literally as well as figuratively. Once, having been up, he lost a game of golf to Asquith because his mind became entirely pre-occupied with a sparkling new form of words. Churchill displayed his gems compulsively, however sharp their cutting edge. Although he admired Lord Rosebery, Churchill felt bound to remark that he diverted himself 'with those exquisite trivialities which titillate the palate of the political epicure'. Like his father, Churchill resorted freely to the picturesque imagery of the countryside thus, in the opinion of refined persons, coarsening the texture of political debate. He compared the Liberal party to a 'toad in the hole' and the German fleet to 'rats in a hole'. However serious the question Churchill found it difficult to repress bubbles of schoolboy levity. When discussing the chance of Joseph Chamberlain's being asked to form a government by the King, Churchill had to cast doubt on whether Chamberlain 'would think such a formality necessary'. Churchill also had an ineradicable fondness for verbal jokes and puns, the more outrageous the better. On his East African safari he remarked, 'sofari, sogoody'. Later he bewildered workmen bringing him some bitumen by asking, 'Oh, is this the bit you mean?' As Prime Minister he refused to see a Greek politician called Kanellopoulos, saying simply: 'Can'tellopoulos'. Indeed he became so enamoured of the expression that he wallowed in his bath throwing the sponge up and down to a chant of 'Kanellopoulos, Can'tellopoulos, Kanellopoulos'.

It was the urchin in Churchill which made the Hooligan acceptable. Just as his speeches revealed the rough, obstreperous side of his nature so they also exposed his charm and zest. His language was so fresh, his manner so rollicking, his ideas so audacious, that he carried audiences along with him despite his abrasiveness. He fascinated them not only by demagogic antics and self-advertising tricks but by beaming personal magnetism. His whole demeanour communicated animal vitality, rich self-approval and wicked good-humour. Invariably when making a joke or coining a phrase he would exhibit symptoms of 'preliminary relish', twitching his feet, cocking his nose, compressing his lips, hugging himself. He seldom laughed. But an impish grin would light up his cherubic features. It was the gleam of the incorrigible schoolboy. In short, the ragamuffin aspect of his personality was always on display. It was this that reminded Wilfrid Scawen Blunt of Lord Randolph. Blunt noted in his diary for 1903 that there was in Winston 'the same gaminerie and contempt for the conventional and the same engaging plain-spokenness and readiness to understand'. Actually the last capacity is doubtful: Churchill was too egotistical to comprehend others or even to take much interest in them. As the journalist A. G. Gardiner wrote: 'He is his own superman and is so absorbed in himself and in his own fiery purposes that he does not pay others the compliment of even being aware of them.' Churchill did not volunteer empathy: he compelled sympathy. In its glow he expanded, his confidence grew more overweening and he began to sway his hearers. He persuaded seventeen Conservative MPs to vote against the government's expensive and impractical scheme for army reform – 'an ill-considered conglomeration of absurdities' – thus effectively killing the measure. Within two or three years Churchill was being described as one of the foremost parliamentary orators. He was likened to Mr Gladstone and discussed as a future Prime Minister.

Certainly Churchill had his eye on the main chance and he later admitted that he would probably have remained a Conservative had Balfour promoted him. But at this stage Churchill seemed to have no chance at all in the Tory party, which became increasingly uncongenial to him. Anyway Conservatism itself seemed bound, after its long reign, to give way to Liberalism. Churchill admired the Hooligan leader, Lord Hugh Cecil, for his fine mind and his bold, uncompromising attitudes. But he also appreciated the essential sterility of that mind and the reactionary nature of those attitudes. Lord Hugh devoted frantic efforts, for example, to resisting the repeal of antique prohibitions laid down in the Prayer Book's 'Table of Kindred and Affinity', so much so that even Churchill briefly allowed himself to become seduced by Cecilian terrors about what would happen if everyone started marrying his deceased wife's sister. But though the knight-errant in Cecil appealed to Churchill, the bigot did not. For he was a pragmatist as much as a romantic. Churchill saw the Hooligans as a means of storming the closet and obtaining office. As befitted Lord Salisbury's son, Lord Hugh was a loyal Conservative at heart. He was unorthodox only in affirming the high-church Tory fundamentalism of a former age. As such he condemned himself to the diehard's fate, perpetual opposition. The sound of Lord Hugh's fluting, pedantic voice caused dogs to vomit and, metaphorically speaking at least, it tended to produce the same reaction in human beings. By 1903 Churchill was detaching himself from this unhelpful ally, who anyway found him impossible to work with on account of his 'lamentable instability'. However, they remained friends and Lord Hugh was to be the best man at Churchill's wedding.

In 1903 Joseph Chamberlain raised the great issue over which Churchill broke with the Conservative party. Chamberlain asserted that Britain should protect her threatened economic pre-eminence behind tariff barriers and bind together her empire in a customs union. Churchill had long sensed the divisive possibilities of such a campaign and he at once entered the fray as outspoken champion of the Tory free-traders. Actually he had little interest in, and less grasp of, fiscal matters. He had earlier voted without any fuss for a minor protectionist measure. In this lack of consistency he resembled his father, but Lord Randolph had finally nailed his colours to the popular mast of free trade and Winston followed suit. Balfour, it was said, 'nailed his colours to the fence'. He devised a compromise policy of 'retaliation', which meant that Britain could impose duties on the imports of those countries which taxed her exports. This formula, intended to preserve party unity, satisfied no one. Churchill in particular ridiculed its ambiguity and disingenuousness. He crusaded against tariff reform throughout the country, even raising his banner in its citadel,

Birmingham Town Hall, where he denounced the claim that protection meant a fairer distribution of wealth as 'unspeakable humbug'. Secure in his conviction that gentlemen make the best political mud-slingers he assailed the devotees of protection within his own party, likening them to topers entering a public house. In March 1904 Conservative back-benchers staged a mass walk-out while Churchill was addressing the Commons, a symbol of the detestation in which he was widely held. Two months later he crossed the floor of the House and joined the Liberals. Tories called him 'the Blenheim Rat'.

Churchill spent the next two and half years beating the free trade drum, establishing himself as one of the foremost speakers on the subject in and out of parliament. But no mere feats of oratory could absorb his terrific energies and he continued the literary work which was to be the rewarding and well-rewarded business of his life out of office. He wrote his father's biography. This fine book, imbued with intense filial loyalty, portrayed Lord Randolph as a tragic hero destroyed by the Conservative party. There was no trace in Winston's two volumes of the 'half-mad' 'arch-fiend' whom, say, Arthur Balfour had known. Instead Winston softened Lord Randolph's more brutal asperities and imposed a consistency on his mercurial course, presenting him as the flail of reactionaries and the champion of a liberalism which almost amounted to Liberalism. Thus the book was also a justification of Winston's own political manoeuvres, especially his secession from the Tories. But Winston's double partisanship, on behalf of his father and himself, was so skilfully integrated into his work that it did not have the air of being propaganda. On publication in 1906 it was widely acclaimed as a masterpiece and it has since been recognised as a classic. Whatever its status, this glowing tribute to Lord Randolph seems somehow to have exorcised the paternal daemon which had long haunted Winston. He now stepped out of the long shadow cast by his father.

During these back-bench years Churchill also developed his huge capacity for enjoying the pleasures of upper-class life. He spent £400 a year equipping himself to hunt foxes. Having once resembled an untidy dissenting parson, he now became something of a dandy. He even bought special silk underclothes from the Army and Navy Stores so as not to chafe his soft, hairless skin. In 1901 he learnt to drive a horseless carriage, a hazardous undertaking for he manoeuvred it like a squadron of cavalry. Churchill also played cards in a dashingly romantic fashion and he savoured the thrill of gambling more money than he could afford: at Deauville casino he was known to stay at the tables until five o'clock in the morning. Wallowing in the lavish hospitality provided at Edwardian country house parties, rich food, copious draughts of brandy, pungent cigars, Churchill became an unashamed hedonist. But he was by no means always a congenial guest.

At balls Churchill danced only with married ladies and at dinners he talked mainly to distinguished men, often ignoring his immediate neighbours, sometimes shouting, even moving his place, in order to do so. If he could not hold forth he might sink into a portentous silence. He was gauche with women, frequently brusque or snubbing, though capable of opening up like a sunflower if his interest was aroused. He liked to invest his histrionic talents in productive themes, preferably grand ones – his own career, for example – and he could not deal in the small change of chit-chat. Beatrice Webb met Churchill at a dinner in 1903 and described him as 'a self-conscious and bumptious person with a certain personal magnetism, restless, shallow in knowledge, reactionary in opinions, but with courage and originality – more the American speculator in type than the English aristocrat. He talked the whole time of his electioneering and himself and seemed interested in other matters to a very minor degree.'

With his snub-nose and his baby-face Churchill was sometimes called ugly. He was short – five foot six and a half – and physically unimpressive though he had beautiful hands, about which he was rather vain. They were soft and ivory-white and looked as though they had never been used. But despite his small stature and his harsh egotism Churchill was not unattractive to women. Some he clearly fascinated, especially those who detected the hidden virtues beneath the obvious faults. However he had too heroic a conception of himself to engage in petty intrigues with married women of his own class let alone in furtive affairs with shopgirls or prostitutes, who might perhaps cause him to go the way of his father. As for young ladies, they were to be revered from afar. (Lady Randolph Churchill herself knew of only two or three girls in society who had not been virgins at the altar.) In fact, his few fleeting romantic attachments apart, Churchill seemed largely oblivious to the possibilities of intimate friendship at all. He even claimed to value friendship less highly than comradeship, the bond between brothers-in-arms. His warm affections were concentrated on members of his own family and he was perhaps closest to the Duke of Marlborough, 'Sunny' by nickname though stormy by nature. Churchill simply ignored the fact that the Duke was ruled, as his second wife said, by 'black, vicious, personal pride like a disease'.

At the end of 1905 the Conservatives, long fixed in a state of 'mesmeric trance', as Churchill said, over the issue of tariff reform, resigned. Sir Henry Campbell-Bannerman formed a new government in which Churchill was appointed Parliamentary Under-Secretary for the Colonies. The Liberals then won a massive victory at the polls. Churchill was elected for a Manchester seat, having fought a characteristically dynamic campaign. It was one that further embittered his relations with the Tories. As the former Minister George Wyndham remarked, 'I would rather sweep the streets than be Winston Churchill.' Even Liberals found him hard to endure. One fellow guest at a Christmas house party wrote of 'Winston making a political speech which lasted without intermission for 8 days. He was the autocrat – not only of the breakfast table – but of the lunch, tea, dinner, bridge and billiard tables.' In the new parliament Churchill was charged with responsibility for presenting departmental policy to the Commons, the Colonial Secretary being a peer. Churchill rightly described his chief, Lord Elgin, formerly Viceroy of India, as an 'unassertive fellow'. But Elgin's excessively assertive subordinate, casting off the frustrations of opposition and throwing himself into his first political job, was by no means allowed to dominate the Colonial Office. Churchill addressed Elgin like a public meeting and sent him long, declamatory minutes. But though he often formulated colonial policy, Churchill could not dictate it. One famous story sums up his relationship with the unimaginative Elgin: Churchill concluded an elaborate memorandum with the flourish, 'These are my views,' to which the Colonial Secretary retorted in the margin, 'But not mine.' Churchill was loyal to his chief and grateful for what he learnt from him. But there were serious strains. A rampageous, high-mettled thoroughbred was yoked to a stolid Scottish plough-horse. Inevitably

Churchill tugged at the reins and champed at the bit.

What made him particularly impatient was Elgin's dourly pragmatic view of colonial responsibilities. Both men believed that the empire was, in Churchill's words, 'a great moral force on the side of progress'. Indeed, what Elgin called the British 'mission as pioneers of civilisation' was an article of Liberal faith, as was the convenient belief that trade was an instrument of peace. But Elgin was prepared to temporise over some of the darker aspects of imperial rule in a way that seemed objectionable to Churchill, who was full of youthful idealism. Elgin was often willing to endorse harsh decisions, particularly over the punishment of 'savages', taken by the 'man on the spot'. Churchill was eager to overrule anyone who sinned against the canons of benevolent paternalism by which he reckoned the empire should be governed. Witness his outraged (and outrageously ironical) protest about the summary detention of the troublesome Bechuana chief Sekgoma:

> If we are going to take men who have committed no crime, and had no trial, and condemn them to life-long imprisonment and exile in the name of 'state policy' why stop there? Why not poison Sekgoma by some painless drug? No argument that will justify his deportation to the Seychelles, will not also sustain his removal to a more sultry clime. If we are to employ medieval processes, at least let us show medieval courage and thoroughness. Think of the expense that would be saved. A dose of laudanum, costing at the outside five shillings, is all that is required. . . . If however, as I apprehend, Secretary of State would be averse to this procedure, the next best thing is to obey the law, and to act with ordinary morality, however inconvenient.

Elgin was merely annoyed by this, and Sekgoma was detained.

Churchill had come a long way from the North West frontier: he condemned 'the disgusting butchery of natives'. He had renounced Hooliganism: indeed he denounced brutally racialist Natal as 'the hooligan of the Empire'. Churchill was categorical about the criterion which should determine colonial policy: 'Let us have only one measure for treating people subject to our rule, and that a measure of justice.' He would not permit justice to be thwarted because of 'the inconvenience inseparable from the reparation of injustice', or to be over-ruled by 'legal technicalities and the pedantries of etiquette'. Nor did he allow it to be obscured by euphemism. He

43

condemned Colonel Lugard's 'pacification' of northern Nigeria in 1906 with biting sarcasm: 'the whole enterprise is liable to be misrepresented by persons unacquainted with Imperial terminology as the murdering of natives and stealing of their lands.'

Churchill discovered that it was less easy to sustain his high ideals in practice. During the election he had stirred up Liberal rage at the treatment of indentured Chinese labourers in South African gold mines. When in government he found that the problem was difficult to resolve. He also asserted, in a celebrated phrase, that the Chinese could not be classified as slaves without some risk of 'terminological inexactitude'. Furthermore, although Churchill deplored the fact that Milner had illegally sanctioned the flogging of coolies, he found himself defending the 'disconsolate Proconsul' from a Commons motion of censure, admittedly in language so patronising that it caused undying resentment. Finally, the first major political achievement in which Churchill had a hand, the granting of responsible self-government to the Transvaal and the Orange Free State, was deeply flawed. For magnanimity towards the Boers involved perfidy towards the blacks.

Churchill acknowledged that the imperial parliament had a moral responsibility towards the Africans who would be treated harshly, if not exploited cruelly, under Boer rule. But he was hampered by the peace treaty with the Boers which prevented Britain from extending the franchise to 'natives' (in other words, to 'all men of colour'). And he was a prisoner of the almost universal European conviction that black men, because they existed on a lower scale of evolutionary development, required white mentors. Churchill never changed his opinion about the stern duty thus imposed on the imperial race or about the essential inferiority of 'niggers' and 'blackamoors'. He continued to use these opprobrious terms all his life, presumably in order to demonstrate his refusal to abandon old-fashioned racial prejudice in the face of what he took to be new-fangled egalitarian cant. Like his father, Churchill would also rail in private against impertinent Indian 'baboos' and at the Cairo Conference in 1921 he wanted Egyptians to be excluded from his hotel. During the early 1930s he refused to meet members of the Congress party because he did not want his views on India 'disturbed by any bloody Indians'. Churchill's view is well summed up in *My African Journey*: the natives were 'lighthearted, tractable, if brutish children . . . capable of being instructed and raised from their present degradation' by the 'impartial and august administration of the crown'.

Churchill's colonial tour started as a 'purely sporting and private expedition' and, to Elgin's somewhat naive surprise, drifted into what was 'essentially an official progress'. His departure in the autumn of 1907 established the tone. Shortly before setting off he accompanied the journalist-politician Charles Masterman to the *Daily News* office and helped to complete his article.

> He ended up with 'where is the statesman to be found who is adequate to the times?' or words to that effect; expecting I think only one answer. But at parting he said, 'If I'm eaten by some horrible tsetse fly in East Africa don't forget this is my last message to the nation!!'

Actually Churchill bombarded the Colonial Office with messages of all kinds, so much so that the permanent Under-Secretary, Sir Francis Hopwood, was to complain to Lord Elgin, 'He is most tiresome to deal with and I fear will give trouble – as his father did – in any position to which he may be called. The restless energy, uncontrollable desire for notoriety and lack of moral perception make him an anxiety indeed.'

Churchill was blithely unconcerned about giving trouble. On the outward voyage he made his devoted secretary Edward Marsh work for fourteen hours a day in the blazing heat of the Red Sea. He kept the Governor of Uganda awake at night by dictating in his bath. He quizzed busy officials about the progress and prospects of their territories. The result of all this toil was a series of recommendations (some implemented, others wildly impractical) which were mainly designed to make the empire pay. Somaliland, for example, was more trouble than it was worth and should be abandoned. Uganda, by contrast, was a pearl of great price. It was ideal for 'a practical experiment in state socialism'. Churchill's plan was beautiful in its simplicity. The labour of the native population should be 'organised and directed by superior intelligence and external capital'. The land would then bring forth a rich crop of cotton which should be sent to Lancashire. There, to the profit of Churchill's own constituency perhaps, it would be manufactured into 'civilized attire' and re-exported to Uganda, thus rescuing the natives from their 'primordial nakedness' and rendering them 'less crudely animal'.

Churchill had to preside over levées at which, he complained, painted 'savages', their heads adorned with feathers and their bodies with shells, danced 'in a monotonous hopping dirge' round his chair. Nevertheless he was determined to enjoy the tour. He and his party travelled from Mombasa to Nairobi on what was envisaged as a spur of the Cape-to-Cairo railway. There was plenty of game. Indeed, man-eating lions had delayed the construction of what they too regarded as a feeder line. So Churchill rigged up a seat on the locomotive's cow-catcher, brought the train to a halt when he saw anything worth shooting and let fly. He slew game of all sorts but his most valued bag was a rhinoceros, 'a peaceful herbivore' as Churchill acknowledged, which he forced into conflict 'by an unprovoked assault with murderous intent'. He later killed several more of the white variety. He was much impressed by the tremendous vitality of 'these brutes', which thundered on like huge engines in spite of the heavy bullets smashing into them. Churchill must have been quite a good shot. At any rate Edward Marsh had enough confidence to accompany him on one rhino hunt armed with nothing more lethal than a pink umbrella.

Churchill was fascinated by Uganda for other than economic reasons. It was a 'glittering Equatorial slum' whose forests he found much more intoxicating than those of India or Cuba. He marvelled at 'the vast scale and awful fecundity of the natural processes'. Even the telegraph poles broke into bud. Of course, such exuberant fertility had its drawbacks and Churchill muffled himself up like an Eskimo, wearing long, soft leather boots and gloves in order to ward off the hordes of mosquitoes. Other insects provided some compensation. Churchill adored the huge gaudy butterflies. He was intrigued by the manoeuvres of the ant armies and could not resist interfering with their columns, jumping nimbly backwards when they attacked him. Still, if East Africa was an exciting playground it was also a tropical estate. Churchill harped on the idea of developing its wealth and harnessing its power. But on his return to England, via the Nile, he was struck by the fact that no might or magnificence abroad could compensate the mother country for 'the effects of misery, squalor, vice and social injustice at home'.

This theme, and the corresponding need for welfare legislation, had been preoccupying Churchill for some time. It was therefore appropriate that he should become President of the Board of Trade in the government which Asquith formed on Campbell-Bannerman's resignation (through ill-health) in April 1908. Newly appointed ministers were then obliged to seek re-election and the Conservatives opposed Churchill in Manchester with all the bitterness reserved for a renegade. He replied in kind ('and when my friend in the gallery says "rot" he is no doubt expressing very fully what he has in his mind') but was defeated. Immediately he accepted an invitation to contest a vacant seat at Dundee. Churchill took his stand on the high ground of principle: 'Socialism seeks to pull down wealth; Liberalism seeks to raise up poverty.' But he addressed himself mainly to males, who had votes – 'men embrace women', he quipped. So some of his speeches were ruined by the Suffragettes. One 'virulent virago' clanged a handbell during his perorations, about whose immaculate delivery he was extremely sensitive. Nevertheless he was safely elected, becoming at the age of thirty-three a fully-fledged cabinet minister.

This was only the second most important event of the year in Churchill's life. In the spring of 1908 he came to know, and to fall in love with, Clementine Hozier. She was beautiful and clever, though her fortune was not equal to her face and her breeding did not match her brains. True her mother Blanche, herself a striking woman of many lovers, was eldest daughter of the tenth Earl of Airlie. But Blanche's husband, Henry Hozier, sprang from humbler stock and worked for Lloyds of London, the insurance under-writers. In any case it is not certain that Hozier was Clementine's father – Wilfrid Scawen Blunt claimed that only he knew the identity of her true sire. Clementine's childhood had been blighted by her parents' quarrels and separation. Her education, something she ardently desired, had been neglected. She had spent much time living abroad in impoverished circumstances and on one occasion Hozier had attempted to kidnap her from Lady Blanche. In consequence Clementine became fiercely independent. On the surface she seemed calm and serene but underneath nerve storms often raged. Seething emotions sometimes defied a strong will. Clementine had already broken off at least two engagements before she met Churchill and she nearly repeated the process with him. However she was dazzled by his daemon. Her reserve and shyness melted in the face of his passionate declarations. He in turn was captivated by Clementine's grace, vivacity, modesty and virtue. Still, his wooing was scarcely well calculated to win her. It was hasty, careless and impetuous, almost another by-election to add to those of Manchester and Dundee. Churchill forgot to send her a promised present, his biography of Lord Randolph. He was late for his betrothal assignation. At the wedding, which took place at St Margaret's Westminster, he talked politics with Lloyd George in the vestry. During the honeymoon he revised *My African Journey* and wrote interminable letters on political matters. It was an unromantic way to conduct a romance, particularly for someone as romantic as Churchill.

Nevertheless Clementine was the rock on which Churchill's life-long domestic happiness was built. His fidelity to her was absolute and her own never really faltered despite a brief flirtation elsewhere during the 1930s. Whatever the triumphs and disasters of his political career Churchill knew that he could always rely on his wife's devotion, courage and integrity. Yet in spite of her sometimes furious partisanship on Churchill's behalf, their political views were essentially at variance. Churchill was an 'aboriginal Tory' who had been drawn into the opposing camp by a mixture of personal ambition and paternalist compassion; Clementine remained, through thick and thin, a Liberal. These and more personal differences inevitably led to rows. But both saw to it that the sun never went down on their wrath. Churchill was often difficult and occasionally impossible, here playing the spoilt child, there the capricious despot. Clementine did not indulge him though she kept him well cosseted. She was also a model of tact. When he shouted her down in argument she imitated Jane Carlyle and sent him reasoned memoranda.

Clementine herself was awkward and prickly. She made plain her dislike for Churchill's raffish friends. She hated the French Riviera and the gambling tables, both of which he adored. She never really reconciled herself to the extravagance of living in Chartwell, the much-loved country house which he bought in 1922. She lacked her husband's energy and at times she acted as a drag on his originality. She was priggish where he was whiggish. Asquith, who preferred spicier company, actually rated her a bore. If so, she was a sane and humane bore. She pleaded against Churchill's inclination to use the iron fist instead of the velvet glove. Only a month after he became Prime Minister in 1940 she fearlessly chided him for the brutal manner he adopted towards colleagues and subordinates. Clementine's influence over her spouse was not great – nobody's was. Churchill was his own man entirely. But through the sweet offices of love she did manage to soften and humanise his personality. Without her he might have become a harsh political calculating-machine. His tender letters are eloquent testimony to the rapture which 'Kat' brought to 'Pug'. Equally expressive in their way were 'Pug's' greetings of 'wow-wow' in the hall when he arrived home and 'Kat's' enthusiastic answering miaows from upstairs. As Churchill wrote at the conclusion of *My Early Life*, 'I married and lived happily ever afterwards.'

CHAPTER IV

YOUNG RADICAL TO

FIRST LORD

WINSTON Churchill liked to say that he was the Board of Trade, for it no longer existed as a board and had a quorum of one. In fact for Churchill the Board of Trade was essentially a springboard. From it he intended to leap to higher offices. As that grey eminence Lord Esher noted, Churchill 'wanted to push to the front of the Cabinet. He thinks himself Napoleon.' Churchill never concealed his intention to reach the top of the greasy pole, though equally he never sought to promote himself by intrigue, being in any case far too transparent to make a Machiavelli. He was as open about his ambitions as he was candid about his capacities. Charles Masterman recorded Churchill as saying in 1908, 'Sometimes I feel as if I could lift the whole world on my shoulders.'

Contemporaries did not rate his abilities quite that high. They were nevertheless amazed and impressed by his initial performance in cabinet. Beatrice Webb, earlier acidulous, now described Churchill as 'brilliantly able – more than a phrasemonger'. In June 1908 Lord Esher considered him 'clever and ingenious, but wild and impractical'; by September he ascribed to the young minister 'real political fire' and endorsed Sir Edward Grey's view that he was a genius whose faults would be forgotten in his achievements. Masterman himself reckoned Churchill 'an extraordinarily gifted boy with genius and astonishing energy'. A. G. Gardiner found Churchill at thirty-four 'the most interesting figure in politics, his life a crowded drama of action, his courage high, his vision unclouded, his boats burned'. J. A. Spender, editor of the *Westminster Gazette*, said that no other man lived 'in such a perpetual state of mental excitement', or entertained 'so many vivid and jostling ideas at the same time', or was able 'to be so honest and brilliant about them'. Others paid tribute to Churchill's flair for exploiting each major political issue as it arose and matching his ambition to the hour. It is true that, as his colleague John Morley said, Churchill now and then mistook a frothy bubble for a huge wave. But he invariably perceived the ebb and flow of the tide. He might ride high or he might plunge to disaster. But, like Phaeton in the chariot of the sun, Churchill always hitched his fate to a mighty cause.

The greatest Edwardian cause was social reform. The Boer War had sparked off terrible fears of incipient national decay, particularly by exposing the inferior physique of the imperial race, many of whom were not fit to fight. Influential books – and Churchill read both academic reports and muck-raking exposés – revealed the misery of the people of the abyss, all the more poignant when contrasted with the fleshpots of the ostentatiously rich. To take but a single instance: malnutrition among the poor had not been so rife since the great famines of Tudor times whereas the gluttony of Edward VII and his circle made Lucullus seem austere. At last, however, it looked as though the long-posed condition-of-England question might be answered. Not that the Liberals were particularly keen on social reform, despite subsequent propaganda. As traditional champions of economic individualism they tended to dismiss Churchill's argument that radical measures would take the wind out of Socialist sails. Nevertheless reform was in the air. Churchill, ever alert to the beat of history's wings, could sense it.

Many people were agitating for improving legislation on 'scientific' lines, most notably the Fabian Society. This was devoted to the gradual infusion of socialist ideas into the policies of all political parties, and its most distinguished members were George Bernard Shaw, H. G. Wells and Sidney and Beatrice Webb. Churchill's objection to being shut up in a soup-kitchen with Mrs Webb is well-known. Less well-known is the fact that ever since 1905 he had attended the suppers she gave at 41 Grosvenor Road, despite the frugality of the fare – Beatrice was 'a rigid anti-flesh-fish-egg-alcohol-coffee-and-sugar-eater' and Sidney Webb only got a square meal when his plate was hidden from her view by a vase of flowers. Later Beatrice claimed that she and her partner had been responsible for converting Churchill to their political creed. As always she exaggerated their influence: in the disillusioned words of H. G. Wells, the Fabians no more 'permeated' the major political parties than a mouse might be said to permeate a cat. Churchill took from them and from other reformers what he wanted, not what they offered. Probably he was most impressed by the example of a flourishing welfare state already in existence. Germany pointed the way out of darkest England. Churchill, pricked on by ambition and convinced that providence had preserved him for a great task, responded ardently to the signs of the times.

The plans which he drew up at the Board of Trade were both more progressive and more comprehensive than those of any other Liberal minister, not excepting his ally Lloyd George. For example, the government was already initiating old age pensions: Churchill wanted 'to rescue the children'. His cardinal aim, however, was to effect a radical improvement, through state action, in the quality of life of those at the base of the social pyramid, so increasing 'the stability of the whole'. This involved establishing a minimum standard of wages and conditions, compulsory education to the age of seventeen, the nationalisation of railways and the setting up of state-run industries such as afforestation to provide work for the unemployed. Above all Churchill was concerned about those who 'fall from the scaffolding of modern life'. He proposed to spread nets over the abyss. Legislation should be passed to prevent exploitation of the financially defenceless, to decasualise labour, to help those out of work find jobs and to insure against sickness and unemployment. Of course, Churchill did not want to remove the spur of competition. But, he argued, the automatic payment of benefits, even to malingerers, would strengthen 'the impulse of self-preservation' by 'affording the means of struggle'. Any 'residieum' [*sic*], Churchill told Asquith in a remarkable statement of his ideas, 'must be curatively treated exactly as if they were hospital patients'. Such policies might almost be labelled socialist, though Churchill, no more friendly than his father to the notion of social equality, intended to impose them *de haut en bas*. At any rate he now seemed to espouse not so much Tory Democracy as radical paternalism.

Whatever its name Churchill's ambitious plans entitle him to be considered one of the founding fathers of the welfare state. But he was only able to complete a small part of his programme. He fixed minimum pay and conditions in various 'sweated' industries. He set up a chain of public labour exchanges which helped men to find work without 'tramping' in search of it. These exchanges were, in Churchill's words, 'the Intelligence Department of Labour', and they were to be a vital element in the defensive system of unemployment insurance which Lloyd George established in 1911. Such martial metaphors sprang easily to Churchill's lips. Certainly he regarded his social reforms as a military campaign fought on several fronts. For example, he employed 'personal discourtesy' as his 'chief weapon' in a cabinet which had known, according to one colleague, 'no electricity' before his arrival.

Churchill contended vigorously against ministers anxious to spend money on the army and navy. Indeed he took the struggle into their camp, the first of many occasions when he interfered with departments not his own and behaved as though the reversion of the premiership was in his pocket. Churchill ridiculed the German 'menace' as 'nightmare nonsense' and proposed a scheme for reducing expenditure on the armed services which the Secretary of State for War, R. B. Haldane, had the utmost difficulty in resisting. As A. G. Gardiner wrote, the whole spirit of Churchill's politics was military: 'The smell of powder is about his path, and wherever he appears one seems to hear the crash of musketry, and to feel the hot breath of battle.'

Churchill's main enemy, of course, was the Conservative party. It was, he asserted, not a party but a conspiracy of the foes of progress, 'old doddering peers, cute financial magnates, clever wire-pullers, big brewers with bulbous noses'. The invective was provoked by the Conservatives' interruption of his programme of reforms. In 1909 they provoked a crisis by rejecting Lloyd George's 'People's Budget' through their majority in the House of Lords. Actually Churchill had private reservations about the budget though publicly he supported proposals to tax the luxuries of the rich in order to supply the necessities of the poor. He was particularly worried about the levy on land – the Chancellor thought he might be happier if the Duke of Marlborough could be exempted. Lloyd George enjoyed teasing Churchill, whose appreciation of jokes at his own expense was much slower than his ready wit and his ironic self-mockery might suggest. At dinner once the Chancellor outlined revolutionary procedures which he intended to adopt after the budget, including barricades, tumbrils and a guillotine in Trafalgar Square. Churchill grew increasingly alarmed and indignant until Lloyd George suggested that he would have a splendid opportunity to figure as a second Napoleon, when he seemed to think that there might be something in the scheme after all. Flights of fancy apart, Churchill was firmly wedded to the social order. The peers seemed to endanger it. By asserting their obsolete right to throw out the lower house's financial measures they had declared a class war. Churchill was ready to join battle at once upon the 'simple issue of aristocratic rule against representative government'.

In the first Peers *v*. People election campaign, precipitated by the Lords' refusal to accept the budget at the end of 1909, Churchill took an especially combative part. He attacked the 'feudal assembly' as 'a prejudiced Chamber, hereditary, non-elected, irresponsible, irremediable and all composed of one class, and that class, as Mr Bagehot said, not the best class'. He ridiculed the peers as heaven-born and God-granted legislators studying ' "Ruff's Guide" and other blue books', resolving 'the problems of Empire and Epsom'. The case for abolishing the Lords' power of veto was so good, he thought, that it should be stated with 'ferocious moderation'. In fact he stated it with moderate ferocity. Only Lloyd George, who compared the aristocracy to cheese (the older it is the higher it becomes), was more outspoken. It was small wonder that the Duke of Beaufort should want to see Churchill and Lloyd George 'in the middle of twenty couple of dog-hounds'. Other peers expressed their revulsion for Churchill's 'nauseous cant'. For this traitor to his caste continued to luxuriate in its feudal perquisites. As usual he spent Christmas at Blenheim, eating off gold plates and served by powdered footmen (all over six feet tall) wearing maroon coats and maroon plush breeches, silver-braided waistcoats, flesh-coloured silk stockings and silver-buckled shoes.

Naturally Churchill became more of a Tory whipping-boy

than ever. But he delighted his own side by a scintillating display of verbal fireworks and his tour of the north west was compared to Gladstone's Midlothian Campaign. The Prime Minister, mesmerised by Churchill's 'zig-zag streak of lightning on the brain' but quite capable of rebuking him for speaking in the government's name, recognised his contribution to the Liberals' victory. In February 1910 Asquith promoted Churchill to the Home Secretaryship.

This post, at a time of mounting industrial unrest and Suffragette violence, was something of a poisoned chalice. Churchill disliked both the officials at the Home Office and the tasks, such as authorising forcible feeding and signing death warrants, which he had to perform there. Later Churchill described a time in his early married life when he was smitten by terrifying, almost suicidal, depression and carried out his duties mechanically without joy or hope. It seems likely that these Black-Dog years were spent at the Home Office. Of course, Churchill's marriage was exceptionally happy. He and Clementine exulted in their first baby, Diana, known as 'the Puppy Kitten', who was born in July 1909 and was the very image, at least in his opinion, of her beautiful father. Lord Esher was a guest at the Churchills' Eccleston Square house on Winston's thirty-fifth birthday, celebrated with cakes, candles, crackers and paper hats. Esher noted that husband and wife sat together on the sofa holding hands, a picture of connubial bliss.

However there were stresses and strains. Churchill was inconsiderate, extravagant and preoccupied. Clementine was given to prolonged worry and sudden flare-ups. She hated his frequent absences. Each autumn he attended military manoeuvres in England, France or Germany, indulging his taste for exotic uniforms and his fantasies about directing great combinations of men in battle. Each summer he camped with the Oxfordshire Yeomanry in Blenheim Park, where the officers gambled all night and generally 'behaved like Regency rakes'. Clementine distrusted his male cronies, adventurers like Baron de Forest and F. E. Smith. And she was jealous of his female friends, fashionable ladies such as Violet Asquith and Venetia Stanley. Her needless suspicions vexed and depressed Churchill. One he chided Clementine for indulging in 'small emotions and wounding doubts'. He assured her, 'your sweetness and beauty have cast a glory upon my life'. For a time at least passing clouds darkened the glory.

Whatever his state of mind Churchill's fanatical industry was not a whit diminished at the Home Office. Having suffered acutely when locked up, he flung himself into the cause of prison reform. Unfortunately he could only effect minor improvements. He planned to better the lot of young offenders and abolish imprisonment for debt. But he would find no parliamentary time for legislative changes and had to content himself with administrative ones. His proposals for reducing the exploitation of shop-workers were thwarted in the Commons, though he did win them a statutory half-holiday. More important was his imposition of new safety standards in coal mines. Finally he planned a fundamental reform of the House of Lords and was quite prepared to abolish this 'lingering relic of a feudal order'. He even threatened to resign on the issue. But when Asquith merely annulled the Lords' power of veto Churchill quickly found himself making passionate speeches in defence of this policy.

He executed a similar volte-face on the Conciliation Bill. This was a measure designed to give the vote to about a million propertied women, a first step towards satisfying Mrs Pankhurst's demands. Churchill was a theoretical suffragist, though he lacked Clementine's vehemence on the subject and refused to be 'hen-pecked' into submission by the Suffragettes. At heart, too, he thought there were enough 'ignorant voters' and did not want any more. So he was easy prey for Masterman, who pointed out the unfairness of the Conciliation Bill which would, for example, enfranchise ladies and prostitutes at the expense of women and housewives. Churchill at once sensed the rhetorical possibilities of this argument. Soon he was marching up and down the room rolling off long phrases and convincing himself that he had always been hostile to the Bill. In parliament he spoke and voted against it, to the fury of suffragist friends like Lord Lytton whose sister was such a zealot that in prison she tried to inscribe the motto 'Votes for Women' on her chest with a needle.

The year 1910 saw a more fundamental change in the direction of Churchill's views. His radicalism had more or less blown itself out and he was beginning to drift towards the right, in many respects his natural home. Partly this was a response to the political posts he occupied – he adapted his arguments to his office, which was now less, and soon not at all, concerned with social reform. Partly it was a reaction, instinctive, aggressive and conservative, against the disorders which were killing Liberal England, not just the outrages of the 'screaming sisterhood' but widespread labour troubles, the looming confrontation over Ireland and the struggle with a militant peerage. After King Edward VII's death in May Churchill took part in negotiations with the Conservatives to see whether the crisis between the two houses of parliament could be resolved by compromise or coalition. Despite his efforts no agreement could be reached and a second election was held that December. At the start of the campaign, which ended with a duplication of the January result, there were two violent civil disturbances. Police clashed with demonstrating Suffragettes in London and with striking miners in south Wales. In both cases Churchill was unjustly blamed. Christabel Pankhurst accused him of ordering police brutality against women, a charge which so incensed him that he seriously considered suing her for libel. The slur that he sent troops to shoot down the miners of Tonypandy lives on in legend to this day. Nevertheless on 'Black Friday' the police had maltreated Suffragettes; and in the end soldiers were sent to south Wales where they exacerbated the unrest. Magnanimity towards the deserving but pugnacity towards the aggressive – these were Churchill's watchwords. Even so now (and as late as the 1930s) he was thinking in terms of 'labour colonies' for 'wastrels', not to mention sterilisation for the feeble-minded. And as the fierce conflicts which plagued Britain before the Great War reached their crescendo he became increasingly disillusioned with the mild panaceas of Liberalism.

A bizarre instance of his combativeness occurred in January 1911 at the famous 'Siege of Sidney Street'. Police had surrounded a gang of foreign 'anarchists', Latvian exiles supposedly led by one 'Peter the Painter', at a house in the east end of London. The anarchists, really terrorist fugitives from tsarist tyranny who had continued to rob banks and kill policemen in London, opened fire with automatic pistols. Churchill was asked to supply troops and gladly obliged. Needless to say, the temptation to visit the scene of action in person was too much for him. He was photographed, wearing a top hat and astrakhan-collared overcoat, peeping from a door-way in the front line. Churchill resisted the impulse to take personal command. Opinions differ about whether he sent for artillery or was merely surprised by its arrival. But there is no doubt that he suggested an assault on the house, the attackers to be protected by a steel shield. And when the besieged premises burst into flames he prevented the fire brigade from putting out the blaze, which duly incinerated the anarchists.

Naturally Churchill's thrusting himself into this affray gave his critics a field day of their own. Balfour derided him in the Commons. His own side was shocked, especially when he sought to make a violent farce the excuse for a sober parliamentary Act – he proposed a thoroughly intolerant Bill (never passed) directed against 'unassimilated aliens'. The press attacked Churchill and though good at delivering abuse he was surprisingly sensitive about receiving it. A. G. Gardiner commented sharply on Churchill's deviation from the pacific Liberal way: 'He sees himself moving through the smoke of battle – triumphant, terrible, his brow clothed with thunder, his legions looking to him for victory, and not looking in vain.' Even Churchill's friends were indignant. Charles Masterman demanded, 'What the hell have you been doing now, Winston?' Churchill lisped, 'Now Charlie. Don't be croth. It was such fun.'

Churchill's conduct was less comic during the violent labour disputes which broke out in the summer of 1911. A combination of strikes by dockers and railway workers seemed to threaten complete industrial paralysis. This was all the more serious because of the simultaneous upheaval caused by the passing of the Parliament Act curbing the Lords' powers and the crisis in foreign affairs, the Agadir incident, which might have led to war with Germany. At the time Churchill claimed to have proof that Hun gold was being used to foment the unrest. Other ministers dismissed this as 'midsummer madness' and in the boiling weather Churchill's incendiary imagination does seem to have overheated. Certainly he saw the labour troubles as an opportunity for conflict rather than conciliation. He became boisterously excited, sent out troops in large numbers to quell disturbances, pored over maps and issued wild bulletins. In the riots four strikers were shot dead in Llanelly and two in Liverpool. Churchill was bitterly condemned for his 'medieval methods' and his 'reckless employment of force'. Even Masterman acknowledged that he displayed a 'whiff-of-grape-shot attitude' towards the strikers and seemed to long for 'blood'. John Burns, President of the Local Government Board, told Churchill that he had mistaken a coffee-stall row for the social revolution. Certainly Churchill gave every indication that he regretted Lloyd George's deft and peaceful resolution of the railway strike. When he heard the news he kicked his model military forces, deployed on the floor, right across the room and exclaimed, 'Bloody hell!' He had wanted to give the strikers 'a good thrashing'.

In the opinion of political friends and enemies Churchill had made the Home Office too hot to hold him. Many on his own side thought he was simply reverting to Tory type. The vigour of his assault on the Conservative Unionists during the struggle over Home Rule for Ireland before the war was partly an attempt to get back into Liberal good graces. Asquith at any rate retained confidence in Churchill though he was probably anxious to detach him from his ally Lloyd George. The Prime Minister, though apt to disparage Churchill for thinking with his mouth and uttering froth, was nevertheless fascinated by his ebullitions of verbal brilliance. These were well described by Sir Almeric Fitzroy:

> Certainly he is a wonderful talker, daring, not to say reckless, but always with a subcurrent of method, striking in phrase, vivid in colour, elegant to the verge of romance, picturesquely vehement, and at the same time persuasive.

Asquith doubtless recognised Churchill's weaknesses as well as his strengths. He was too loquacious to be a good negotiator. He was too impetuous to be a good administrator. He was too bellicose to be a good politician on the home front – where the only war to be waged was the class war. What Churchill needed was an office which would excite his imagination, employ his inexhaustible energies, exploit his unrivalled power of initiative and satisfy his martial cravings. The Admiralty was just such an office and as it happened the Agadir incident, Germany's essay into gunboat diplomacy in Morocco, had exposed the inadequacy of naval war planning. Accordingly, in October 1911 Churchill swapped places with Reginald McKenna and became First Lord of the Admiralty. Soon all his talk was of oil, boilers, armaments and armadas. Lloyd George complained that he had turned into a sea creature and forgotten that the rest of humanity lived on land.

The years before Armageddon, like those before the French Revolution, are traditionally supposed to have seen the privileged classes enjoying an exquisite *douceur de vivre*. Certainly Churchill's peace-time spell at the Admiralty was one of the happiest periods in his life. In June 1911 Clementine had given birth to a handsome boy, named Randolph and nicknamed 'the Chumbolly', in whom Churchill rejoiced. Unlike his own father Churchill loved playing with his children, even indulging them. They became very wild and no nanny or nursery maid would stay with the Churchills for long. As the children grew up he invented uproarious games. Growling like a bear or shambling like a gorilla, he would chase them round the room. He revelled in charades. And he took the greatest delight in digging on the beach, not so much building sandcastles as constructing water-works, dams, rivulets and cascades. Sir George Riddell, Churchill's golfing friend, summed up his domestic state in 1912: 'Winston is charming in his home life and Mrs W. a most attractive person.'

At the Admiralty Churchill found both the staff and the work congenial. Naval pomp and circumstance appealed to him. He loved being whisked about in gleaming launches and piped aboard mighty ships. Churchill valued the service camaraderie and consorted freely with everyone from admirals to stokers. He tried to restore the Nelsonian 'band of brothers' spirit after the feuds of Admiral Fisher's era and held friendly wardrooms enthralled into the night-watches with extravagant nautical rhapsodies. Moreover the post offered him delicious opportunities for extra-mural enjoyment, all in what he persuaded himself was the line of duty. In 1912, for example, as founder of the Royal Naval Air Service he lost (as he later put it) his aetherial virginity. Flying was then an extremely hazardous business and Churchill had a number of more or less serious accidents and close calls. But the occupation added a new zest to his life and he resisted Clementine's attempts to make him give it up.

Another wonderful perquisite of the First Lordship was the 4,000-ton Admiralty yacht *Enchantress*. She became Churchill's mobile office and playground. He spent months aboard her visiting dockyards and naval bases. He also sailed off on summer cruises to the Mediterranean in 1912 and 1913, ostensibly on naval business. He took Asquith and friends, binding the Prime Minister more tightly under his spell in the process. A famous cartoon showed the two men lounging in deck-chairs on the yacht. Churchill: 'Any home news?' Asquith (from behind a paper): 'How can there be with you here?' In one respect the cartoon was misleading. Even on holiday Churchill was incapable of relaxation. When Violet Asquith marvelled at the beauty of the Adriatic coast-line Churchill was assessing it as a target for six inch guns. While other members of the party admired the temples at Paestum Churchill was organising a lizard hunt, enrolling Admiral Beatty and his secretary as beaters and urging, 'We must be more scientific about our strategy. There is a science in catching lizards and we must master it.'

Edward Marsh said that at the Admiralty the First Lord's new commandment ordained that on the seventh day 'thou shalt do all manner of work'. Unlike his civilian predecessors Churchill took every aspect of the navy as his province – men, ships, ordnance, administration, all was made to conform to his will. He offended the Admiralty by the frequency, urgency and brusquerie of his minutes. They requested information on every subject and probed into the senior service's most sensitive places. Advised by Admiral 'Jackie' Fisher, the volcanic and eccentric former First Sea Lord, Churchill was soon refusing to accept the opinions of naval experts, even on technical matters. He interfered in everything and his unpopularity grew apace. During target practice he capered about the deck, elevating, depressing and sighting the guns. During the naval manoeuvres of 1912 he issued wireless instructions to the Commanders-in-Chief and afterwards lectured flag officers on the performance of their duties. When inspecting a ship's company he was quite capable of subjecting officers to a curt inquisition in front of their men. He left at least one wardroom in a state of 'choking wrath' over his dictatorial behaviour. Sometimes he solicited the advice of junior officers in order to overrule their seniors. Once his gross meddling with naval discipline almost provoked the resignation of the entire Admiralty Board and the Commander-in-Chief of the Nore fleet. The latter was finally placated with the argument that the First Lord was 'so much off his head' that admirals need take no notice of him. In fact Churchill, living for the limelight, could never be ignored. Disgruntled admirals had to content themselves with embroidering yarns about his budding megalomania. A favourite concerned his penchant for Ruritanian uniforms, in this case that of an Elder Brother of Trinity House. Churchill was said to have told the French ambassador, 'Je sweeze oun frair ehnay de la Trinnitay.' The ambassador supposedly congratulated him on having such distinguished relations.

Actually the First Lord's pretensions were not divine, rather Napoleonic. When Morley told him that he would finish his days in St Helena, Churchill was 'more flattered by the comparison than dismayed by the prospect'. At the Admiralty Churchill doffed the mantle of peace and put on the panoply of war with a clear conscience. He entirely changed his tune on the issue of military expenditure. And he found in the Agadir incident the perfect justification for fighting his own corner with such vehemence. After it Churchill could claim that Armageddon was imminent, as many of his countrymen had long believed – Admiral Lord Charles Beresford's invariable greeting was, 'Good morning, one day nearer the German war.' While the Agadir tension was at its height Churchill had found the Admiralty 'cocksure, *insouciant* and apathetic'. Thus his policy as First Lord and the excuse for all his meddling was the paramount need to prepare the Royal Navy for battle. On his success the nation's survival depended. Churchill rose to this daunting challenge with incomparable vigour and self-confidence.

These characteristics were precisely the ones to which he owed both his failures and his successes as First Lord. For, as Admiral Bacon said, Churchill's vices were simply his virtues in exaggerated form. Dash became rashness, assurance became cocksureness. Churchill's overflowing energy was difficult to harness. His overwhelming faith in himself closed his mind to the opinions of others. Consequently as he began to lick the navy into shape the First Lord sacrificed long-term efficiency for short-term readiness. Sometimes this was deliberate, more often inadvertent. Frequently trials were skimped so that production could begin. Thus when the war came British shells and torpedoes were inferior to those of Germany. There were no efficient mine-layers and British mines were 'squibs' (Fisher's word), so unreliable that they were more of a danger to those who sowed them than those who hit them. Magazines and turrets in the new fast battle-cruisers were inadequately protected; this was disastrous in modern naval warfare, which Churchill likened to 'a battle between two egg-shells striking each other with hammers'. British gunnery was inaccurate and there were no anti-aircraft guns at all. There was a lack of night-fighting equipment.

In their tactics many British admirals remained in the days of sail. They looked back to Nelson and beyond – as Fisher said, they might as well have looked back to Noah. No proper provision had been made to combat two major new factors, effective German mines and submarines. These were to place Britain's Dreadnoughts on the defensive, despite Churchill's heedless urge to mount a close blockade of Germany. Indeed, because Scapa Flow and other naval bases were vulnerable to submarine attack the Grand Fleet had to sail the high seas for long periods at the outbreak of war, a dangerous and exhausting procedure. In short, by 1914 the Royal Navy was deficient in many vital particulars and Churchill's claim that British ships were superior unit for unit was wide of the mark.

What then did he achieve at the Admiralty? How was it that a detached observer like the German Naval Attaché could conclude that although Churchill had caused friction in the navy because of his 'stubborn and tyrannical character', he had earned the service's gratitude by inspiring and accomplishing unprecedented improvements? First, and most important, Churchill developed fast and heavily armed (fifteen inch gun) battleships in such numbers and at such speed that Britain's fleet increased its superiority over Germany's during his tenure of office. Without this superiority Britain would surely have lost the war, probably from starvation, possibly from invasion. Secondly, Churchill pushed ahead with the change from coal to oil fuel. This meant that a speedier fleet could stay at sea for longer periods (though despite establishing the Anglo-Persian Oil Company Churchill omitted to build up sufficient stocks of oil and there was a severe shortage in 1917). Thirdly, Churchill created a War Staff, in the teeth of naval opposition, which enabled proper war plans to be laid for the first time. Unfortunately it had not developed the requisite skills by 1914 and during the war much of the Admiralty's staff work was deplorable. Nevertheless Lord Esher considered this to be 'the most pregnant reform which has been carried out at the Admiralty since the days of Lord St Vincent'. Finally Churchill improved the morale of the navy. He increased its meagre pay, revised its archaic disciplinary code, gave senior posts to officers of ability and made it possible for men to rise from the ranks. Even so the navy continued to obstruct promotions in certain branches of the service. With mordant sarcasm and inimitable logic Churchill returned to the issue during his second spell at the Admiralty in 1939: 'If a telegraphist may rise, why not a painter? Apparently there is no difficulty about painters rising in Germany.'

Even though most of his innovations were improvements, many officers found it impossible to forgive Churchill for his cavalier disregard for naval tradition. 'Don't talk to me about naval tradition' was his famous reply, 'it's nothing but rum, sodomy and the lash.' Churchill scarcely troubled to disguise his patronising attitude towards sailors. They were simple souls, he thought, and certainly none of them was a match for him in debate. Fisher, by no means inarticulate, was to complain that although he knew he was right Churchill consistently 'out-argued' and 'miasma-ed' him. Captain 'Blinker' Hall, had the same experience. During an argument with Churchill lasting into the small hours he was reduced to muttering to himself, like Kipling's Kim, 'My name is Hall, my name is Hall,' because he feared that the First Lord would convince him otherwise. Churchill considered, with some justification, that the silent service was mute because its officers were ill-educated even in professional matters. Sailors responded by damning him as an ignorant civilian. Unfortunately Churchill sometimes provided a good target for his naval critics by advocating impractical schemes like 'bulging' the hulls of vessels in order to protect them against torpedoes. Contrary to what he claimed in *The World Crisis*, Churchill also continued to favour airships after their military inferiority to aeroplanes had been demonstrated.

Yet if he was something of a crackpot inventor Churchill was also a visionary of startling prescience. His early support for aircraft-carriers and 'landships' (tanks), his inauguration of a force of naval aeroplanes and his remarkable forecast, made in 1911, of the early strategic developments of the war show him a true prophet. Nor was he without honour in progressive echelons of the navy. Admiral Bacon concluded that it was 'impossible not to be captivated by his dynamic qualities, and his disregard for time-honoured red-tape methods'. Admiral Keyes reckoned that his maddening interventions were often 'pure gain' for the navy: his 'quick brain and vivid imagination were invaluable'. Despite their ferocious quarrels Admiral Fisher gave Churchill his greatest accolade: 'he was a war man'.

Before August 1914 the only war which seemed imminent was a civil war over the issue of independence for Ireland. For now that the Tory Lords had lost their power of veto the Liberal Commons were slowly pushing a Home Rule Bill through all its parliamentary stages. Unable to block it constitutionally, the Conservatives and Unionists encouraged the Protestants in northern Ireland to express their 'loyalty' to Britain by means of treason. If all else failed they were determined to keep the kingdom united by force. Churchill hoped that the prospective civil war would evaporate into 'uncivil words', 'far more congenial to Orange gentlemen and the yellow press'. He also looked for a compromise by which Protestant Ulster could remain in the United Kingdom while Catholic southern Ireland achieved self-government under the crown. But he spoke and acted in a characteristically provocative manner. In 1912 he and Clementine paid a hazardous visit to the capital of violent 'loyalism', Belfast. There Churchill hoped that Irish nationhood would stem from the reconciliation of races and turned his father's watchword inside out, urging that Ulster would be right to fight for 'the dignity and honour of Ireland'. As the Unionists resorted to more extreme measures Churchill challenged them to disclose their 'sinister revolutionary purpose'. 'Let us go forward and put these grave matters to the proof.'

When in March 1914 it seemed as though armed Ulster Volunteers would seize British military stores Churchill dispatched a flotilla to the Clyde, from where it could intervene. As mutiny loomed in the British armed forces the naval orders were hastily withdrawn. Nevertheless the Unionists were furious that Churchill seemed willing to use their own violent methods against them. He had declared, in what Morley despairingly called 'a Tory cliché', that there were 'worse things than bloodshed'. If Belfast showed fight, the First Lord had fulminated, his ships would reduce the city to ruins within twenty-four hours. Understandably, therefore, Unionists maintained that Churchill was planning a 'pogrom' in Ulster. It was something they never forgot or forgave. Meanwhile they tried to pass a parliamentary motion condemning the government. This proceeding, as Churchill sharply remarked, was 'uncommonly like a vote of censure by the criminal classes on the police'.

If Churchill's embattled stance hid his conciliatory intentions over Ulster the same was true over the vexed question of naval estimates. As usual Churchill wanted to impose moderation from a position of strength. Several times he offered a 'naval holiday' whereby Britain and Germany would both call a halt to their construction programmes. The effect was spoilt by his brutally frank assertion that Britain, for whom a strong fleet was a necessity, was now building against Germany, a land-power for whom ships were a luxury. Nor did Churchill's pacific offers cut much ice with his economical colleagues. For when Germany failed to respond he had every excuse to increase the naval estimates. The struggle was one that he was well equipped to win, even against an opponent as wily as Lloyd George. Churchill had a monopoly of technical information which he deployed to suit himself. He possessed elephantine stamina as well as smashing power in debate. He dominated cabinet discussions with a volubility which exhausted and demoralised his opponents. He was resourceful in manoeuvre and unscrupulous in manipulation. By turns he was charming and sulky, wheedling and aggressive. In January 1914 he came close to resigning and bringing the government down with him. By February he had got nearly everything he wanted.

Strife was Churchill's element, his salamander's fire. It was also his fate. Churchill was convinced that he had been marvellously preserved in order to save the navy. In the middle of the estimates crisis he told Riddell, 'I believe I am watched over. Think of the perils I have escaped.' From the first the Admiralty had been a consummation of his desires. When he was offered the post, as Violet Asquith said, 'the tide of happiness and realisation was too deep even for exuberance'. When the world crisis suddenly overtook that of Ulster in the summer of 1914 Churchill's sense of fulfilment became sublime. His ecstasy, indeed, was tinged with guilt. On 28 July he wrote to Clementine:

> Everything tends towards catastrophe and collapse. I am interested, geared up and happy. Is it not horrible to be built like that? The preparations have a hideous fascination for me. I pray to God to forgive me for such fearful moods of levity. Yet I would do my best for peace.

At the same time that 'splendid *condottiere* at the Admiralty', as Morley called him, made every preparation for war. He was determined that no last-minute surprise would prevent his labours from bearing their fruit. Bellicose to the point of euphoria, he pleaded with his colleagues for authorisation to order full mobilisation. It was to Churchill's eternal credit, as Kitchener said, that on 4 August 1914, when Britain's ultimatum to Germany expired, the fleet was ready.

CHAPTER V

ARMAGEDDON

A S CHURCHILL acknowledged, he liked things to happen and if they did not happen he liked to make them happen. Now he was at the centre of history's stage, overlord of the mightiest navy in the greatest war that the world had ever seen. Yet he was not completely satisfied. Napoleon-like, he yearned not only to direct operations but to participate in them as well. This accounts for his frenetic restlessness at the Admiralty. Not content with usurping many of the operational functions of his naval advisers, he also strove to get to grips with the enemy more immediately. It was this impatience for action which led him into the fire-eating enterprises that eventually caused his downfall. Nevertheless no one in the cabinet contributed more fortitude, zest and energy to the business of war. Asquith described the way in which Churchill's eyes lit up with the glow of genius when anything excited his interest. In October Edward Grey, the Foreign Secretary, told Clementine that he was warmed by the thought of 'sitting next to a Hero. I can't tell you how much I admire Winston's courage and gallant spirit and genius for war. It inspires us all.'

The Admiralty was more incensed than inspired. On 5 August Churchill remarked to Captain Richmond: 'Now we have our war. The next thing to decide is how we are going to carry it on.' This was worthy of Disraeli's question to his first cabinet, 'And now, gentlemen, what shall we do?' and it set the tone of improvisation which characterised so much of Churchill's war work. The First Lord's initial behaviour caused widespread disquiet among the sailors and Richmond thought it tragic that the Admiralty was in such 'lunatic hands' at such a time. True, the navy transported the army to France successfully. And the seven seas were swept clear of German ships, though not without grave losses, delays and embarrassments. Setbacks such as the escape of the battlecruiser *Goeben* to Turkey were partly caused by poor Admiralty staff work, work sometimes helped and sometimes hindered by the First Lord's ceaseless interventions. Moreover Churchill kept pressing for offensive action, closer blockade of Germany, perilous Baltic expeditions, the capture of the German island of Borkum. The last scheme was described by Richmond as '*quite mad*' but it seemed eminently feasible to Churchill. As another naval officer remarked, if the First Lord was not interrupted he could take Borkum in twenty minutes.

Churchill's lust for battle took many forms. 'With a courageous stroke of the pen' (as Balfour remarked) he had begun by dismissing the respected old Commander-in-Chief Admiral Callaghan, appointing in his stead Jellicoe, who was untried but supposedly Nelsonian. As in the Second World War, Churchill had little respect for the position of neutrals and he proposed to take the unhelpful Dutch government 'by the throat'. He was fond of martial jaunts, the point of which escaped his naval subordinates. The First Lord found frequent excuses to rush across the channel by destroyer in order to visit General French and see the conflict at close quarters. Churchill was eager to have additional military units at his command. He dispatched marine contingents to France in London buses (his much criticised 'Dunkirk Circus'), and sent armoured car detachments to guard his air squadrons. To the intense dismay of the Royal Naval Volunteer Reserve he conscripted most of it into an 'Admiralty Army' to fight on land. 'It will be a fine force,' said Churchill. 'We will have artillery, and why not cavalry too?' 'Ye Gods!' exclaimed one disgusted RNVR Commander, 'the Horse Marines at last.'

More than most politicians Churchill hated to admit that he had been wrong. But he did later come close to apologising for the inept transformation of the RNVR into the Royal Naval Division. The new force of soldier-sailors (which continued to measure time by bells in a pathetic attempt to retain its esprit de corps) was ill-trained and ill-equipped to take part in Churchill's first great adventure of the war. This was his attempt to save Antwerp, the vital port on the left flank of the Allied line. When it looked as if Antwerp would surrender Churchill, already on his way to France, was authorised to visit the city and try to stiffen its resistance. The commission fired his blood. Dressed in one of his spurious uniforms and accompanied by a naval entourage, he arrived on 3 October in a large dun-coloured touring car, its horn blaring. Like the hero in a melodrama he announced to the burgomaster that the city would be saved.

Churchill established himself in the principal hotel, met the King, interviewed ministers and promised reinforcements. Soon he had persuaded the Belgian government and army to 'hurl themselves with revived energy into the defence'. As the monstrous German howitzers stamped with 'iron footprints' on the fortifications Churchill set about organising Antwerp for a siege. He animated resistance, inspected trenches, positioned guns and deployed his naval brigades. He also remained supremely indifferent to the enemy's bombardment, posing for photographers and cinema cameras with shells bursting near him. Churchill was particularly inspired by the spectacle of a soldier monarch 'preserving an unconquerable majesty amid the ruin of his kingdom'. To the amazement and amusement of the cabinet he telegraphed Asquith offering to resign his post as First Lord in order to take formal charge of the British forces at Antwerp. The only minister not to laugh this bizarre proposal out of court was Kitchener, who was prepared to make Churchill a lieutenant-general on the spot.

The Prime Minister merely wanted him to come home and do his job. But Churchill reiterated his offer on his return from Antwerp, when Asquith gave Venetia Stanley a vivid account of the First Lord's mood:

> Having, as he says, 'tasted blood' these last few days he is beginning like a tiger to raven for more and begs that sooner or later, and the sooner the better, he may be relieved of his present office . . . . His mouth waters at the sight and thought of K[itchener]'s new armies. Are these 'glittering commands' to be entrusted to 'dug-out trash', bred on the obsolete tactics of 25 years ago, 'mediocrities

who have led a sheltered life, mouldering in military routine?' etc. etc. For about ¼ of an hour he poured forth a ceaseless cataract of invective and appeal, and I much regretted that there was no shorthand writer within hearing – as some of his unpremeditated phrases were quite priceless. He was, however, quite three parts serious, and declared that a political career was nothing to him in comparison with military glory.

Such flamboyant irresponsibility helped to discredit Churchill at the Admiralty. Indeed, Antwerp was a disaster for him in terms of public esteem, not least because he was gratuitously rude to the press. Forgetting his former profession he ordered two war correspondents back to Britain, thumping the table to emphasise his displeasure. The city fell after only a few days, with the loss of many of Churchill's raw naval soldiers. The fact that his intervention had held up the German advance at a crucial moment and helped to secure the channel ports for the Allies was ignored. In the popular view Churchill had deserted his post to direct what the *Morning Post* called 'a costly blunder'.

Asquith continued to think that a resourceful and inventive civilian like Churchill was a good master of expert servants at the Admiralty. But the press outcry was augmented by a chauvinist clamour against the First Sea Lord (operational head of the navy), Prince Louis of Battenberg, on account of his German ancestry. In an effort to protect himself Churchill therefore sacrificed the Prince, who resigned with dignity and sorrow. The seventy-three-year-old Lord Fisher was, as he put it, '*Resurrected! Resurrected! Resurrected! Again!*' Fisher's prestige was colossal and he seemed to many an inspired choice to replace the Prince. He was the founder of the modern British navy. No one had a clearer vision of the strategic implications of new weapons. Unimpaired by age his explosive vitality and fecund imagination matched Churchill's own. Their methods of work were complementary: Churchill did not retire until the small hours and Fisher rose well before dawn. Each believed in the other's genius, though not without reservation. Fisher, for example, maintained that Churchill so idolised power that he had surrounded himself at the Admiralty with '3rd class sycophants'. But Fisher, in the First Lord's view, was 'built on a titanic scale'. He appealed to Churchill's grandiose worldview, being 'in harmony with the vast size of events'.

Fisher at once justified his appointment. He speedily dispatched Admiral Sturdee's strong flotilla which arrived just in time (December 1914) to destroy von Spee's squadron off the Falkland Islands. But he also quickly vindicated those who had forecast that the presence of two dictators at the Admiralty would lead to friction. Fisher was a classic illustration of the cliché that genius and madness are akin. His grasp of essentials was uncannily sure yet his mind was a rag-bag of tags, puns, mottoes and riddles, all of which, as Margot Asquith said, might have come out of Christmas crackers. Fisher had prophesied Armageddon (his dates were always precise though seldom the same) but he was convinced that the British would win because they were the lost ten tribes of Israel. His energy was volcanic but it sometimes ran to waste – Fisher liked to stick red labels marked RUSH on anyone he caught loitering in the corridors of the Admiralty. He created the Dreadnought fleet but his rancorous vendettas and serpentine intrigues had caused civil strife in the navy.

Fisher's missives, written in violet ink, couched in violent terms and spattered with every kind of stylographic emphasis – underlinings, capitals, exclamation marks – were eccentric to the point of lunacy. They were full of wild invective, extravagant endearment, ringing exhortation, breathless confidences, jackdaw adages and paranoid egotism. In *The World Crisis* Churchill made light of these letters which began 'My beloved Winston' and ended 'Yours to a cinder', 'Yours till Hell freezes' or 'Till charcoal sprouts'. But when writing that book he was still in the grip of his bizarre infatuation – the attraction of similars – with Fisher, who had himself fallen 'desperately in love' with Churchill at their first meeting in 1907. Of course they had quarrelled. Churchill knew that in 1915 Fisher had told Clementine, maliciously and mendaciously, that her husband was not conferring with General French but cavorting in Paris with a mistress. But Churchill, in some ways an evergreen innocent, did not realise in the early 1920s how unstable Fisher was. He did not appreciate that in the Admiral's eyes he was a 'Hero' one moment and a 'Poltroon' the next, now an angel, now possessor of satanic attributes. Not only was Churchill ignorant of the full measure of Fisher's duplicity and megalomania, he was also anxious to vindicate the appointment of a brilliant sailor with whom he had later co-operated in trying to exonerate the Admiralty of blame for the Dardanelles fiasco. Only when he read Bacon's *Life of Fisher* (1929) did Churchill give a more considered, and a more just, verdict on the Admiral:

> Harsh, capricious, vindictive, gnawed by hatreds arising often from spite, working secretly or violently as occasion might suggest by methods which the typical English gentleman and public-school boy are taught to dislike, Fisher was always regarded as the 'dark angel' of the Naval Service.

After an autumn honeymoon, during which Fisher inaugurated a huge new ship-building programme, the two autocrats of the Admiralty began to cross swords. Fisher aspired to be a warlord like Kitchener but Churchill monopolised all naval initiative. In the public mind the First Lord was the Admiralty and when German vessels bombarded east coast towns it was Churchill who denounced 'the baby-killers of Scarborough'. Fisher's prescriptions, which including boiling prisoners in oil and shooting admirals on their quarter-decks, were not then to Churchill's taste. He resisted Fisher's plan to execute enemy males in reprisal for Zeppelin raids, though the Admiral tried to resign over the issue. He also prevented Fisher from taking disciplinary action against officers responsible for allowing enemy ships to escape in what ought to have been a complete victory off the Dogger Bank in January 1915. After a month or two Fisher was complaining about Churchill's incessant meddling. The First Lord sat in his great bed at the Admiralty, an enormous Corona Corona in his mouth, a pad on his knee, his counterpane littered with multi-coloured despatch boxes, dictating to a stenographer. Telegrams, letters, memoranda on every conceivable subject and minutes by the basketful fell from his lips. Fisher was amazed by his capacity for work but furious that he and the other Sea Lords were being reduced to nobodies. Fisher's comments on reading operational telegrams, about which the First Lord proposed to consult him after they had been sent, were sulphurous.

Finally, and disastrously for both of them, Fisher and Churchill fell out over the question of taking the offensive. In theory Fisher agreed with Churchill that some vigorous naval

initiative was desirable. In January 1915, for example, he sent
this explosive message to the First Lord: 'DO SOMETHING!!!!!
We are waiting to be kicked!!!!' But when it came to the point Fisher
instinctively plumped for keeping 'the fleet in being'. In practice he balked at the Borkum project, which he had long
cherished. Churchill, on the other hand, rebelled fiercely
against the passive strategy of blockade. He surveyed the
bloody 'slogging match' that was being fought in the trenches
of the western front. And he persuaded Asquith that there
must be 'other alternatives than sending our armies to chew
barbed wire in Flanders'.

Soon his imagination was vaulting over mundane obstacles
into golden realms of victory. Looking back into history he saw
the dramatic possibilities of amphibious action offered by
command of the sea. He dreamt of a world-shattering
Mediterranean coup like that of his hero Napoleon. He projected splendid visions of forcing the Dardanelles, capturing
Constantinople, knocking Turkey out of the war, rallying
Russia, turning the enemy's front on a continental scale, taking
Europe in the rear and winning not only the war but huge
colonial prizes. The Dardanelles enterprise was not originated
by Churchill but he breathed life into it. Churchill invested it
with plausibility. He pushed it forward against all obstructions,
overwhelming doubters with torrents of eloquence. He
galvanised the cabinet with an apocalyptic passion. It was well
expressed in his discourse, recorded by Margot Asquith in
January 1915:

> My God! this is living History. Everything we are doing and saying
> is thrilling – it will be read by a thousand generations, think of
> that!! Why I would not be out of this glorious delicious war for any-
> thing the world could give me.

His eyes were glowing but he paused and, fearing that the word
'delicious' might be misunderstood, asked the Prime Minister's
gossipy wife not to repeat it.

As always Churchill's argumentative skills were pressed into
the service of his imagination. He persuaded himself, and he
tried to convince everyone else who mattered, that his vision
could be translated into reality. He contradicted hostile
opinions even when they were his own. In 1911, for example,
he had told McKenna: 'It is no longer possible to force the

Dardanelles, and nobody could expose a modern fleet to such perils.' And as late as 1915 he had reminded Fisher, 'Germany is the foe, and it is bad war to seek cheaper victories and easier antagonists.' Churchill ignored the fact that an early naval bombardment of the Dardanelles defences had alerted the Turks. He secured Fisher's reluctant acquiescence and took it for approval. Otherwise, he scarcely consulted his own staff and overruled experts who repeated the traditional warning that ships, the shells of which had a flat trajectory, were no match for forts. Churchill secured the support of Admiral Carden, the Mediterranean commander in whom neither he nor Fisher had any faith, by the simple expedient of asking a question which begged the answer yes. However the First Lord evidently had little idea of what the fleet would do on its own even if it managed to burst through to Constantinople. Like the hussar officer he was, Churchill concentrated on the charge and assumed that once the enemy's line was broken the remnants could be mopped up at leisure. He was fond of quoting Napoleon's maxim to this effect: 'Frappez la masse et tout le reste vient par surcroît.'

Meanwhile, the more Fisher thought about the Dardanelles plan the less he liked it. Churchill being, as Fisher said, a 'subtle dialectician' who could 'talk a bird out of a tree', he would argue the old admiral round or at least reduce him to silence. But Fisher was stubborn as well as erratic. He kept coming back to the belief that it was dangerous and futile to commit the navy on its own. The army's support was essential he asserted, backing up his ineffectual protests with equally ineffectual moves to resign. However Fisher's opinion was endorsed by others, and Churchill himself accepted it shortly before the naval bombardment began on 19 February 1915. Unfortunately by then his relationship with Kitchener had again deteriorated, largely owing to the First Lord's compulsive interference in France and his supposed intrigues with General French. To Churchill's 'immense and unconcealed dudgeon', Asquith wrote, Kitchener convinced the cabinet that no troops were immediately available for the Dardanelles. So for several weeks the naval assault went on alone. Churchill urged Admiral Carden to press forward and take risks, even told him how to accomplish his task.

However the minefield, commanded by Turkish batteries,

could not be cleared properly and in March five old battleships were sunk or damaged. Churchill was sure that victory was imminent at little further cost. 'Not to persevere,' he said later, 'that was the crime.' But Admiral de Robeck (who had succeeded Carden) and Fisher refused to take further risks until army units arrived. These were released by Kitchener on 10 March. Churchill hoped desperately that the operation could be salvaged. When Colonel Hankey, Secretary of the Committee of Imperial Defence, warned that opposed landings would be extraordinarily difficult Churchill snapped back that he could see no difficulty at all. Anyway the enterprise was now out of his hands. As it happened the inordinate delays, combined with every sort of ineptitude, turned the Dardanelles into a major military disaster. But as late as June Churchill was still prophesying 'a victory such as this war has not yet seen'. He never forgave those responsible for the final withdrawal.

Opinions differ about whether the Dardanelles was a superb strategic conception which was sadly bungled or a military miscalculation with no chance of success from the start. Nor is there agreement about how much responsibility Churchill bore for the episode. At the time politicians, press and public were in no doubt that attacking the Dardanelles had been a terrible blunder for which the First Lord's impetuosity was chiefly to blame. The Dardanelles Commission included Asquith and Kitchener in its indictment. Later historians, shocked by the carnage on the western front, looked more favourably on an eastern assault. Impressed by Churchill's apologia in *The World Crisis*, they praised him for possessing more military inspiration than all the generals put together (not such a compliment when one considers those generals). Authorities like Sir Basil Liddell Hart and Professor Arthur Marder endorsed Attlee's view that the Dardanelles plan was 'the one strategic idea of the war'.

But historical fashions change and it now seems that contemporaries were not far wrong in their judgement after all. The Dardanelles venture was badly planned and executed. For this Churchill, who combined visionary extravagance with a passion for laying down the law about minute details, must bear a significant part of the guilt. Victory was never as close as he claimed. It was a mistake to divert such huge resources to an

Lord Randolph Churchill (1849–1895)

Lord Randolph Churchill aged thirty

Jennie – Lady Randolph Churchill dressed for a ball, 1872

Winston Churchill aged seven

Lady Churchill with her two sons, 1889

Churchill at Harrow

Churchill in full-dress uniform of the Fourth Hussars, 1895

Churchill as a subaltern in India

Churchill, prisoner of the Boers, November 1899

Churchill addresses Durban crowd after his escape, December 1899

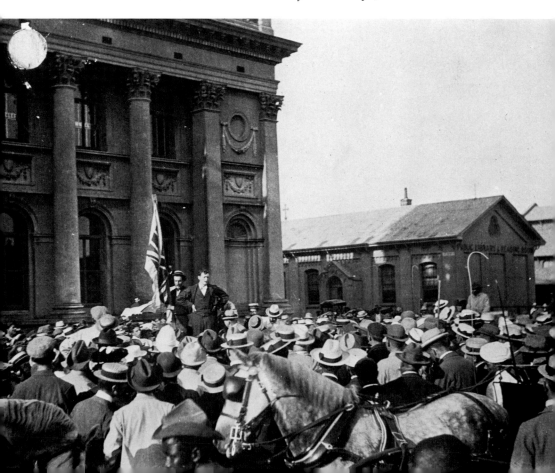

The young politician, 1904

Betrothed couple – Churchill and Clementine, 1908

From left to right: 9th Duke of Marlborough, Viscount Churchill,
Winston, Jack – on Territorial Army Camp

Churchill and the Kaiser

Churchill attends manoeuvres with the German Army, 1909

Churchill, First Lord of the Admiralty, learns to fly

Churchill at the Battle of Sidney Street, 1911

Churchill and Lord Fisher

*Churchill and Lloyd George in
Whitehall, 1915*

*Colonel Churchill and his second-in-command, Sir Archibald
Sinclair, in combat dress – Armentières, 1916*

exposed and subsidiary theatre of operations. Moreover even if the Dardanelles had been forced, the gains which Churchill anticipated would probably never have materialised. Germany herself triumphed in the east and lost the war in the west. This is not to say that the western strategy as implemented by Haig – a strategy which produced blood-lettings like the Somme and Passchendaele – was correct. It is to suggest that the fundamental reason why the Allies won was that they subjected the Kaiser's Reich to slow strangulation. Germany collapsed at a time when her unbroken armies were everywhere fighting on foreign soil. It was Churchill's tragedy that his cavalryman's qualities were irrelevant to this grim siege warfare. Indeed they were a positive handicap. He was impatient with defensive stratagems, deep shelters, convoys, distant blockade. Yet, as Richmond had said in August 1914: 'We have the game in our hands if we sit tight, but this Churchill cannot see!'

What Churchill's naval advisers could not see was that they might have exploited the talents and energies of their headstrong overlord if only they had adopted his own dialectical methods. The technique was learnt and to a considerable extent applied by service chiefs during the conflict with Hitler and it was an important debt which the Second World War owed to the First. Churchill described his mode of argument as the mounting of 'a mental reconnaissance-in-force'. Instead of putting forward an idea and discussing it on its merits, Churchill proceeded in a way that was essentially military. He hit on an objective and directed a polemical foray towards it. Stating his case in extreme and tendentious terms, ignoring or belittling obstacles, he endeavoured to turn an exploratory charge into a devastating rout. The correct response of his professional experts, assuming that they thought the notion a bad one, was to repulse this first assault in no uncertain terms. Churchill seldom minded plain speaking: in 1942 he brushed aside an apology from Sir Charles Portal, 'You know, in war you don't have to be nice, you *only* have to be right.' Preferably, too, his advisers had to use the sort of vivid phraseology which would stop Churchill dead in his tracks, thus allowing them to focus his attention on some more worthwhile project. For if he met anything less than total resistance Churchill would muster rhetorical reinforcements and proceed to blast his way through. Soon all his reserves of eloquence would be deployed and his prestige would be so committed that it was almost impossible for him to retreat.

Few civil servants and fewer military men were strong enough or articulate enough to withstand this onslaught. Fisher might have done so in his prime. But now old, unbalanced and frustrated, he preferred to rely on the weapons of intrigue and resignation. Outraged by Churchill's proposal to send two more submarines to the Dardanelles the Admiral resigned, for the ninth and final time, on 15 May 1915. In order not to come under Churchill's magic spell and retract once again, Fisher pretended that he had gone to Scotland. In fact he lurked in London, dodging between his locked and curtained house, the Charing Cross Hotel, Westminster Abbey and the Athenaeum Club, in order 'to escape from Winston'. Asquith ordered him to stay at his post 'in the King's name' – George V thought Fisher should be 'hanged at the yardarm for desertion . . . in the face of the enemy'. Churchill pleaded with Fisher to return, even offering him (without authorisation) a seat in the cabinet as an inducement. The Admiral was adamant, though he professed entire loyalty to the First Lord. Behind Churchill's back Fisher informed the Conservative leader Bonar Law (under a seal of secrecy patently meant to be broken) that he had 'rejected the 30 pieces of silver to betray my country', Churchill being 'a bigger danger than the Germans by a long way'.

The mad mid-May of 1915 was an extraordinary moment in history. It was a time of crisis when all the leading figures seemed to lose their equilibrium, including Asquith who was anguished by the wreck of his romantic pen-friendship with Venetia Stanley, shortly to marry Edwin Montagu. On 14 May *The Times* reported on the shortage of high explosive shells on the western front, a revelation which some politicians believed to have been inspired by Churchill. This scandal, together with Fisher's resignation, brought the last Liberal government to an end. While negotiations were proceeding to form a coalition with the Tories, the German fleet put to sea. For a few hours it seemed as though a decisive battle would be fought. Churchill was almost alone at the Admiralty. His proposed replacement for Fisher as First Sea Lord, Sir Arthur Wilson, had not been confirmed in office. Fisher himself skulked at home, convinced that the German navy was merely trying to find out whether the British had occult means of reading their codes. In fact they were covering a mine-laying operation and quickly scuttled back to port. Churchill was thus deprived of the chance to save himself by a dramatic last-minute coup. Fisher burnt his own boats by sending Asquith a memorandum amounting to an ultimatum. This remarkable document guaranteed 'the successful termination of the war' if six conditions were met and made public, among them Churchill's exclusion from the cabinet and Fisher's own promotion to supreme suzerain at the Admiralty. As Hankey succinctly remarked, in a verdict which Asquith and Churchill both endorsed, 'Jackie had got megalomania and done for himself.'

Churchill's struggle to stay on at the Admiralty was humiliating and hopeless. He tried to persuade Asquith that he was indispensable and could bring 'this vast Dardanelles business safely through'. 'It is no clinging to office . . . which seizes me,' he urged, 'I am clinging to my *task and to my duty*.' Asquith persisted in his dismissal. Encouraged by Sir Arthur Wilson's unexpected refusal to serve under any First Lord but himself, Churchill failed to realise how discredited he had become in the popular estimation. Nor, apparently, was he aware of the deep loathing in which he was held by most Conservatives. Churchill actually appealed for support to Bonar Law, who thought him clever but unbalanced and much more of a danger to his own side in any conflict than to his enemies. Having first declared that he would only accept a military department Churchill told Asquith that he would serve in any capacity however humble. Thus in the coalition government he was made Chancellor of the Duchy of Lancaster. This was a virtual sinecure, but Churchill did remain a cabinet minister and a member of the Dardanelles Committee, the effective council of war.

Nevertheless Churchill's fall from high executive office was the greatest setback in his career. It was a crushing blow to his pride as well as to his ambition. John Burns considered Churchill's expression 'demoniacal' as he left the Admiralty. Others observed him sitting silent for hours with his head bowed in his hands. Edward Marsh reckoned that Churchill's being torn away from his naval work was 'a horrible wound and mutilation . . . it's like Beethoven deaf'. Churchill's friend Max Aitken, soon to be Lord Beaverbrook, described him as 'a lost soul'. Clementine thought her husband would 'die of grief'.

Churchill himself found the most vivid image to convey his agony: 'Like a sea-beast fished up from the depths, or a diver too suddenly hoisted, my veins threatened to burst from the fall in pressure.'

For the first time witnesses observed a strange characteristic in Churchill, that he altered physically according to circumstances. At forty he was already balding and podgy, slope-shouldered and bulldog-jowled. Despair made him appear older and greyer than his years. He thought he was finished and seemed to shrink and crumple under the shock. In defeat he was also gentler and more considerate. As Lord Beaverbrook wrote, on the top of a wave Churchill had in him the stuff of which tyrants are made. In the wave's trough, by contrast, he showed the sweet and sympathetic side of his nature. He could not hide his bitterness, remarking that 'if he was Prime Minister for 20 years it wouldn't make up for this fall'. But as Austen Chamberlain wrote in 1915, 'Winston is never seen to such advantage as in adversity. It will only be temporary, but he is showing great dignity and good temper.' It was only temporary for Churchill spared no effort to climb to the crest again. In these endeavours he was chiefly buoyed up by his own rhetoric. Lord Northcliffe said that Lloyd George had the 'faculty of auto-stimulation by conversation to a degree that I have never seen in anybody else'. Churchill regenerated himself by means of monologue. He seemed to expand as he spoke, inflated by the heroic nature of his conceptions. As he warmed to his theme he would slough off his cares like a shrivelled skin, his pink baby-face glowing with renewed vitality.

But however quick the pace of his thought, Churchill could not for long shake off the Black Dog of depression in that hideous summer and autumn of 1915. For though he was still in government he was out of power. Still voluble in council and prolific in memoranda, he tried to impose continuing pressure on events. Above all he refused to admit defeat in the Dardanelles. As late as October Churchill believed the Narrows could be forced. A friendly journalist noted, 'The idea had become a regular obsession – a fetish which had gained possession of his mind, blinding him to facts and filling his brain with illusions.' Churchill also demonstrated the futility of frontal assaults in France, urged the necessity of tanks ('mechanical elephants'), pleaded for the dismissal of Kitchener and the introduction of conscription.

To his intense chagrin Churchill's efforts were frustrated. Nothing could assuage his melancholy or dull his pain – until he made a great discovery. He had never visited an art gallery in his life but his sister-in-law Gwendeline Churchill (known as 'Goonie'), herself an enthusiastic amateur, suggested that he should paint. Soon he was daubing away in oils and (for once) in silence, totally absorbed. He never learnt to draw well and the composition of his pictures was always shaky. But he had a dramatic sense of colour. Disliking 'the sepulchral finality of black' he especially rejoiced in the rich and brilliant tones which he found in the south of France. In a graphic essay on painting Churchill proposed to spend his first million years in heaven getting to the bottom of the subject. Orange and vermilion would be the darkest colours on his celestial palette. Thus painting, which began as an anodyne, ended as a delight. It was to become his chief leisure activity, a marvellous source of solace and relaxation.

However, painting was not the kind of action Churchill craved in war-time. Nor was holding a post without power. When it became apparent that, despite his efforts, Gallipoli would be evacuated Churchill resigned. The decision was made reluctantly, in view of the fatal effect which relinquishing office had had on his father's career. But there was no real alternative. Churchill resolved that if he could not direct the war he would tear himself away from 'the Senate and the Forum to fight in the battle-fields of France'.

Before his departure Churchill made a long, vigorous speech to the Commons in defence of his stewardship, though he spoilt the effect by describing the Dardanelles as 'a legitimate gamble'. That phrase and the cry 'What about the Dardanelles?' taunted him for years to come. Meanwhile 'the escaped scapegoat', as Major Churchill called himself, was made to feel his unpopularity by front-line officers who despised politicians anyway. Despite their ostentatious coolness Churchill was happy. He was attached to the Grenadier Guards with a view to gaining experience of the trenches before being given a brigade of his own and he found a new peace of mind amid the shambles of war. Danger stimulated him and discomfort he ignored. He preferred the front line, wet in every sense, to battalion headquarters where no alcohol was served. Clementine kept him well supplied with brandy, not to mention cigars and other luxurious necessities from Fortnum and Mason. As always Churchill was fascinated by war and quite immune to fear. He actually enjoyed the noise made by the whizz-bangs. His fertile mind found plenty of exercise in devising 'variants of the offensive', trench-bridgers, bullet-proof waistcoats, shields and other novel means to break the deadlock. He quickly earned the Guards' respect and was even made second-in-command for a short time, an honour he valued highly. However General Haig, who had succeeded French as Commander-in-Chief, did not share his subordinates' high opinion of Churchill's military capacities. And Asquith was not prepared to incur hostility among his Conservative allies by confirming the former naval person as a brigadier-general in the army. Churchill was profoundly hurt and disappointed. He had to rest content with promotion to colonel of the 6th Battalion Royal Scots Fusiliers, a post he took up at the beginning of January 1916.

The hundred days which Churchill spent in command of this battalion can be seen as a microcosm of his whole life. He applied exuberant energy to intractable problems with mixed results, though his efforts were finally hailed as successful. The colonel's appointment was greeted in a mutinous spirit and he began by telling his assembled officers that he would break anyone who opposed him but look after those who gave him their support. Soon, however, Churchill's charm won round those not to be intimidated by threats. He smartened up the men and 'declared war' on lice. As Captain A. D. Gibb of the Scots Fusiliers recorded, Churchill delivered such a lecture on the louse's 'origin, growth and nature, its habitat and its importance as a factor in wars ancient and modern, as left one agape with wonder at the erudition and force of its author'.

Once in the line, near Ploegsteert, Churchill held forth with equal assurance on the art of laying sand-bags. Here he was fallible. So were certain other military ideas which he propounded. For example, he issued the impractical order that each officer should be everywhere accompanied by his batman who was to act as a bodyguard. Churchill did not hesitate to make 'trouble', waking up soldiers to warn them that the wind was in the right direction for a gas attack. He also called up huge artillery bombardments for no obvious reason and with no result other than to provoke German retaliation in kind. Still, though he never ducked at shells or bullets Churchill did appreciate the value of fortifications, or at any rate he enjoyed constructing them. As Captain Gibb wrote, one officer was instructed to devise 'shelters and scarps and counter-scarps and dug-outs and half-moons and ravelins . . . in some ludicrously inadequate time'. Churchill inspected his thousand yards of front three times a day and made periodic sorties into No Man's Land at night, crashing around in the shell holes and barbed wire like 'a baby elephant'. He had several narrow escapes.

The colonel imposed a lenient discipline on his men despite his theoretical belief that 'strict justice' should be meted out to them. On the other hand he took a very tough line with staff bureaucrats who held up promotions or medals ('the poor man's escutcheon'). Churchill was generous, allowing officers to use his tin bath. He was forthcoming in the mess, unafraid to discuss delicate political matters. He was comical: though fond of odd hats he tried on the Fusiliers' glengarry, looked in the mirror and exclaiming 'Christ!' quickly removed it in favour of his French steel helmet. All told, Churchill was the very model of the charismatic colonel, right down to the rhetoric, never more sincere, with which he attempted to inspire his doughty Scotsmen: 'War is a game that is played with a smile.' Captain Gibb's equally sincere conclusion was that 'no more popular officer ever commanded troops'.

Paradoxically the war was too peaceful for Churchill. He had found calm and balm amid shot and shell. But he hungered for the vertiginous thrills of Westminster. He called Clementine 'My dearest soul', the form of address used by the Duke of Marlborough in his letters to the Duchess during Queen Anne's war. But Churchill craved the combination of political and military power such as the Duke had exercised and, deprived of it, he suffered, like a drug addict, from withdrawal symptoms. His impatience to return to high office was clearly indicated by the speech he made to parliament while on leave in March 1916. In it he trounced A. J. Balfour, his successor as First Lord, for his impotent regime at the Admiralty. But he laid himself open to a devastating counter-attack by proposing the return of none other than Admiral Fisher. This astonishing instance of bad judgement was prompted by good personal motives. Churchill magnanimously desired to show that he had buried the hatchet with Fisher and that the past should not govern the future.

Clementine was less forgiving towards 'the fiend', as she called Fisher. But she did try to revive good relations with Asquith, to whom she had written 'the letter of a maniac' (his verdict) in May 1915 pleading for her husband's political life and asserting that only he possessed 'the power, the imagination, the deadliness to fight Germany'. Churchill himself felt that he had been betrayed by the Prime Minister. But he desperately needed Asquith's help in order to regain his political credit. For only by an official investigation into the Dardanelles imbroglio could Churchill present his case to the public and try to show that he did not bear responsibility for the disaster. It was with the intention of pressing for the Dardanelles Commission that Churchill took the opportunity, presented by the amalgamation of the 6th and 7th Scots Fusiliers and the consequent loss of his command in May 1916, to come back to civilian life. Clementine felt an aching ambivalence about his return. She was delighted to have him safely home but fearful that he was sacrificing the prestige he had so perilously won abroad. Her indomitable spouse was a prey to no such doubts. Churchill felt driven by destiny to abandon the 'rough, fierce life . . . under the hammer of Thor' where he had experienced such contentment and enter once again into the political fray.

CHAPTER VI

WARMONGER AND

PEACEMAKER

FOR over a year after his return from the front, between
May 1916 and July 1917, Churchill was in limbo. His faith
in his own judgement was not shaken. Indeed, as he and Fisher
collated the evidence they would present to the Dardanelles
Commission, Churchill became even more certain that the
operation could have succeeded and that its failure was not his
fault. But to watch from the side-lines while Asquith's administration pursued its nerveless course, while Haig supervised his
disastrous offensive on the Somme, and the lackadaisical
Balfour permitted – as Fisher said – grass to grow in the corridors of the Admiralty, all this was torment to Churchill.
Balfour's feebleness was clearly demonstrated by his inviting
Churchill to draft a reassuring report on the battle of Jutland
after his own too pessimistic communiqué had damaged
national morale. But Churchill had no other official task to
occupy him during these terrible months. His personal
occupations, writing for money and painting for pleasure,
brought little real satisfaction. He fretted his soul away, damning
fate that his gift for war was not being used, that his treasure
was spurned, that he was banished from the scene of action and
denied scope to serve his country in its hour of need. He longed
to plunge into action once more but he found himself 'simply
existing' while golden opportunities slipped past.

Privately he thought the government 'rotten to the core' but
his public criticisms were muted. This was partly because the

Dardanelles still hung round his neck like an albatross, partly because he would not give comfort to the Germans. True he did press for more efficient conduct of the war, especially for more aid to the men in the trenches whose plight he explained to a largely uncomprehending House of Commons. But although he helped to discredit Asquith, Churchill took no part in the intrigue by which Lloyd George superseded him in December 1916. Churchill, who had supported Lloyd George during the Marconi scandal, fondly expected to be found a place in the new ministry. But even the Welsh Wizard could not dispel the hatred and mistrust which Tories felt for Churchill. Senior Conservatives refused to serve with him. They insisted that, brilliant though he might be, there was a fatal flaw in his make-up which caused him to destroy anything he touched. The whirring cogs of his mind, they thought, were prevented from running true by some hidden defect. Lloyd George instructed that busy go-between Max Aitken to hint that Churchill would be excluded and thus lessen his disappointment. Aitken did so at a dinner given by F. E. Smith. When Churchill grasped Aitken's message he was livid. 'Smith, this man knows I am not to be included in the new government,' he exclaimed and stormed out of the house carrying his hat and coat. Churchill later said that this was the 'toughest moment of his life'.

The report of the Dardanelles Commission, issued early in 1917, largely exonerated Churchill without entirely rehabilitating him. It held him culpable for not reporting the advice of his naval experts to the War Council and for being carried away by his own enthusiasm for the project. But though it swept away what Churchill called 'many serious and reckless charges' made against him, some of the mud stuck. Still, he now shared the blame with others, particularly Asquith and Kitchener. In this respect the report, which Churchill subjected to minute and effective criticism in the Commons, was 'an instalment of fair play' despite its 'ungracious' language. However it was not this partial restoration of Churchill's reputation which caused Lloyd George to give him employment. Churchill had continued to disparage the current war policy, advocating an end to 'those dismal processes of waste and slaughter called attrition', ridiculing the possibilities of a cavalry break-through, calling for machines as a substitute for men and for brains to save blood. It was obvious to the Prime Minister that Churchill himself would break through somewhere, 'like a geyser bursting through a crack'. Lloyd George therefore determined to enlist Churchill's argumentative and executive vigour on his own side. In July 1917 he appointed him Minister of Munitions without a seat in the war cabinet. Rather than have Churchill against him Lloyd George was prepared to flout his Tory supporters and risk the dangers implicit in allying himself with so powerful and volatile a political force.

Lloyd George's true opinion of Churchill is difficult to gauge. Privately he was apt to remark that Churchill was eaten up by egotism and vanity, ruined by reading about Napoleon, would 'make a drum out of his mother's skin if he could use it to sound his own praises'. Above all 'reckless impatience has been his besetting curse through life'. In public he paid tribute to Churchill as 'a man of dazzling talents', possessing 'a forceful and a fascinating personality', fertile, courageous, indefatigable. Certainly Lloyd George was amused and stimulated by Churchill, fond of him even in spite of his oft-repeated assertion that there was no friendship at the top. He found in Churchill a kindred spirit, one whose quicksilver cleverness and passion for politics matched his own. Lloyd George appreciated Churchill's capacities and by 1917 he no longer regarded him as a rival. The Prime Minister knew that 'Men of his ardent temperament and powerful mentality need exceptionally strong brakes.' But Lloyd George reckoned that if anyone could control Churchill's wayward impulses and check his erratic judgement he was that man. On the whole, though not without long and maddening struggles, Lloyd George was right.

For his own part Churchill had to accept the fact that his relationship with Lloyd George was now that of servant and master. He was less inclined to cavil at this because of his admiration for the Prime Minister's spell-binding political gifts, his unrivalled ingenuity as a negotiator, his mongoose quickness, his uncanny foresight and his supreme mastery of 'the art of getting things done'. Churchill never acknowledged it but he may well have regarded Lloyd George as his superior at the business of politics. In fact Lloyd George by no means eclipsed Churchill as a war minister. It has to be said that the Welshman suffered from grave disadvantages. In particular he wanted the authority which came from being leader of a great party. Churchill's own chief handicap perhaps stemmed from the fact that as warlord he had too much authority, which permitted him to indulge his obstinate vices of impatience and interference. But Churchill possessed moral qualities which Lloyd George lacked and to them in large measure the smoother and more efficient direction of British efforts during the Second World War was due. Churchill never had the guile which enabled Lloyd George to wriggle out of some difficulties but enmeshed him firmly in others. Churchill's attempts at dissimulation would scarcely have deceived a child. Not that he made many. He was boldly straightforward, would not intrigue against his subordinates, never betrayed them in secret. There were naturally rows and antipathies during the Second World War. But they were nothing like the treacherous vendettas, especially between 'Frocks' and 'Brass Hats', which so hampered the British high command in the Great War.

Churchill was shocked and, for a time, chastened by the howl of protest which greeted his appointment to the Ministry of Munitions. But he soon absorbed himself in the heavy work of the department, improving efficiency in every sphere. He simplified the bureaucracy and galvanised the forces of labour. He tried to reduce strikes, first by raising wages, by conciliation and exhortation; and later by threatening to conscript those who would not cooperate. Very soon he had increased production and was organising what he afterwards called 'gigantic agencies for the slaughter of men by machinery'. He manufactured 'masses of guns, mountains of shells and clouds of aeroplanes'. His civil servants, initially hostile, were astounded by his energy and captivated by his charm and eloquence. Less pleased were the Admiralty and the Ministry of War in whose affairs Churchill could not resist meddling. Needless to say this 'ironmonger', as Lord Derby contemptuously called him, claimed that such interference was all part of his duty. He behaved, in effect, as though the tail of armaments should wag the dog of war.

Now that America had entered the conflict Churchill was looking for victory on the western front. Not that he had altered his view about the futility of assaults in the style of the Somme and Passchendaele. But he thought that sheer weight of munitions, especially in the form of 'dreadnoughts on land' – tanks – could smash German resistance. In this belief he was both over-optimistic and ahead of his time. Of course, the generals were unimaginative in their use of tanks. But in fact these mechanical monsters were too slow and cumbersome to make any appreciable difference in the First World War. Not until the Second did tanks come into their own as a decisive weapon.

Churchill studied to meet the army's needs, which gave him every excuse for gadding backwards and forwards to France, latterly by aeroplane. He managed to witness every major battle between July 1917 and the end of the war. The front acted on him like a powerful magnet. Once, as his secretary Edward Marsh observed, Churchill simply started walking towards the trenches from well behind the line, attracted by the sound of shell-fire. In this passion for danger Churchill was only matched by the French premier Clemenceau. On a tour of the front which they made together, vividly described in Churchill's book of essays *Thoughts and Adventures*, the British Bulldog found himself remonstrating with the French Tiger about the unwisdom of exposing himself to such risks. He received the splendidly Churchillian response, 'C'est mon grand plaisir.'

Churchill's most frequent companion on his expeditions to France was the third Duke of Westminister, known as 'Bendor'. The Duke suffered from moral as well as physical halitosis. He was, for example, an ardent anti-semite. But he was also the sort of raffish crony whom Churchill liked. Bendor – always stimulating, often charming – was immensely rich and Churchill enjoyed hunting boars on his magnificent estate in Normandy. In the Duke's opinion Churchill, because of the polite reception he got in France, did not realise how unpopular he was among the soldiers. Perhaps, but Haig and the generals certainly appreciated Churchill's efforts on their behalf. During the final German offensive in the spring of 1918 one of his staunchest critics, General Sir Henry Wilson, exclaimed, 'Winston is a *real* gem in a crisis.' Lloyd George even accused Churchill of changing his tune and 'echoing the sentiments of GHQ'. This was not quite the case. But he was sufficiently *persona grata* with the military to have a château put at his disposal in France. It was near a place called Fouquienbergue, which Churchill christened 'Fuck and bugger.'

Such language, of course, was taboo in front of the ladies. Nevertheless Clementine feared that the war, with its accumulation of terrible incidents, had had a coarsening and brutalising effect on her husband. Snug in her Sussex 'country basket' – she had insisted that 'the babies must keep rabbits' – 'the Kat' was preoccupied with her growing brood of 'kittens'. While Churchill was in Antwerp their third child Sarah ('the Mule') had been born and shortly after the armistice another daughter Marigold ('the Duckadilly') appeared. Between these joyous events Churchill had become, as Clementine said, 'a Mustard Gas fiend, a Tank juggernaut and a flying Terror'. She longed for him to be a 'reconstructive genius' in the new world which was struggling to be born after the swift and unexpected German collapse of autumn 1918. Churchill was nothing loth. But his first goal was to secure himself a prominent place in the coalition government which Lloyd George hoped to re-form after the general election. Indeed Churchill's support for this ministry was conditional upon his personal advancement. Edwin Montagu penned a comic description of how Lloyd George hooked Churchill. The latter began the interview by being 'sulky, morose and unforthcoming'. Then he poured forth a 'torrent of turgid eloquence' to the effect that he could not bear the burden of responsibility without having the power to determine policy. The Prime Minister, exerting all his fascination, seemed to indicate that Churchill would have a seat in an enlarged cabinet. At once 'the sullen looks disappeared, smiles wreathed the hungry face, the fish was landed' – though not without further ineffectual struggles to obtain more positive guarantees.

On the evening of 11 November 1918 Winston and Clementine drove through cheering crowds to congratulate the Prime Minister on his triumph over Germany. During dinner Lloyd George expressed a wish to shoot the Kaiser. Churchill disagreed. As always after victory he sought reconciliation. Admittedly during the subsequent election Churchill made some concessions to those who wanted to make Germany pay. But in general he campaigned for a comprehensive programme of 'peaceful reconstruction', including the nationalisation of railways, the regulation of capitalism and the establishment of 'a decent minimum standard of life and labour'. These policies, designed in part to steal the clothes of his left-wing opponents, can be seen as the final sparks from the embers of Churchill's young radicalism. Henceforth, foreseeing the death of Liberalism and decrying the birth of Bolshevism, he moved unashamedly rightwards. This political shift was made easier by the office to which Lloyd George appointed him, Secretary of State for War (and Air), in January 1919.

'What is the use of being War Secretary if there is no war?' Churchill fretted, while trying to make up his mind whether to accept the post. Bonar Law answered crushingly: 'If we thought there was going to be a war we wouldn't appoint you War Secretary.' Actually, of course, there was a war. Tsarist forces were fighting against the Red Army in Russia and British troops had been peripherally involved for almost a year. They had been stationed in Murmansk and Archangel to prevent military stores from falling into Bolshevik or German hands. Churchill was anxious to reinforce them, being intent on ridding the world of 'the plague bacillus of Bolshevism' even if it meant using poison gas. One of his first acts at the War Ministry was to send out a secret memorandum to army commanders asking whether their men would 'parade for draft' in Russia. The response was discouraging. Indeed, war-weary British soldiers were themselves close to revolution as the result of a demobilisation scheme which one general described as 'organised anarchy on wholesale lines'.

Churchill immediately scrapped this scheme and nipped mutiny in the bud. Within a month he had returned a million men to civilian life and he brooked no unnecessary delay in releasing the rest. As always the bureaucrats were swept along in the comet's train. Beaverbrook gave a vivid picture of Churchill at the War Office in 1919, striding up and down his room on little feet,

> tingling with vitality. Bold and imaginative in the sweep of his conceptions, prolific of new ideas, like a machine of bullets and expelling his notions in much the same manner. Fertile, resourceful, courageous, he was always tolerant, though in this age occasionally wanting in prudence.

Imprudence could scarcely have been taken further than to advocate intervention in a foreign civil war in the immediate aftermath of Armageddon. Yet Churchill became devoured by the notion that the British lion in all his victorious might should confront the Russian bear so foully metamorphosed by what he called 'the baboonery of Bolshevism'.

Churchill developed an obsession about Bolshevism. Lloyd George reckoned that his ducal blood revolted at the murder of so many Grand Dukes. Certainly Churchill was outraged by the atrocities of the Bolsheviks who 'hop and caper like troops of ferocious baboons amid the ruins of cities and the corpses of their victims'. As Lloyd George's secretary and mistress Frances Stevenson wrote, he raved about Bolshevism 'almost like a madman'. True, Churchill had an immediate insight into Bolshevik baseness because British cryptographers had broken Russian codes. And, though secret intelligence so fascinated him that he was apt to make a fetish out of it, Churchill was not alone in being outraged by the deciphered revelations. Thus it was that Lord Curzon refused to shake hands with the leader of the Russian Trade Delegation in 1920 until the Prime Minister appealed to him to 'be a gentleman', and Churchill inquired: 'Did you shake hands with the hairy baboon?' However Churchill regarded Communism as more than just a novel form of tyranny. In his view it was a virulent contagion which threatened to destroy civilisation. Bolshevism would turn the evolutionary clock back and reduce human society to the level of an anthill. This explains the violence of his language: 'One might as well legalize sodomy as recognize the Bolsheviks,' he expostulated. It also accounts for his determination to implement the policy which he summed up in this trenchant formula: 'Kill the Bolshie. Kiss the Hun.'

Churchill's persistence in trying to step up British intervention in Russia was almost sublime. He was opposed by the Prime Minister, by nearly all his colleagues, by most MPs, by the bulk of the press and by the vast majority of the population. Yet he argued, cajoled, exhorted and manoeuvred. He threatened resignation. He took his case to the public in newspaper articles. He simply would not give up. In fact Churchill employed his dialectical technique of the 'reconnaissance-in-force' to its utmost, striving desperately to build up some sort of attacking momentum as he had done during the Dardanelles operation. When overruled in cabinet he asserted that the only safe way to extricate British troops from Russia was for them to advance in order to cover their retirement. For a time he even induced the cabinet to accept this bizarre strategy. When forced to concede the army's unequivocal withdrawal, he agitated for the employment of the navy and proposed a scheme for annexing the Caspian Sea. Churchill insisted that 'surplus' war materials should be sent to the Tsarists. He urged support for Poland in her fight against Russia. When the Tsarists got close to Moscow he talked of 'going out there to ride a white charger into the city, at the head of the victorious forces'. When the Red tide turned he called for the evacuation of White Russian refugees in British ships. He kicked against receiving the Bolshevik Trade Delegation. Even his fine speech condemning General Dyer for the massacre of nearly four hundred unarmed Indians at Amritsar became an opportunity to attack the Bolsheviks. 'Frightfulness is not a remedy known to the British pharmacopoeia,' he pronounced, whereas 'bloody and devastating terrorism' was the hallmark of Bolshevism.

Churchill's struggle against 'Red Bruin' annoyed Lloyd George who begged and commanded him to abandon it. In private the Prime Minister even declared that Churchill was more trouble than he was worth in government. Their relationship suffered accordingly and a new sharpness marked their mutual ragging. 'Don't you make any mistake,' jeered Churchill, 'you're not going to get your new world. The old world is a good enough place for me, and there's life in the old dog yet. It's going to sit up and wag its tail.' Lloyd George then accused him of being 'the only remaining specimen of a real Tory'. At least this meant, Churchill retorted, that he would always have to be included in Lloyd George's all-party administration. 'Oh no!' said Lloyd George, 'to be a party you must have at least one follower. *You* have none.' This cut was close to the bone. For after almost twenty years of political prominence Churchill had no body of supporters. He was independent in the sense that no party could depend on him. This 'very clever bright-haired angel', as Sir Alfred Mond called him, was a lone voice and a personal force. He owed allegiance only to his star; no one owed or offered allegiance to him. He induced apprehension, not adhesion. Indeed Churchill's 'private war' in Russia had revived fears, brutally expounded in the press, that he was an adventurer determined to write his name on the pages of history in letters of blood.

Yet Churchill did have Pied Piper qualities which, though he was not fond of 'new people', he sometimes chose to display. In November 1920, for example, he visited Oxford to speak at the Union and his young host Victor Cazalet waxed rapturous about the occasion:

> Winston is a great man, full of energy and drive, vigour, knowledge and push. He was charming and delightful to all the young men I introduced him to, so interested in their war experiences, so sympathetic, so simple. I asked him how he liked writing his review of Mrs Asquith's *Memoirs*. He said: 'Have you ever seen an elephant do an egg dance?'

When the mood took him Churchill radiated warmth, geniality, fun and affection. Some like Lord Riddell found him 'lovable'. But as Cazalet and others learnt to their cost, Churchill expected unswerving loyalty in return for his benevolence. When it was not forthcoming he would switch off his smile and switch on his scowl. The diarist 'Chips' Channon later recorded that when Churchill met someone he disliked 'he seems to contract, suddenly to look smaller and his famous charm is overclouded by an angry taurine look'. In such a situation Churchill could be extraordinarily ungracious and unattractive. His eyes rolling, he would back and sidle away like a restive horse. He would frown and glower and grunt.

Churchill had much cause for ill-temper during his thirteen-month tenure of the War Office. His recognition of Russian Communism as a potent new threat to world peace may now be deemed far-sighted. But it was apparent to contemporaries that his interventionist crusade had proved a fiasco. Similarly his attempt to combat Irish terrorism with English coercion was not meeting with the success for which he had hoped. As the Republican campaign for independence grew more violent Churchill endorsed the vicious counter-measures taken by the 'Black and Tans'. He apparently favoured retaliatory murders, though there was some argument about whether reprisals should be 'authorised', 'official' or 'responsible'. Churchill also advocated the bombing and machine-gunning of Sinn Fein meetings from the air. And he proposed sending seven battalions of Ulstermen to the south, a sure-fire method of provoking a massacre. Luckily his more blood-thirsty initiatives were stifled. Clementine prudently advised him to try to achieve his goal – a just and generous measure of Home Rule – by moderate means, avoiding 'the rough iron-fisted "hunnish" way'.

The trouble was that everything was coloured by Churchill's fanatical hatred of Bolshevism. He saw all acts hostile to Britain, whether in Ireland, the Middle East or India, as part of an international revolutionary conspiracy directed against the victorious empire. Why else, he asked, 'should the Egyptian extremists give money to the Socialist *Daily Herald*? Why does Lenin send them money too? Why does he also send money to Sinn Fein?' This was not pure paranoia. The Communists did think that world revolution was imminent and they were not averse to acting as midwives of the inevitable. On the other hand the British Labour party loathed Bolshevism (a fact appreciated by Lenin, who proposed to support its leaders as a rope supports a hanged man) and there has never been a significant revolutionary tradition among the British proletariat. Churchill knew nothing about the working class; indeed, he was shocked to discover that there were starving children and men with bare feet in his own Dundee constituency. But he scented subversion everywhere and believed that it should be met by force. The extremes which he was prepared to countenance were apparent even in his jokes. At a dinner party he told the Secretary for India, Edwin Montagu, that Gandhi 'ought to be laid, bound hand and foot, at the gates of Delhi and then trampled on by an enormous elephant with the new Viceroy seated on its back'.

In February 1921 Churchill was glad to exchange the frustrations of conducting the War Ministry in peace time for the challenge of becoming Colonial Secretary at a moment when the empire had just about reached its furthest territorial limits. In this office he altered course, seeking to achieve his country's ends by negotiated settlement rather than by force of arms. True, he was not squeamish about employing the RAF, whose future as an independent service he had secured after the war, to drop mustard gas on colonial dissidents. But he aimed to divide and rule by diplomatic means.

So in the Middle East, one of his two major headaches, he supported Zionist aspirations. He hoped thus to wreck what he took to be Bolshevik plans for the creation of an 'international Soviet', or global Communist state, run by Jews. At the same time, with the assistance of T. E. Lawrence, he endeavoured to allay the fears of Arabs, though he was privately convinced that they were barbarians who ate little but camel's dung. Out of territories mandated to Britain at the Treaty of Versailles he carved an independent Trans-Jordan. And he established an Arab government in Iraq, reducing costly British defence forces at a stroke. Lord Curzon, who resented Churchill's inter- ference in foreign affairs, was apt to mock his colleague's Middle Eastern efforts. In March 1921, when Churchill set off to try to solve the problems of the region in person (accompanied by Clementine and a mountain of luggage, including five hat boxes) the Foreign Secretary remarked, 'He will be under irresistible temptation to declare himself King of Babylon.' (It was perhaps an echo of Riddell's suggestion that if Churchill went to Russia in pursuit of his anti-Bolshevik campaign he 'might become Tsar'.) Churchill's sovereign attribute was, of course, his tongue and he employed it in a temporarily success- ful, though ultimately doomed, attempt to reconcile Jew and Arab. Still, his policy, presented to the House of Commons with incomparable power and grandeur, did much to wipe out the stigma of failure at the War Office.

Churchill's other main headache was Ireland. Here again he helped to arrive at a conciliatory settlement. Of course it satis- fied no one at the time and to this day the Irish problem apparently remains insoluble. What Churchill said in 1921 about the 'medieval hatreds and barbarous passions' rampant in Ulster is still lamentably true. But at least the compromise of 1921/2 ended the immediate conflict between British and Irish forces. And after the civil war within Sinn Fein, which followed the treaty, it provided northern and southern Ireland with a relatively peaceful *modus vivendi* for half a century. By the spring of 1921 it had become clear that coercion was merely breeding terror. A truce was agreed and Churchill took a prominent part in the subsequent negotiations with Nationalist leaders. One of them, Michael Collins, was hostile to him at first: 'Will sacrifice all for political gain . . . Inclined to be bombastic. Full of ex-officer jingo or similar outlook. Don't actually trust him.' He soon changed his mind. Shortly before his assassination Collins sent Churchill a message saying that they could have achieved nothing without him. Churchill insisted that Ulster should determine her own destiny and that the rest of Ireland should remain under the crown and within the empire. This apart he was willing to concede an almost complete measure of independence. Once an agreement had been reached he became its most vociferous exponent. Drawing on his experience of conciliating the Boers, he pleaded for mutual tolerance and understanding. He wisely urged that the only mode of progress for Ireland was the creation of 'a gulf between the past and the future'. He pointed out the tragic alternative – Ireland degenerating into 'a meaningless welter of chaos and confusion'.

Churchill's standing rose almost to pre-war heights during his time at the Colonial Office. His efforts at conciliation (backed, admittedly, by threats of force) made it impossible for opponents to sustain the charge that he was an irresponsible warmonger – or, at any rate, *always* an irresponsible warmonger. There were many tributes to his statesmanship. Officials like Richard Meinertzhagen, though often driven to distraction by his 'fulminations', acknowledged his 'brilliant brain', sure instincts and Trojan industry. Churchill rightly regarded the parliamentary session of 1921/2 as one of unprecedented personal success. This did not mean that he was entirely contented. He seethed with rage in April 1922 when Sir Robert Horne was promoted over his head to the Chancellorship of the Exchequer. His grumblings about Lloyd George almost culminated in resignation on several occasions. He particularly disliked the Prime Minister's squalid traffic in honours. It was a blatant scandal of which Churchill could not be unaware, despite his innocent assumption that his own probity was matched by that of others. The Prime Minister himself complained that he could 'never rely on Winston in a crisis'. Lloyd George ruefully recalled the occasion in 1909 when he had entrusted his £100,000 budget fighting-fund to Churchill who, with casual lordliness, went off and spent most of it in his own constituency.

Churchill's own financial position improved at the beginning of the 1920s. He was writing his six-volume *World Crisis* at half-a-crown per word and doing similarly remunerative journalism as well as receiving his ministerial salary. Of course, his income was matched by his expenditure, for Churchill's sybaritic tastes were not cheaply satisfied. A Rolls Royce motor car, polo ponies, gambling, holidays in the south of France, 'pigging it at the Ritz' – all this drained his exchequer. But on the death of a distant relation in 1921 Churchill received a large legacy producing an annual income of £4,000. With it he was able, the following year, to purchase (and rebuild) Chartwell Manor, his country house near Westerham in Kent – the 'Garden of England' about which his nanny Mrs Everest had excited his childish imagination. However, his prosperity counted for little beside the personal losses which Churchill suffered at this time. In April 1921 Clementine's brother committed suicide. In June Lady Randolph Churchill (by now actually Mrs Montagu Porch) suffered a fatal haemorrhage after having her leg amputated as the result of a fall. Winston mourned her deeply, though he could never regard as tragic the deaths of those who had reached the end of full lives. Worse was to come. In August little red-haired Marigold, 'the Duckadilly', died of septicaemia. Both her parents were grief-stricken. Clementine could scarcely be comforted even by the arrival of Mary, the last and best of her brood, who was born in August 1922.

A few weeks later, quite out of the blue, a crisis in foreign affairs sprang up which smashed Lloyd George's government and threw Churchill into political outer darkness. The Turks, deprived of large tracts of Asia Minor by the peace settlement, had revived under the leadership of Mustapha Kemal, had driven the Greeks into the sea at Smyrna and menaced British garrisons on the neutralised straits. Churchill, reacting vigorously against this new threat to his beloved Dardanelles, abandoned his pro-Greek policy and, with Lloyd George, ardently sought to resist Turkish incursions. He sent reinforcements to Chanak. He tried to engage the empire, but unfortunately released news of his appeal before dominion governments had

had time to decode it, causing them to look even more sourly on the enterprise. Finally, Churchill and Lloyd George instructed General Harington on the spot to issue an ultimatum to the Turks: withdraw or be fired on. Harington sensibly ignored their telegram and instituted negotiations. The crisis was resolved peacefully, much to the chagrin of Churchill who was anxious to teach the Turks a lesson and longed to exchange paint brush for sword. But the nation was shocked at having been so nearly pitchforked into war on a minor issue. Conservative back benchers, led by Bonar Law and Stanley Baldwin, withdrew their support for the coalition, which duly collapsed.

At the height of this turmoil Churchill himself collapsed, entering hospital with acute appendicitis. Clementine, the infant Mary still at her breast, had to defend his Dundee seat in the ensuing election. Wearing pearls she was spat at by working women as she canvassed. Undaunted she harped on the Irish treaty and tried to contradict renewed assertions that her husband was a daemonic warmonger. 'I am exhibiting you as a Cherub Peace Maker with little fluffy wings round your chubby face.' Churchill did little to sustain this beatific image when he at last appeared, an angry invalid, a few days before the poll. He attacked his left-wing opponents with a barrage of invective: 'Mr Gallacher is only Mr Morel with the courage of his convictions, and Trotsky is only Mr Gallacher with the power to murder those whom he cannot convince.' Such charges did him no good. Liberalism was doomed and Churchill was defeated. 'In the twinkling of an eye', to quote once again Churchill's justly celebrated assessment of his fall, 'I found myself without an office, without a seat, without a party and without an appendix.'

CHAPTER VII

CHANCELLOR OF

CHARTWELL

WITH his future uncertain Churchill sought to live down his past. He spent the six months after his defeat (until May 1923) in the South of France working on *The World Crisis*. That vivid history of his time was also a massive exercise in self-vindication (though not vindictiveness – Churchill bore little malice and no rancour). The book, which was dictated, is really a brilliantly sustained Churchillian monologue, shaped by chronology and supported by carefully chosen extracts from official documents. It is a Mississippi of rhetoric, sweeping along with great narrative power though little interpretative depth – Churchill always preferred anecdote to analysis. But its waters sometimes burst their banks as the majestic style becomes swollen with bombastic phrases. For example Churchill described the approach of Armageddon in 'a world of monstrous shadows moving in convulsive combinations through vistas of fathomless catastrophe'. On the other hand no one else could have told such a story with such vitality. Churchill's account, although flawed, is informed by an authentic vision of a heroic past. His writing, although imitative, is a genuine expression of a flamboyant personality. All told, *The World Crisis* is just what it was designed to be: a mighty monument to a patriotic states-man. It helps to explain how, 'with the most plentiful crop of political wild oats ever sown' (to quote the acidulous A. G. Gardiner), Churchill was to become within a couple of years 'easily the foremost figure in parliament'.

Churchill's move to the political right was brought to an abrupt halt in 1923. Stanley Baldwin, intent on strengthening the second-rate government which he had inherited on Bonar Law's death, unexpectedly went to the country on the issue of protection. Having deserted the Conservatives to further the cause of free trade, Churchill could only stand as a Liberal. But at the election campaign in West Leicester it became clear that he was fighting against Socialism rather than for Liberalism. The hostile crowds, he said, behaved 'more like Russian wolves than British workmen'. Both Churchill locally and Baldwin nationally suffered defeat and were thus thrown together. Though lacking an overall majority, Labour was the largest party in the new parliament and the Liberals allowed it to take office for the first time. Churchill, who had consistently declared that Socialists were unfit to govern, was horrified by the Liberals' treason. It was, he said, like missionaries assisting cannibals. He announced that Labour's accession to power was 'a serious national misfortune'. Then he girded himself up for a crusade against these 'un-English', 'foreign-minded' Socialists who possessed 'not the slightest idea of fair play or sportsmanship'.

In February 1924, after gaining the benevolent neutrality of Baldwin (who had renounced protection), Churchill stood as a 'Constitutionalist' or anti-Socialist candidate in a by-election for the Abbey Division of Westminster. Though opposed by an official Conservative, he had much Tory support, especially from highly-placed friends like Balfour and Lord Birkenhead (as F. E. Smith had become). Churchill was also assisted by a motley crew of dukes, prize-fighters, jockeys, courtiers, chorus-girls and press barons. After ten days of barn-storming, which included a well-trumpeted tour of the constituency in a coach-and-four, Churchill lost by a mere forty-three votes. For a time he despaired. But luck was on his side for the Conservatives were determined that this formidable freebooter should fight under their colours. Although he kept the 'Constitutionalist' flag aloft it was really as a Conservative that he was elected when the Tories returned to power in October 1924. Victory so delighted him that he had a commemorative medal struck. It bore the words 'Union and Freedom' and Churchill gave one to each of the workers in his new constituency, Epping (later re-named the Wanstead and Woodford Division of Essex), which he was to represent for the next forty years. It was a congenial place with a couple of well-situated hotels, in each of which he kept a private stock of champagne, brandy and cigars. Thus Churchill negotiated the arduous road back to his first political home. Anyone could 'rat', he remarked complacently, but it took a certain ingenuity to 're-rat'.

Baldwin looked on Churchill with a mixture of awe, admiration and fear. Toryism's newest old recruit was a wild beast who could wreck the party unless he was tamed and domesticated. After much stolid cogitation the pipe-smoking premier offered Churchill the Chancellorship. 'Of the Duchy of Lancaster?' Churchill is supposed to have asked. 'No, of the Exchequer.' Churchill's watery eyes, always prone to overflow, filled with tears and he apparently replied: 'That fulfils my ambition. I still have my father's robe as Chancellor. I shall be proud to serve you in this splendid office.' So, aged almost fifty and clutching the seals which he was reluctant to entrust to anyone less than a Permanent Secretary, Churchill marched into the Treasury. No. 11 Downing Street was to be his official residence for the next five years. P. J. Grigg, his Principal Private Secretary, had been accustomed to regard his own existence as a series of events. Now he found it pervaded by 'a single dominating personality', 'the most brilliant and versatile individual who has lived in our age'.

Grigg penned a lively sketch of his new master. What struck him most was the degree of freedom which Churchill permitted his civil servants. They were encouraged to speak their minds with the utmost frankness. Indeed, the Chancellor bore no resentment if, when fighting their corner, they bested him. But this happened seldom, even when Churchill was in the wrong, for his argumentative potency was such that he usually defeated his subordinates where he did not cow them. Churchill treated his officials with candour amounting to indiscretion. Within a few weeks of his arrival he was giving Grigg a mordant commentary on his cabinet colleagues, only to conclude with a grin: 'But who am I to criticize the selective capacity of the Prime Minister.' Churchill's fund of humour was immense. He once solemnly told Grigg that he proposed not to apologise for his unpopular betting tax but to address his audience on major political issues. ' "In fact I shall take a high moral line" – and then with that urchin's look over his spectacles that I got to know so well, "You be buggered and that sort of thing." ' As usual Churchill worked with words, and he was always inclined to think that a problem dealt with oratorically was a problem solved. He dictated countless minutes, everything from important state papers to complaints about the office of works supplying Czechoslovakian matches to a British government establishment. As Churchill later acknowledged, he never understood the technical or 'bucket-shop side of the Treasury'. He talked himself into a superficial knowledge of economics, though he thought economists spoke Persian. He argued passionately for his many original schemes, some of them sound, some of them hare-brained, most of them ingenious ways of robbing Peter to pay Paul.

Actually Churchill was not interested in high finance. As his Parliamentary Private Secretary Robert Boothby said, the essence of Churchill's genius was vitality, fecundity and versatility. His budgets, fiscal soufflés whipped up and presented with marvellous panache, were a triumph of manner over matter. Churchill's aim was to make the same sort of splash as Lloyd George had done at the Treasury. To some extent he succeeded, reducing direct taxes and improving pensions. But he was gravely handicapped by two circumstances. First, as a virtual outsider he could not persuade the Conservatives to support the cuts he now demanded in military expenditure. Indeed he provoked deep resentment by working overtime on the affairs of other departments. Secondly, there was what he came to regard as the greatest political blunder of his life – the return to the gold standard in April 1925. Orthodox economists of all parties wanted to tie the value of sterling to gold. But Churchill was not entirely convinced by the experts, especially as both Keynes and Beaverbrook contradicted them. Probably his real motive for making the change had to do with prestige. It was inconsistent with Britain's greatness, which he wanted to restore after the war, to have a fluctuating currency. If the pound was based not on faith or hope but on reality, it could look the dollar in the eye. Unfortunately the return to gold involved the over-valuation of sterling, which meant that British exports became more expensive and less saleable. As a protective (though not, Churchill claimed, a protectionist) measure he re-imposed duties on some luxury imports such as motor cars. But this did little to help British manufacturing as a whole. The coal industry, depressed by renewed German competition, faced a particularly sharp crisis.

This in turn precipitated the general strike of May 1926. Churchill in fact sympathised with the miners and had supported a government subsidy to maintain their wages. But stiff economies were essential if his second budget was to be balanced. And Churchill responded aggressively to the challenge of a general strike. It was understandable, he thought, for the miners to withdraw their labour in protest against the imposition of longer hours for lower pay. But for the Trades Union Congress to organise a sympathetic strike by other workers . . . this was to transform a trade dispute into a revolution. Churchill's volcanic imagination boiled over at the prospect: the country would be starved into submission, parliament would be coerced by a *sans-culotte* mob, aristocratic gore would flow in the gutters. All his bellicose instincts were aroused. He wrote Baldwin flaming letters announcing that 'we are at war'. 'A little bloodshed would do no harm,' he considered, and he wanted to combine the police and the Territorial army. Churchill curtly refused an offer from the trades unions to organize food distribution, an offer which belied the insurrectionary nature of the stoppage – it failed, indeed, because its leaders were so half-hearted. Churchill organised armed food convoys which amazed and amused east enders. Despite the singular absence of sedition Churchill favoured intimidation, a display of force, the deployment of tanks and machine-guns. Baldwin, who was 'terrified' of what Churchill might be like, sensibly channelled the energies of his headstrong colleague into the prosecution of a paper war rather than a real war.

During the strike, which lasted for ten days in most industries and pretty well paralysed Fleet Street, Churchill presided over the government's newspaper, the *British Gazette*. He flung himself into the enterprise with piratical zeal, occupying the *Morning Post*'s premises, improvising a staff, requisitioning newsprint and being outrageously rude to Lord Beaverbrook when he withheld it. With his mercurial temperament, his capacity to dictate pungent prose at breakneck speed, his willingness to instruct experienced (and infuriated) printers in the fundamentals of their craft, his delight in tearing the paper to pieces minutes before the deadline, Churchill was the very model of a press magnate. He himself rejoiced in the *British Gazette*, pushing its circulation up to nearly 2½ million. It seemed a marvellously exciting conflation of his twin enthusiasms, politics and war, 'the combination of a first-class battleship and a first-class general election'. Unfortunately it was neither and Churchill's noisy broadsides backfired. He stirred up needless hostility by expressing the government's uncompromising determination to break the strike and defeat 'the enemy'. He made the necessary task of conciliation more difficult by refusing (until Baldwin's more moderate counsels prevailed) to report news of a football match between strikers and police or to print an appeal for peace from the Archbishop of Canterbury – while finding space for paragraphs on love-birds, monkeys and bearded lizards. He even nursed ambitions to commandeer the BBC, which under the direction of the tall, beetle-browed Sir John Reith (disparaged by Churchill as 'that Wuthering Height') made a thin pretence of neutrality while really being on the government's side.

The same was true of the *British Gazette*, though its veneer of objectivity was quite transparent. For Churchill utterly declined, in his famous phrase, to be impartial as between the fire engine and the fire. His journalistic ideal was an old-fashioned one, harking back to the time when newspapers were merely the adjuncts of political parties. The *British Gazette* feigned independence in order to make its official propaganda more plausible. Churchill was never really to understand the role of newspapers as fourth estate of the realm. 'As to freedom of the press,' he remarked dismissively, 'why should any man be allowed to buy a printing press and disseminate pernicious opinions calculated to embarrass the government?' Such views and such behaviour during the general strike commended Churchill to west end theatre audiences – he received a warm ovation when attending a musical. Churchill also gained a 'complete stranglehold on young reactionary Tories'. In Beaverbrook's exaggerated opinion, he practically was the government, keeping Baldwin in 'a padded room of his own'. On the other hand Churchill's flagrant provocations secured his place in Socialist demonology. The mere mention of his name was a signal for tumult at Labour meetings for years to come. Opposition members of parliament, exposed to Churchill's bantering good humour, found it harder to bear malice. There was a touch of affection in Ellen Wilkinson's suggestion that Churchill's invincible 'superiority complex ... should somehow be embalmed for the awe of future generations'. Emanuel Shinwell said that there was 'a grace about Churchill' which could not be denied. His opponents roared with laughter at Churchill's reluctance 'to cast my pearls before ... those who do not want them'. They were convulsed by his bathetic conclusion to this ominous threat: 'Make your minds perfectly clear that if ever you let loose upon us again a general strike, we will let loose upon you – another *British Gazette*.'

After the 'unconditional surrender' of the trades unions, which had been demanded by the *British Gazette*, Labour MPs also recognised the fact that Churchill made every effort to resolve the pay dispute in favour of the miners, who remained on strike. He even went so far as to try coercing the pit-owners. But, scenting victory, they were now wholly intransigent; and anyway the Conservative cabinet would not tolerate such radical behaviour. Similarly the miners resisted Churchillian attempts to bully them into submission. However, they did submit to starvation. During the autumn and winter of 1926 they gradually drifted back to work on the owners' harsh terms. Their humiliating defeat left a long legacy of bitterness. And in the popular mind Churchill's early pugnacity blotted out the memory of his later magnanimity. The best that Labour could say of him was that Churchill was invariably generous to those he had wronged. The worst, expressed by the left-wing *New Statesman*, was that Churchill should be hanged. He scarcely went out of his way afterwards to conciliate radical opinion. During the course of his winter holiday in the Mediterranean at the end of 1926 Churchill visited the Pope and Mussolini. His audience with the Pontiff was awkward until the two men discovered common ground in their mutual loathing of Bolshevism. Churchill's interview with the Duce went smoothly. He professed himself 'charmed' by Mussolini's 'gentle and simple bearing' and declared that in Italy he would have been a Fascist.

The industrial turmoil of 1926 had cost the revenue over £30 million and in his next budgets Churchill had to repair this deficit. He set about the task with characteristic exuberance. According to P. J. Grigg he behaved as though he were conducting a military campaign, here erecting fortifications, there massing reinforcements, mining and counter-mining, and employing all the techniques he had learnt at Sandhurst and from his reading about Napoleon. By imbuing the drear intricacies of economics with the glory of war Churchill gave them urgency and excitement. He held financial conferences at Chartwell, discussed fiscal measures at the dinner-table, dictated budget proposals in his bath – wallowing, gurgling, turning the taps on and off with his toes, and surfacing with a noise like a whale blowing. He strode up and down his room, his head thrust out, his thumbs stuck in the armholes of his waistcoat, conjuring up a host of dramatic strategies, illuminating them with the lights and colours of his imagination, and finally choosing the one which held the most appeal – from an artistic as much as a military point of view.

Churchill's budget speeches were those of a showman of genius. But the content of the entertainment never matched the style of the performance. There was simply too much financial juggling, too many mountebank dodges. Churchill's betting tax was a fiasco: it even prompted a bookmakers' strike. His service cuts damaged the country's defences, something he liked to forget in the 1930s. His windfall taxes, like shortening brewers' credit, only produced short-term gains. Churchill raided the road fund, imposed duties on wines and spirits, reduced rates at the expense of a tax on petrol, pinched and scraped and saved without ceasing. But he introduced no great new constructive measure – though he hoped his de-rating scheme would be such. Moreover, he had to keep interest rates high in order to prevent the pound from sliding away from parity with gold. This naturally did nothing to promote industrial growth or to banish the scourge of worklessness. Even so world trade did increase slightly, unemployment did fall a little and there was some economic revival by 1928/9. This brief recovery before the slump was one factor which disguised Churchill's inadequacies as Chancellor. The other was simply his overwhelming personal magnetism. Churchill was, as Harold Macmillan wrote, 'unique, wayward, exciting, a man with a peculiar glamour of his own, that brought a sense of colour into our rather drab political life' during the Baldwin era.

Meanwhile Churchill's personal life grew in happiness with every year that passed. In 1924 the family moved into Chartwell, which became his (though not Clementine's) pride and delight. The old manor house, riddled with dry rot, had been completely reconstructed. Occupying a splendid position high on a hill near Westerham, it had faced west. In order to take advantage of the marvellous views over the South Downs a new, four-storey wing had been built. Its main feature was the drawing-room, which Churchill called 'my promontory'. House and garden were as much as possible made an elegant whole by means of many French doors. Clementine created a comfortable home though, because of the public life Churchill lived, it was never cosy. She also embarked on an ambitious scheme of re-planting the grounds. Churchill concentrated on more dramatic ventures. He excavated ponds, lakes and a swimming pool, constructed waterfalls, built a tree-house and a garden cottage for the children, put up walls, laying the bricks with his own hands and – a well-publicised coup – demonstrated his *bona fides* by joining the Building Workers' Trade Union.

Churchill also nursed romantic notions about establishing himself as a gentleman farmer and living off the land. Earlier he had developed a passionate though ephemeral interest in growing potatoes. Now he purchased live-stock. They were an expensive failure (paid for by the £20,000 a year which he earned from his late-night writing). The chickens became infested with red mite, the pigs got lice and one of the rams butted its indignant owner. More successful were his pets: the marmalade cat, goldfish and golden orfe (later segregated at considerable cost to stop piscine cannibalism), ruddy sheldrakes, varieties of geese, black and white swans. Feeding these birds was a great pleasure to Churchill though even that was liable to become a military exercise. His friend Lady Diana Cooper recollected an occasion when, using a basketful of bread as ammunition, Churchill attempted to start a war between geese and swans: 'We must make a policy,' he said. 'You stone them and we will get the five flying fools on their right flank.' In fact he was very attached to them. At one celebrated meal he had to ask Clementine to carve because 'this goose was a friend of mine'.

Churchill presided over the dinner table like a great potentate sitting on his throne. With a feast of talk and a flow of champagne, meal-times were an incomparable source of stimulation. Churchill felt an epicurean disdain for intemperate self-denial. Food was a gift of the gods. Drink made everything look happier. It was an invaluable adjunct to oratory and social intercourse. As Churchill was fond of remarking, he had always taken more out of alcohol than alcohol had taken out of him. So, glorying in self-indulgence, Churchill would hold forth. His discourse invariably careered towards monologue and anecdote. Clementine sometimes succeeded in creating a general conversation. Churchill himself was willing to let favoured guests such as T. E. Lawrence occupy the centre of the stage. Moreover he was proud of his children, especially the handsome and precocious Randolph. He liked to see this adolescent shine in adult company. Having been ignored by his own father, Churchill made the mistake of paying his *enfant terrible* too much attention. The spoilt boy, though not without flickers of wit, charm and ability, thus became a tragic parody of Churchill's more brutal characteristics, with a dash of Lord Randolph's profligacy thrown in for good measure. At Eton Randolph was caned for being 'bloody awful all round', 'the kind of comprehensive verdict', according to Michael Foot, 'which others who had dealings with him were always searching for'. It was later said of this hectoring bully that he should not be allowed out in private – indeed, he said it himself. Randolph's spiky friend Evelyn Waugh made a more profound comment, which applied in some degree to Churchill himself. Waugh compared conversation as he loved it – apt repartee, spontaneous reminiscence and quotation, argument based on accepted postulates, a fantasy growing in the telling – with Randolph's own brand of talk, an unsubtle recapitulation of old stories, *bons mots* and jokes mainly by or about his father.

WINSTON CHURCHILL

Of course Randolph made himself look ridiculous, a pygmy assuming the airs of a giant. But part of his trouble, as Churchill himself acknowledged, was that he tended to hear at home only the reactionary opinions of his father's rich friends, who were ever strong upon the stronger side. The most frequent visitor to Chartwell, for example, was Professor Frederick Lindemann, the Oxford physicist. 'The Prof', as he was always called, was a crashing snob who courted the mighty and regarded the lower orders as sub-human. He disliked Jews and blacks. He loathed the ugly and the stupid. Lindemann rightly thought himself hated at Oxford where he pursued the normal college squabbles with abnormal ferocity – he once took counsel's opinion about what place he was entitled to occupy at high table in Christ Church. Worse still, from Churchill's point of view, 'the Prof' was a teetotaller and a vegetarian. Nevertheless, from about 1922 onwards he was one of Churchill's closest friends.

Churchill admired his courage: having solved theoretically the problem of 'spin' in aeroplanes Lindemann had learnt to fly and proved himself right in practice. Lacking personal followers Churchill welcomed the Prof's unswerving devotion: Lindemann subscribed to 'the moral code of an elephant – unremitting loyalty to his friends and implacable hostility to his enemies'. Above all Churchill appreciated the Prof's outstanding intelligence, his lucid yet racy vocabulary, full of words like 'bull-dozing' and 'four-flushing', his blistering invective – Lindemann once expressed the wish to castrate an Oxford colleague, adding quickly, 'not that it would make any difference'. The Prof excelled at elucidating complicated scientific ideas in concise lay terms, an attribute that was to be of immense importance during the Second World War. Churchill liked to challenge him to explain the quantum theory in five minutes at the dinner table, a feat he accomplished with ease. Whipping out his slide-rule the Prof would make lightning calculations about anything from economic statistics to the volume of water Churchill would need to make an impressive cascade. Lindemann once worked out how much champagne his friend had drunk in his life-time – Churchill was disappointed to learn that it was only enough in bottles to fill half a railway carriage.

CHANCELLOR OF CHARTWELL

Unlike many of the guests at Chartwell, Lindemann found favour in Clementine's eyes. He was charming to women and took endless trouble with children. Moreover he was a first-class player of tennis, a game which Clementine enjoyed. Perhaps too she recognised that this unlovable man yearned for affection. Wearing his bowler hat like a helmet, Lindemann was armoured by convention and prejudice. But he was inwardly tense and vulnerable. At any rate he did not provoke Clementine to outbursts of temper and temperament. Sometimes she would let fly at a visitor who made an arrogant or illiberal remark and then storm out of the room. One who particularly roused her ire was the financier, newspaperman, MP and busybody, Brendan Bracken. During the early 1920s this red-haired, thick-spectacled Irishman, who made a mystery of his humble origins, attached himself to Churchill with such fidelity that he was rumoured to be his illegitimate son. Churchill was amused by the story and did not bother to deny it. Clementine was furious and tried to ban Bracken from the house.

Churchill clung to Bracken, relishing his indiscreet gossip, his bizarre sense of humour and his pungent epithets on their enemies – he called the pious Lord Halifax 'Baldwin's bugger-boy'. Churchill also appreciated the distinct whiff of charlatanism that emanated from Bracken: as a journalist said, everything about him was phoney, even his hair which looked like a wig and wasn't. Churchill liked fast friends, in every sense of the word. He was bored by the respectable and the sober. He was depressed by people of low vitality. He yearned for the kind of rakehell excitement with which his father had imbued each living minute. The effervescent Bracken was a tonic. Of course the two men quarrelled at times, but the good-natured Bracken could forgive and forget as easily as Churchill. In any case fascination swallowed up exasperation. Bracken told an acquaintance:

> Being friendly with him is like being in love with a beautiful woman who drives you mad with her demands until you can bear it not a minute longer and fling out of the house swearing never to see her again. But next day she smiles at you and you know there's nothing you wouldn't do for her and she crooks her little finger and you come running.

111

WINSTON CHURCHILL

A man is known by the company he keeps, and in his choice of friends, as in everything else, Churchill liked to live dangerously. His boon companion (until his death in 1930) was F. E. Smith, later Lord Birkenhead, who correctly described himself as a 'verbal gladiator'. Churchill was always somewhat in awe of Birkenhead whose barrister's knack of thinking on his feet he could never quite match. During an altercation in court, for example, the judge rebuked Smith: 'You are extremely offensive, young man.' 'As a matter of fact we both are,' retorted Smith, 'but I am trying to be and you can't help it.' Birkenhead was not only quick, he was so brutal that his ripostes were quite capable of reducing companions to tears of mortification. Such was the intellectual arrogance of this 'most fluent and plausible bounder' (Raymond Asquith's characterisation) that his brains were said to have gone to his head. He was an unfortunate model for his godson Randolph, who could equal his rudeness if not his wit. Still, Churchill found Birkenhead a wonderfully stimulating crony. Their taste for luxury was the same and both lived wildly beyond their means. They were equally fond of drink though Churchill remained its master while Birkenhead became its slave. They shared a liking for rough, clubbable, male society and the kind of humour that went with it. Each adored the extravagant romance of politics and revelled in the thrill of single combat. Churchill described their friendship as perfect.

By contrast his relations with Lord Beaverbrook went up and down like a yo-yo. Clementine detested the press baron, regarding him as a bottle imp to be exorcised, a microbe from which her husband's blood must be purified. Churchill himself recognised Beaverbrook's capacity for wickedness but found it impossible to rid himself of a craving for his company. Ernest Bevin summarised their association pithily by likening Churchill to 'a man who's married a whore; he knows she's a whore but he loves her just the same'. 'Some people take drugs,' Churchill himself remarked, 'I take Max.' Churchill found the conversation of this Presbyterian hobgoblin almost as exhilarating as his own monologues. The feeling was not reciprocated – at home Beaverbrook would drown Churchill in mid-flow by switching on the wireless. The two men, so alike in their love of mischief (though Beaverbrook's was combined with a malice quite foreign to Churchill's nature), often came into conflict over politics. Yet each was anxious to make amends. After the general strike, for example, when Churchill in 'one of his fits of vainglory and excessive excitement' had insulted Beaverbrook during 'a terrible scene', there was soon a reconciliation. Victor Cazalet was disgusted to see Churchill licking Beaverbrook's boots in order to get back into his, and the *Daily Express*'s, good graces. For his own part Beaverbrook extended the olive branch in the shape of presents. He sent Churchill a refrigerator. Churchill was delighted: he no longer had to dilute his champagne with ice.

Churchill was attracted to Beaverbrook because he was such an extraordinarily entertaining mixture. An earthly power with heavenly aspirations, Beaverbrook conducted unscrupulous crusades here below yet sang Calvinist hymns when drunk, scrambling up the bookcase like a monkey at any reference to being 'bound for glory'. Beaverbrook's behaviour was secular to the point of depravity. But his language was that of a latter-day Nonconformist. It was in religious terms that he described Churchill: 'He is born to trouble for like Jehovah in the hymn – "He plants his footsteps in the deep and rides upon the storm." ' Yet it was not merely because Beaverbrook was as complex and fascinating as a Chinese puzzle that Churchill liked him. He admired the Canadian's bursts of superabundant energy. When Beaverbrook dramatised himself as a titanic natural force, the dangerous wave called 'rage' which beats upon the New Brunswick shore, Churchill did not find it incongruous. Beaverbrook was, as he claimed, a 'victim of the furies', a driven man, one who could move mountains. It was for this reason, as much as because he was an old crony, that Churchill appointed him to the vital post of Minister of Aircraft Production in 1940.

Yet if the press baron did the Prime Minister incomparable service at the beginning of the war he helped, by encouraging attacks on 'National Socialists' in the Labour party, to lose him the election at its end. So those who regarded Beaverbrook as Churchill's evil genius were not altogether wrong. At their worst both men belonged to the ignoble freemasonry of bullies (Birkenhead was also a prominent member) and encouraged each other in the practice. Beaverbrook liked to induce apoplexy in his editors and sought out his journalists' weak points in order to exploit them. Churchill, though not calculatingly malevolent, was prone to fits of fury. When roused he would curse subordinates and swear at servants. One called his behaviour 'piggish'. The smallest domestic upsets, the soup too cold or the bath water too hot, could produce a storm of abuse. Nor was Churchill above creating petulant scenes with his social equals, the Duff Coopers, Cranbornes, Archie Sinclairs, Bonham Carters and other visitors to Chartwell. Clementine herself was not immune, though she could defend herself and even counter-attack – she once threw a dish of spinach at Winston's head. (It missed.)

Wits liked to say that there was a streak of humility in Churchill, expressed in his fervent devotion to the monarchy, which had somehow escaped the scrutiny of his friends. There was also a streak of cruelty. As Churchill's Parliamentary Private Secretary during the 1920s, Robert Boothby, recalls:

> I always felt like a toy in the hands of a mischievous boy. I never knew whether he was trying to break me to pieces or to mend me. All I could be sure of was that it was one or the other. I once told him that he was a bully by nature, but that he could never bully me.

Certainly Churchill respected those who stood up to him and sometimes his incivility was not an expression of spleen so much as a test of character, a moral equivalent to his argument-ative 'reconnaissance-in-force'. But outbursts of black bile were a perennial feature of Churchill's temperament and they helped to make him the formidable politician he was. They also emphasised the fact that in general his character was benign and his disposition sunny.

By 1929 Churchill's rich personality, with its starkly con-trasting tones, had become something of a handicap. Lloyd George apart, Churchill had by now occupied a central place on the Westminster stage for longer than any of his colleagues or rivals. He was beginning to seem an old-fashioned figure, a gorgeous survival from an earlier age. His flamboyant notions, swashbuckling mannerisms and archaic language belonged to a more gaudy epoch, an era of chivalry and romance. Churchill was an artist, actor and rhetorician at a moment when trust was inspired by more prosaic characters. He wore out the patience of the cabinet with his wayward schemes and the terrible pertinacity with which he pressed them forward. He roused their suspicions by his continuing association with irresponsible immoralists like Beaverbrook and Lloyd George. Churchill's political ideas were antique. He opposed giving the vote to women under the age of thirty ('flappers') and insisted that the Labour party was the local branch of an international revolutionary conspiracy. As Leo Amery (who had known Winston since Harrow) said in 1929: 'in essentials he is still where he was twenty-five years ago . . . . He just repeats the old phrases of 1903 and no argument seems to make any difference to him.' Churchill's extravagant oratorical displays, so different from Baldwin's colloquial chats, were equally out of date. In the age of the cinema his rolling periods and stately gestures belonged to the days of the music hall. Hero or villain, Churchill was too melodramatic a performer for contemporary taste. Everyone paid tribute to the marvellous quality of his entertainments but few took him seriously as a political leader.

Thus Churchill's position grew increasingly uncomfortable and by the end of the 1920s he contemplated leaving parliament altogether. Nothing could disguise the fact that he was out of place in Baldwin's government. Churchill's conception of political life was to initiate some action calculated to stagger humanity. Baldwin was a ruminant who liked to sit in the House of Commons sniffing the order paper; he only moved during a crisis. On the other hand, more than most politicians Churchill relished office – not for the spoils but for the opportunity of making his mark on the tablets of history. The prospect of a Labour victory at the general election of 1929 filled him with despair. During the campaign he paid little heed to Baldwin's reassuring slogan 'Safety First'. Instead he conducted a bitter assault on the Socialists. Having perpetuated a 'constitutional outrage' in the shape of the general strike, they remained unfit to govern. Yet they were advancing, under 'the banner of plunder', to destroy the tranquillity of the nation. The votes were cast on 30 May and that night Churchill went to 10 Downing Street in order to hear the results. As the Conservatives began to lose seats, he kept rising and going into the passage to glare at the machine which was printing out the score. Sipping whisky and soda, he grew redder and redder as his fury mounted, hunching up his shoulders and lowering his head like a bull about to charge. As the news got worse Churchill confronted the machine, tore the sheets from it and, as Tom Jones, Deputy Secretary to the cabinet, wrote, 'behaved as though if any more Labour gains came along he would smash the whole apparatus. His ejaculations to the surrounding staff were quite unprintable.' Well might he curse, for that apparatus was tapping out a message that would consign Churchill to the barren wastes of opposition for ten painful years.

CHAPTER VIII

DESERT DECADE

CHURCHILL left office just as the see-saw of history was tilting from the aftermath of the First World War to the prelude of the Second. The gay twenties turned into the gloomy thirties and the shadow of Nazism darkened Europe. The Bright Young Things were succeeded by the Auden generation and everywhere aesthetic preoccupations gave way to political ones. Oxford undergraduates laughed at Churchill when he waxed sentimental about 'our island home' and they passed a motion in the Union refusing to fight for King and Country – an 'abject, squalid, shameless avowal' which he found 'nauseating'. At Westminster, Conservatives and Socialists put forward, respectively, appeasement and disarmament as their panaceas, while as early as 1930 Churchill condemned the 'spirit of defeatism in high places'. Pacifism and Communism became fashionable creeds, and fellow-travellers wished 'death to the old gang'.

No one appeared more of an old gangster than Churchill. The impression was reinforced during the 1930s when he associated himself with policies which Tories themselves considered reactionary. In particular, modern liberal-minded Conservatives were alienated by Churchill's attempt to hold back the tide of self-rule in India. Engaged in this doomed struggle he became isolated, more out of joint with the times than ever. Churchill seemed, in Lord Beaverbrook's graphic phrase 'a busted flush'. Or as the writer Christopher Sykes put it, he was a 'disastrous relic of the past, a dangerous has-been'. Observing his 'great round white face like a blister' in 1930, Harold Nicolson thought him 'incredibly aged', 'an elder statesman'. Churchill's calls for rearmament, for martial virtue, for revival of 'the spirit of the British race', sounded cracked and tinny, like a record played on an Edwardian phonograph. Throughout the 1930s his was an ancestral voice prophesying war. But his warnings, like Cassandra's, were discredited simply because they were his. Until history caught up with him – or rather, reverted to him – at the end of the decade, Churchill was a prophet without honour in his own country.

Abroad, by contrast, he was regarded as a political giant. Churchill discovered this on the holiday tour of North America which he made shortly after the Conservative defeat, in the summer of 1929. Everywhere he was greeted with enthusiasm and heard with respect. His trip was a whirl of speeches, meetings, dinners and receptions, combined with much sightseeing. In Canada Churchill harped on the 'mighty ties, incomprehensible to Europeans', which bound the British empire together. In the United States he emphasised the indissoluble links between the English-speaking peoples. He was especially impressed by the enormous industrial strength of the New World. When Randolph commented on the lack of Canadian culture Churchill responded fiercely, 'Cultured people are merely the glittering scum which floats upon the deep river of production.'

In the United States Churchill's small family party stayed with the press magnate W. R. Hearst, the model for *Citizen Kane*, at his fairy-tale castle of San Simeon. Churchill found Hearst, with his Mormon appearance and his Oriental extravagance, both interesting and likeable. He even tactfully deferred to Hearst and arranged to contribute to his newspapers. Randolph was less tactful: in night-time pursuit of a female guest he mistakenly climbed through the window of his father's bedroom. Hearst and his mistress, Marion Davies, mounted lavish entertainments and introduced the Churchills to Hollywood's film stars. Churchill was most delighted with Charlie Chaplin who, despite his 'bolshy' politics, later became a welcome guest at Chartwell. It was then that Chaplin told Churchill he proposed to play the part of Jesus Christ in his next film, prompting the immortal retort: 'Have you cleared the rights?'

Churchill travelled back across the United States, visiting Civil War battle fields *en route*, during the boom immediately preceding the slump in November 1929. His confidence in the stockmarket was boosted by bad advice and he invested large sums which he had earned, or would earn, from his writing. Churchill arrived in New York just as the bubble burst and he actually witnessed the chaos caused to pedestrians and traffic when a ruined stockbroker threw himself out of a skyscraper window. Churchill's own shares sank in value by tens of thousands of pounds, and he spent much of the 1930s recouping his losses.

Between the ages of fifty-five and sixty-five, when human energies normally begin to wane, Churchill seemed to defy nature. He became a literary industry run on Stakhanovite lines. Living, as he put it, from mouth to hand, Churchill kept his secretaries busy with incessant dictation, beginning in the mornings as he sat up in bed and finishing in the small hours as he paced up and down his study. He wrote countless newspaper articles, the best of which were collected in *Thoughts and Adventures* (1932). His biographical essays appeared as *Great Contemporaries* (1937). In 1930 Churchill published *My Early Life*. He completed *The World Crisis*, the sixth volume of which, published in 1931, dealt with the war on the eastern front. His major enterprise, the biography of his great forbear the Duke of Marlborough, fell from the presses in four thick volumes during the decade. He toyed with the idea of embarking on a life of Napoleon and worked on a film script of George V's life (never produced). Finally he wrote much of his *History of the English-Speaking Peoples* though the work was not to be completed until the 1950s.

Churchill was a thoroughly professional journalist who earned the high fees which he demanded. He wrote fast and always met his deadlines, though he sometimes left articles to the last minute. Like others in the inky trade, he made good copy out of his personal experiences and was not above reworking previously published material. Character sketches of famous people he had known were also a regular resource. Here again he tended to repeat himself and, though readable,

119

his biographical essays were superficial. He was better at telling what his subjects had done than at saying what they were like. However, Churchill was extremely versatile, and during the 1930s he turned his hand to anything from rehashing 'The World's Great Stories' to rehearsing 'Great Deeds that Gave Us Our Empire'. Nor was he ashamed to pen answers to such flagrantly journalistic questions as 'Shall We All Commit Suicide?' and 'Are there Men in the Moon?' In fact he was particularly interested in popular science, the more apocalyptic the better. With Lindemann's help he produced a number of startlingly accurate forecasts about the shape of wars to come. He predicted, for example, the development of chemical weapons and the employment of rockets containing bombs of immense power.

Of course, Churchill also used the press to transmit his current political opinions. His rightward drift was plainly apparent in a series on 'The Abuse of the "Dole" '. More sinisterly, some of his writing seemed to be inspired not so much by nostalgia for a Whig past, or even by disgust for a Socialist present, as by hopes of a Fascist future. Churchill deplored the absence of able leaders, bred and trained for the task, who 'feel themselves to be uplifted above the general mass'. Not that he wanted a return to the 'ridiculous airs and graces of periwigged potentates'. But, he said, 'we miss our giants'. 'Standardized citizens . . . equipped with regulation opinions' now asserted that one man was as good as another, if not better. And 'blameless mediocrities . . . strutted conscientiously around the seats of the mighty decked in their discarded mantles and insignia'. There were no monarch peaks on the 'democratic plateau'; there was no 'venerated "El Capitan" or "Il Duce", casting its majestic shadow in the evening light'. In the face of such sentiments it was easy for Churchill's enemies, Conservative as well as Labour, to charge him with aspiring to be Britain's Mussolini.

However, although Churchill (like many others) did flirt with totalitarian ideas in the 1930s, his imagination was chiefly preoccupied with the patrician splendours of former days. In *My Early Life*, for example, he drew a rose-tinted 'picture of a vanished age', a time when Britannia ruled the waves and the aristocracy ruled Britannia. This autobiography, so light-hearted and so steeped in heroism and adventure, is perhaps

Churchill's finest book. Certainly it is his most enjoyable one. It bubbles with ironic humour as the mature Churchill casts a sardonic eye on the brash doings of his former self. Witness the account of his behaviour at Government House in Poona where, as a newly arrived young subaltern, he was entertained by Lord Sandhurst.

> His Excellency . . . was good enough to ask my opinion on several matters, and considering the magnificent character of his hospitality, I thought it would be unbecoming in me not to reply fully. I have forgotten the particular points of British and Indian affairs upon which he sought my counsel; all I can remember is that I responded generously. There were indeed moments when he seemed willing to impart his own views; but I thought it would be ungracious to put him to so much trouble; and he very readily subsided.

My Early Life bears the imprint of the man rather than the orator. It is more intimate and conversational in tone than Churchill's other literary declamations. But even here the diapasons roll out as he evokes the glamour and glitter of late-Victorian high society. In particular he contrasts the brilliant parties given by the few hundred families who had taken England to 'the pinnacle of her glory', with the glum public hospitality dispensed by Labour governments, who were presiding (in 1930) over the decline of their country and the fall of its empire. In the short space of his own lifetime, Churchill declared, a silent English revolution had taken place and the traditional governing class had lost its power. Churchill had no illusions about restoring an oligarchy, let alone about establishing a dictatorship. But his political views in the drab 1930s were almost entirely coloured by his vision of a glorious past.

Nowhere was this vision more spectacularly projected than in his *Life of Marlborough*. Churchill identified with his ancestor completely and portrayed him as a demigod. In the pages of his huge biography Marlborough becomes a statesman who guided the destiny of his nation with unerring wisdom and defeated that great menace to Europe's freedom, Louis XIV. As a soldier he was not only a wholly victorious commander in the field but a strategist of genius. Churchill actually makes this superman cast a radiance over lesser mortals, especially

121

when he can find a good phrase in which to enshrine his hyperbole. Thus his dull sovereign, Anne, becomes 'a great Queen championed by a great Constable'. Marlborough's distinctly secular association with Prince Eugene of Savoy is dignified as the 'Holy Alliance'. Even the Duke's marriage to that stormy termagant Sarah, who helped to ruin his credit with the Queen, is viewed through a golden haze. In short, what Churchill conjured from the past was not history but romance.

However, as with his other books, it was romance alloyed with calculated partisanship. To the astonishment of his research assistant, Maurice Ashley, Churchill started dictating his biography before he had really begun to read about Marlborough – he knew nothing about his subject but he knew what he wanted to say. Not that Churchill was averse to historical knowledge. In fact, he collected it eagerly, if not comprehensively, and he checked it meticulously. But information must always be subordinate to opinion. 'Give me the facts, Ashley,' Churchill said, 'and I will twist them the way I want to suit my argument.' Consequently much of this book was very special pleading indeed. There was, for example, the awkward question of Marlborough's avarice – Eugene said that the Duke was so mean that he left his 'i's undotted in order to save ink. This was a characteristic difficult to reconcile with Churchill's portrait of the Duke as a generous-souled *preux chevalier*, and Churchill was inconsistent in accounting for it. Sometimes he admitted Marlborough's greed as the fault of a great man; sometimes he defended it as the understandable product of an impoverished youth; and sometimes he transformed it into wholesome thrift.

Churchill also tried to place Marlborough's morally dubious early life in the best possible light, though he found it impossible completely to justify his desertion of James II in 1688. In making his case for the Duke, Churchill encountered all sorts of difficulties. For example, he found himself defending Marlborough's strategy of fighting the French where they were strongest, in Flanders, an argument which ran directly counter to his own preference for attacking Europe in its 'soft underbelly'. Churchill resolved such incongruities with panache. Indeed the whole biography is a triumph of panache. Churchill sustains his story with tremendous bravura. His battle scenes are marvellously vivid and exciting. His hero receives heroic treatment. All told, it is a grand book about a great man. Churchill proves once again that history can be vitalised by an injection of myth and illuminated by the glare of propaganda.

Churchill's literary successes during the 1930s afford a stark contrast to his political failures. The greatest of these was over India. At the beginning of the decade Churchill declared his total antagonism to the policy of 'casting away that most truly bright and precious jewel in the crown of the King, which more than all our other Dominions and Dependencies constitutes the glory and strength of the British Empire'. To cut India adrift would be a 'hideous act of self-mutilation'. From such a catastrophe, he proclaimed, there could be no recovery. Making concessions to Gandhi was like feeding cat's meat to a tiger: he would never be satisfied. His movement must be crushed and the British mission to develop India and defend all her inhabitants must be pursued. Many Tories agreed, though only a small number of back-bench MPs would vote with Churchill. After the death of Birkenhead in 1930 Churchill was the only prominent Conservative to oppose the extension of self-rule in India.

In January 1931, already alienated from senior colleagues who were hankering to protect Britain from the economic blizzard by means of tariff barriers, Churchill quitted Baldwin's shadow cabinet. His Indian campaign was interpreted by many as a bid for personal power. Others deplored his incendiary language. One passage in particular echoed round the world. This was Churchill's reference to the 'nauseating' spectacle of Gandhi, 'a seditious Middle Temple lawyer, now posing as a fakir of a type well-known in the East, striding half-naked up the steps of the Vice-Regal palace'. Churchill doubtless hoped, by appealing to the atavistic imperialism of the Conservative party, to oust the torpidly liberal Baldwin. But his five-year struggle to preserve the Raj was also inspired by concern for untouchables, Muslims and other minorities, whom he rightly saw as the potential victims of independence. Nevertheless, when he conceded defeat in 1935, after the Government of India Act had been passed, Churchill's high-minded motives were forgotten. He had branded himself as an unscrupulous opportunist and a blimpish reactionary.

At first Churchill had talked blithely about smashing the Conservative party over the Indian issue and having the government out in a fortnight. In practice he was not even accepted as leader by the 40-strong rump of Tory back-benchers who voted with him. He made sporadic efforts to charm and cajole them, but it was apparent that he regarded the Commons as an assembly to be dominated rather than conciliated. His parliamentary habits were not endearing. When out of the limelight he would yawn loudly, whisper audibly, crack jokes, laugh, mutter, fidget, snort. He refused to listen to 'the dreary drip of dilatory declamation'. In fact, the only member to whom he listened with consistent attention was himself. Moreover he was inclined to appear in the chamber solely in order to speak and deny his opponents the courtesy of staying to hear their replies. True, his speeches were coruscating set-pieces. But Harold Nicolson's comment indicates why Churchill remained, even in the eyes of those who agreed with him over India, an untrustworthy political renegade. Nicolson found Churchill not only 'the most interesting man in England' but 'a phenomenon, an enigma', and he wondered how so versatile and so brilliant a man could avoid being considered volatile and unsound.

He could not. In 1931 an entire book, entitled *The Tragedy of Winston Churchill*, was published to explain him away as a brilliant failure. Forging an image to be employed by Baldwin, its author V. W. Germains concluded that at Churchill's birth the good fairies came trooping in, each with her gift: 'Imagination, Daring, Energy, *Guts*'. Then two bad fairies arrived to deny him Patience and Concentration, so confusing the other gifts that this wonder-child grew up always in a desperate hurry and never able to do a single job thoroughly. Many of Germains' criticisms were inept: he did not realise, for example, that the pendulum of opinion about the Dardanelles was swinging in Churchill's favour. But he was shrewd enough to see that Churchill had no home to go to in politics.

He could not follow Sir Oswald Mosley, whom he anyway regarded as a 'gilded butterfly', into the jungle of Fascism. The Socialists were anathema. The Liberals were moribund. Churchill would have to stick to the Tory party, and he proposed to do so with 'all the loyalty of a leech'. This adherence

was certainly not enough to secure him a position in the
National Government, formed in mid-1931 to stop 'the run on
the pound'. Ironically, although Churchill always hankered
after coalitions of the centre and could do no other than regard
this one with 'discriminating benevolence', he was excluded
from it as an extremist. Worse still, the National Government
abandoned the policies with which he was identified – the de-
rating scheme, the gold standard, free trade – and so acute was
the economic crisis that Churchill felt unable to utter more
than a token protest.

The bad year of 1931 ended with a serious personal setback.
Churchill went to America in December on a lecture tour, and
he was knocked down by a car in New York. The impact almost
killed him. As it was he made a painfully slow recovery, convalescing in the Bahamas. Then, manfully struggling against
the after-effects of the shock, he completed his well-paid
engagements in the United States. Churchill's friends celebrated his escape and his return to England by presenting him
with a Daimler motor-car.

His travails were not over. Churchill spent 1932 working on
Marlborough and in the summer he visited the Duke's battle-
fields, re-peopling them with 'ghostly but glittering armies'.
He did not like the current scene in Germany, which was full of
'bands of sturdy Teutonic youths', their eyes alight with
nationalism, their hands eager for weapons. He always sympathised intensely with the sufferings of others and he particularly loathed Nazi persecution of the Jews. Although he
never met Hitler, Churchill did send him a personal message
through his creature Putzi Hanfstaengl: 'Tell your boss from
me that anti-semitism may be a good starter, but it is a bad
sticker.' Actually Churchill himself was not averse to a mildly
anti-semitic joke, but his horrified condemnation of the later
holocaust was unequivocal. Churchill did no more than sense
the new mood in Germany for he was soon struck down by
paratyphoid fever. He shook it off for a time but he suffered
from a recurrence of the illness later in the year.

When Hitler came to power in January 1933 Churchill saw
no immediate 'likelihood of a war in which Great Britain would
be involved'. Indeed, during the 1930s he was by no means as
consistent about the imminence of war, about the necessity of

rearmament, even about the wickedness of Hitler, as he afterwards liked to maintain. At the time, his political enemies, who
had listened throughout the 1920s to his harangues on the
need for military economies, assumed that Churchill was
merely using these issues as a stick to beat the government –
which he hoped to join. Certainly when there seemed a chance
of office in 1935/6 Churchill's bellicose tones were muted.
However, despite occasional quavers and some discordant
notes, Churchill's trumpet-call grew in strength and certainty
as the thirties progressed. Made in the teeth of every sort of dis-
couragement, it was a triumph of political fortitude.

From 1933 onwards, almost alone, despised and rejected of
men, described by Sir Herbert Samuel as 'a Malay run amok',
Churchill agitated for arms to prevent war. He reiterated his
message with such urgency that he became worse than a
menace – a bore. Only from a position of strength, he urged,
could Britain remain great, deter aggression, and remedy just
grievances consequent on the treaty of Versailles. Disarmament would no more bring peace than an umbrella would prevent rain. Appeasement from weakness was both stupid and
craven. It would lead first to threats which the victim was
powerless to resist and then to the very thing it was supposed to
preclude – war. And without preparation defeat was inevitable.
As early as March 1933 Churchill pointed to 'the tumultuous
insurgency of ferocity and war spirit' raging in Nazi Germany.
He warned that these savage passions, now expressing themselves in 'the pitiless ill-treatment of minorities' inside Hitler's
Reich, might soon be vented on Europe and the world. Germany
had 'abandoned her liberties to augment her might'.

As the evidence of German rearmament grew more obvious
Churchill's warnings grew more strident. Yet the year 1934
probably marked the lowest point since the Dardanelles in the
switchback of his public fortunes. For he seriously discredited
himself in the spring by mounting an ill-starred attack on Sir
Samuel Hoare, Secretary of State for India, and his influential
ally Lord Derby. Documents were brought to Churchill
indicating that these two prominent Tories had induced the
Manchester Chamber of Commerce to submit testimony
favouring the government's devolutionary policy to the
Parliamentary Committee on Indian Reform. Churchill knew

that, in fact, Lancashire wanted greater British control of the sub-continent in order to increase cotton exports which were being blocked by a protectionist India. So he took the bit between his teeth and accused Hoare and Derby of breach of parliamentary privilege. In the Commons he professed that the charge was one of political impropriety not personal corruption. But it was widely interpreted as a vicious assault designed to ruin the defendants, destroy the Indian reforms and wreck the government. Churchill's excitable behaviour and violent language in private gave substance to this view. 'I will break this bloody rat Hoare's neck,' he growled, acknowledging the risk to his own.

In the event his own neck was wrung but not broken: Churchill strained every nerve but he was unable to prove his case before the Select Committee which examined it. Hoare and Derby were unanimously exonerated while Churchill was universally execrated. In spite of the Committee's findings Churchill was sure that the truth was on his side. He was correct. Correspondence which has only just come to light shows that Hoare and Derby did influence witnesses and did tamper with evidence put before the Parliamentary Committee. What is more, during the subsequent enquiry they withheld facts which would have established their guilt. Churchill had relied on imagination, offensive spirit and élan to fill the yawning gaps in his argument, applying the techniques of a cavalry charge to a complex legal exercise. No wonder that he was routed and that another 'blunder' was chalked up on his crowded slate.

Churchill's life was further darkened in the summer of 1934 by the death from cancer of his beloved cousin 'Sunny' Marlborough. By now, too, his own family, so long a source of happiness, was causing him anxiety and vexation. Randolph in his early twenties was quite out of control and caused mayhem wherever he went. His idea of a compliment was to tell a dowager that he was sure *her* daughters would commit 'adultery with the utmost discretion'. When he actually meant to be offensive the brawling did not always stop at words. Randolph worshipped his father, organising, for instance, a splendid party at the Ritz in November 1934 to celebrate his sixtieth birthday. But Randolph was rash even by Churchillian standards and his partisanship was so furious that it embarrassed his father. Early in 1935, for example, Randolph stood in a by-election as a Conservative opposed to the India Bill, split the Tory vote and let a Socialist into parliament. There were further escapades of this kind and frequent rows, exacerbated by alcohol, as a consequence.

Clementine, who found life in the titan's wake enough of a struggle when domestic peace prevailed, increasingly took to going on long holidays apart from her family. For the first four months of 1935, for example, she travelled to the Dutch East Indies on board Lord Moyne's luxurious yacht *Rosaura*, a converted channel steamer in which Winston and Clementine had already enjoyed one Mediterranean voyage. Moyne (*né* Walter Guinness) was a typical Churchill friend, a vastly rich, astonishingly brave individualist with eccentric habits and rakish tastes. Among his guests on the Indonesian expedition was not only Moyne's current consort, Lady Broughton, but a certain Mr Terence Philip. He was a glamorous art-dealer with whom Clementine, in her daughter Mary's words, 'fell romantically in love'. The romance petered out on their return but it must have caused Churchill some heart-burning.

Nor were the affairs of his two elder daughters satisfactory. Diana was a neurotic, unstable creature whose first marriage was ending in misery. Sarah scandalised her parents by going on the stage as a chorus girl. Then she outraged them by running off to America and marrying (in 1936) the star of her first show, the comedian Vic Oliver. Family reconciliations were slow, painful and incomplete. Churchill always loved his grown-up children, but sometimes he found it difficult to like them, and often he loathed what they did.

Churchill refused to let his domestic worries interfere with his political exertions. After a fierce struggle at the last ditch he conceded defeat over India. In a way this was a relief. For he could now concentrate on Europe and on the one fact which put all others in the shade, German rearmament. Churchill emphasised in particular the rapid expansion of the Luftwaffe and the corresponding weakness of the RAF. He pictured the 'incalculable conflagration' which might be unleashed by an incendiary-bomb attack on London. He visualised three or four million people being driven into the open countryside and eventual conquest by Germany. Baldwin accused him of alarmism and exaggeration. But he promised to maintain parity with the German air force and was embarrassed in March 1935 when Hitler claimed that it was already equal to the British. Actually Hitler himself was exaggerating the speed of its growth. But in the face of his boast the government had to re-define parity as meaning air power in general rather than specific numbers of aeroplanes. Baldwin confessed that he had been 'completely wrong' in his estimates of Germany's future air strength. In fact Churchill's figures, many of them leaked to him by worried officials like Ralph Wigram, were also wrong. Churchill mistakenly included trainer planes in his statistics and he did not realise how weak Germany was in reserves – almost all the Luftwaffe was in the front line. Nevertheless he was supremely right in sensing the danger and pressing for British rearmament. The government, still obsessed by the depression, dallied and vacillated.

Partly because the need for arms was so urgent, partly because he was miserable when deprived of office, partly because the Indian issue was out of the way, Churchill abated his criticism of the National Government in 1935. Baldwin responded by making him a member of the secret sub-committee on air defence research, a post Churchill accepted on the understanding that he would not be gagged. He loyally supported the coalition during the summer general election despite the Prime Minister's pledge that 'there will be no great armaments'. After Baldwin's victory Churchill was deeply mortified not to be given a cabinet job, though later he thought this a marvellous piece of luck: 'Over me beat the invisible wings.' At the time however he continued to live in hope and did not rock the boat. Thus Churchill deplored Mussolini's Abyssinian adventure. But he stayed painting and writing in the Mediterranean sunshine when the government tottered after the revelation of the Hoare–Laval pact. This was the plan proposed by the English and French Foreign Ministers to give Mussolini what he wanted in return for peace. Such was the outcry in Britain that Hoare was forced to resign in December 1935. Churchill was unwilling to exploit the government's weakness and press for serious action against Mussolini. He believed, in any case, that Abyssinia was 'not a fit, worthy, and equal member of a league of civilised nations'.

Similarly he more or less condoned the Japanese invasion of Manchuria. And when civil war broke out in Spain he favoured 'non-intervention', a term which (as Talleyrand had said) roughly corresponded in meaning to 'intervention' – in this case on the side of General Franco. Churchill refused to shake hands with the Republican ambassador, turning away and muttering, 'Blood, Blood, Blood.' He repudiated tyranny in all its forms though if forced to a choice he would still say that Communism was worse than Fascism. But ideology was an ugly word, he considered, for an uninteresting thing. The truth was that he was wholly taken up with the overwhelming danger of German aggression. A sinister portent of this was provided by Hitler's reoccupation of the de-militarised Rhineland in 1936.

Throughout that year Churchill's warnings grew more plausible and the government's hesitations became less defensible. It was now difficult to dismiss Churchill as a disruptive scaremonger or an irresponsible warmonger. But if his ruthless ability to focus on a single issue was a massive source of strength it could also be a crippling handicap. For when his one-track mind was derailed great was the smash that followed. This was precisely what happened at the end of 1936 when Churchill destroyed much of his painstakingly reconstructed prestige in the few days of the abdication crisis. It seemed almost as if he had a political death wish. But it was not this, nor even his abstention from brandy for twelve months, the result of a bet with Lord Rothermere, which led him to espouse Edward VIII's forlorn cause with such self-destructive zeal. It was sentiment.

Admittedly there was something in Conservative suspicions that Churchill was scheming to put himself at the head of a King's party in order (as his ally Beaverbrook supposedly said) 'to bugger Baldwin'. But Churchill was more soft-hearted than hard-headed. He was a man of intense feeling. He wept indiscriminately, while contemplating the immense tragedy of human existence or watching a trite film. Unable to tell one tune from another, he was deeply moved by cheap music. He could not bear to hear 'Keep Right on to the End of the Road'. Churchill's response to an emotional appeal was always generous, and when it came from his sovereign he succumbed at once. Romantic visions of a great monarch being saved by a great minister must have swum before his eyes. All his quixotic instincts were aroused. Clementine called him the last believer in the divine right of kings.

At any rate Churchill exerted himself to delay the choice which Baldwin was trying to rush the King into making – abandon plans to marry the unsuitable Mrs Simpson or abdicate. Churchill whimsically suggested that Edward should lock himself in Windsor Castle and station royal doctors at both gates to repel intruders. More seriously he pleaded on the King's behalf for 'time and patience' in order to work out a solution. Churchill, who was tolerant in the easy-going Whig fashion, entirely misjudged the puritanical mood of the nation. For two generations or more, certainly since the odd newspaper had jested that there was nothing between Edward (VII) Prince of Wales and Lily Langtry, 'not even a sheet', the press had treated the monarchy with respect bordering on reverence. Fleet Street had maintained a conspiracy of silence about Edward VIII's affair with Mrs Simpson. So when the news broke of his wish to make this American divorcée his Queen the public was shocked and outraged. Churchill's attempt to postpone a decision was howled down in the House of Commons, whose temper he also misjudged. It was one of the most brutal parliamentary rebuffs he ever suffered and he emerged from the chamber shaken, muttering that he was 'finished'. Other observers also thought him 'done for' and his supporters over rearmament complained bitterly about his unreliability as a leader. When Edward left the throne Churchill grieved for the 'poor little lamb'. But he soon conceived an aversion for the exiled Duke of Windsor's 'court of dagos' and concluded that George VI was the sounder sovereign. At his coronation Churchill rejoiced in 'the ceremonial, the splendour and the pageantry that are associated with the Crown'.

Churchill's isolation in 1937 was almost complete and his fires burnt low. He referred to himself now as 'a very old man' and thought that he was in the last lap of life. He even came close to selling Chartwell, for the kittens had become cats and his finances were failing – the house was only saved through the generosity of one of Brendan Bracken's rich friends. In May Baldwin was succeeded by Neville Chamberlain, who was even more sternly determined to exclude Churchill from the government. Nothing should interfere with Chamberlain's policy of appeasement, not even flagrant acts of aggression by the dictators. Nevertheless Chamberlain was rearming, albeit stingily and tardily. Churchill, who continued to receive much secret information about the comparative military strength of the European nations, tried to impress ministers privately that British preparations were too little and too late. In public, however, he expressed support for the government's 'policies of defence and world peace'. He even announced that he did not take the German danger as seriously as before.

This was a momentary aberration. Churchill's lonely voice rose again to its accustomed pitch in 1938, as his terrible prophecies were steadily fulfilled. In February he deplored the resignation of Anthony Eden, a Foreign Secretary who had at least given the impression of standing up to the dictators. In March Churchill denounced Hitler's annexation of Austria and reiterated his pleas for a strong military deterrent combined with collective security – 'arms and the covenant'. In May he condemned Britain's abandonment of her right to use naval bases in Eire. Throughout the spring and summer he warned against Hitler's designs on Czechoslovakia and urged resistance. In September he asserted that the cession of Sudetenland involved 'the prostration of Europe before Nazi power'. In October nearly everyone in the Commons and the country cheered Chamberlain, who had conceded virtually everything to Hitler at Munich but returned home bringing 'peace with honour'. Churchill declared that 'we have sustained a total and unmitigated defeat'. He predicted that the remains of Czechoslovakia would soon be devoured and that Hitler's appetite would grow with eating. The western democracies were now at the mercy of a Nazi regime 'which vaunts the spirit of aggression and conquest, which derives strength and perverted pleasure from persecution, and uses, as we have seen, with pitiless brutality the threat of murderous force'.

After Munich it was impossible to dismiss Churchill's speeches as picturesque sabre-rattling. Many MPs still reckoned that he was more moved by bitterness than conviction, evidenced perhaps by his threat to vote with the Socialists. He remained an object of deep hostility, though he managed to preserve a façade of personal civility towards ministers – despite his private conviction that the Tory party had never been led by a more purblind, obstinate and cowardly crew. His message was also unpopular in the country and his own constituency organisation tried to repudiate him. But by the beginning of 1939 it was clear that Munich, which Chamberlain represented as a just concession, was really, as Churchill had said, a humiliating capitulation. In March Hitler engulfed the remnant of Czechoslovakia. This was, of course, a complete abrogation of the Munich agreement and Churchill was justified in stating that 'practically everything' he had forecast 'has already proved true'.

Chamberlain, who had supposed that he could control Hitler, 'the commonest little dog' he had ever met, was furious at this betrayal. He now made a show of resolution, effecting a thoroughly impractical alliance with Hitler's next obvious victim, Poland, and hastening preparations for war. However, cold-blooded pragmatist that he was, Chamberlain still hankered for a negotiated settlement with Germany. In spite of growing popular pressure at home, he would not provoke the German leader by including Churchill in the government. Nor would he, as Churchill urged, clinch a defensive alliance with Communist Russia. Hitler took advantage of this reluctance, stepped in himself and in August concluded the Nazi–Soviet pact. His eastern flank secure, he invaded Poland on 1 September. Chamberlain and his Foreign Secretary Halifax searched frantically for some last-minute compromise. None was forthcoming. Even so the Prime Minister would not sanction the evacuation of London's children as this might be 'provocative'. At last on 3 September 1939 he mournfully announced that Britain was at war with Germany. Having invited Winston Churchill to join the government, and kept him in suspense about his office for two days, Chamberlain appointed him First Lord of the Admiralty.

Churchill had not yet become the inspiring symbol of the nation's will to resist dictatorship. His promotion to the war cabinet was chiefly an acknowledgement that he possessed *par excellence* that surprisingly rare political commodity – courage – the quality which, as Churchill wrote, guarantees all the rest. Others had recognised Hitlerism for what it was, but among

British leaders only Churchill had opposed it steadfastly and without flinching. Eden by comparison had been feeble. In public and in private Churchill had stood up to be counted. When, for example, the American ambassador Joseph Kennedy predicted defeat for Britain in any war with Germany, Churchill unleashed a cascade of impromptu indignation:

> It may well be true that this country will . . . be exposed to dire peril and fierce ordeals. It may be true that steel and fire will rain down upon us day and night scattering death and destruction far and wide. It may be true that our sea-communications will be imperilled and our food supplies placed in jeopardy. Yet these trials and disasters . . . will but serve to steel the resolution of the British people and to enhance our will to victory.

Churchill's confidence in himself was matched only by his faith in the patriotic spirit of the nation. Back at the Admiralty, which he had 'quitted in pain and sorrow almost a quarter of a century before', Churchill felt a blissful serenity of mind:

> The glory of Old England, peace-loving and ill-prepared as she was, but instant and fearless at the call of honour, thrilled my being and seemed to lift our fate to those spheres far removed from earthly facts and physical sensation.

After a decade in the desert – the years that the locust had eaten – Churchill girded himself for office and for battle.

CHAPTER IX

FINEST HOUR

'WINSTON is back' was the famous signal by which the Admiralty notified the fleet of the identity of its new chief. His return was an emotional one. Everything was as it had been before. The discipline, style, ceremony, routine, even the ships were the same. But a new generation of men filled the uniforms. 'It was a strange experience,' he wrote, 'like suddenly resuming a previous incarnation.' Churchill told the assembled board what a privilege and an honour it was to be sitting once again in the First Lord's chair. He promised that together they would overcome the many difficulties ahead. Then he dismissed them with the words: 'Gentlemen, to your tasks and duties.'

Churchill went about his own tasks and duties with characteristic gusto and zeal. He was acutely conscious of being within two months of his sixty-fifth birthday, nearly an old-age pensioner, 'almost the only antediluvian' in the cabinet. To compensate for his age he made a prodigious effort of will. Also, of course, his combative instincts were roused and he would stride up and down 'flaming out his soul' with eagerness to come to grips with the foe. As always his being thrilled to the clash of mighty forces. Indeed he complained that it was a dull war with 'only Germany to fight' and looked forward to the day when Italy and Japan joined in to liven it up. Still, for the time being one enemy kept him fully engaged. Perhaps as an earnest of his commitment he went so far as to overcome his love of opulence and banish the First Lord's splendid four-poster bed, which rose to a height of sixteen feet from a sea of gold dolphins and tritons. Instead, in austere campaigning spirit, he slept on a narrow, curtainless pallet-bed.

There was little time for sleep. Indeed, when senior naval officers were dropping with fatigue in the small hours Churchill would put off going to bed in favour of a final visit to the map room. Here he would pore over the beflagged charts which showed the disposition of every ship in the fleet. Churchill worked with furious concentration. He dictated memoranda, discussed strategy, instigated plans, inspected naval installations, visited ships, interviewed officers, addressed ratings. Churchill effervesced with ideas. Everywhere he stimulated, galvanised and invigorated. The navy responded to this strong hand on the tiller. Men were inspired by Churchill's personality. They were amazed by his energy, which was sustained by frequent infusions of whisky – he endeared himself to one sailor by refusing tea on medical grounds: 'My doctor has ordered me to take nothing non-alcoholic between breakfast and dinner.' Morale rose. Those who saw and heard him were convinced that the right man was in the right place. The stolid, somnolent First Sea Lord, Admiral Sir Dudley Pound, expressed the 'greatest admiration' for Churchill's 'good qualities' and for his overwhelming desire to 'hit the enemy'.

Yet though Pound felt inclined to kiss Churchill's feet one minute, he was eager to kill him the next, for the First Lord's habits were, if anything, more infuriating during his second spell at the Admiralty than they had been during his first. He interfered constantly in operational matters, always with the aim of making the navy take the offensive. Pound's technique was to give way to him in everything except vital matters. Even in these Pound was reluctant to confront Churchill with a flat negative. Instead he tried to show that the First Lord's schemes were impractical. This naturally provoked ferocious argument. As Admiral Godfrey wrote, Churchill's battery of dialectical weapons included 'persuasion, real or simulated anger, mockery, vituperation, tantrums, ridicule, derision, abuse and tears'. All these he would direct at anyone who opposed him, sometimes over quite trifling matters. Furthermore, Churchill did not hesitate to send ungracious messages direct to naval commanders. He accused admirals of lacking fire. He dismissed officers who contradicted his views: one who correctly asserted that by 12 November Britain had sunk six out of fifty-seven submarines, as against Churchill's absurd claim that half the U-boat fleet had been destroyed, was sent to sea at ten minutes' notice. He even called Pound 'yellow'. So it was that Churchill came to dominate his service advisers. Exhausted by his 'midnight follies', they obeyed the call of the First Lord's 'morning prayers', those importunate minutes which began 'Pray . . .'.

Churchill's ascendancy was never complete. For example, Pound was able to prevent him from dictating the dispositions of Commodore Harwood's flotilla, which accomplished the first triumph of the war, the destruction of the pocket battle-ship *Graf Spee* off the River Plate in December. Moreover, Pound managed to postpone (and thus to cancel) Churchill's madcap enterprise in the Baltic. Churchill wanted to send ships there primarily in order to cut Germany off from Scandinavia and to stop her receiving vital iron ore supplies from Sweden. Had this fleet been dispatched it would have been a sitting target. Despite having been the champion of air power throughout the 1930s, Churchill, like the Admiralty itself, still thought the battleship was a match for the aeroplane. Also like the Admiralty, he put too much faith in the submarine detection system Asdic and failed to appreciate how vulnerable surface vessels were to U-boats. However, Churchill had learnt some caution from the Dardanelles episode, which bore certain sinister resemblances to his proposed Baltic operation. So although he out-argued the cautious Pound, Churchill did not over rule him. But throughout the war he never ceased to hanker for what General Ismay called 'an Arctic Gallipoli'.

Not all the First Lord's ventures were as giddy as the Baltic scheme. He successfully mobilised the navy's resources to cope with the magnetic mine. Churchill increased the production of small destroyers to combat U-boats, which had already scored some notable successes and would, he expected, grow in numbers towards the end of 1940. He made Scapa Flow impregnable to submarine attack. Unhappily this was just a day too late to prevent the torpedoing of the *Royal Oak* – 'a wonderful feat of arms' for which he could not restrain his admiration.

Churchill was always excited by unconventional developments in the art of war, the odder the better. He was intrigued by military stunts and conjuring tricks, cloak and dagger work, special units and sabotage operations, dummy ships and Q-ships, fluvial and aerial mines, espionage and the spreading of 'Münchausen tales ... to confuse and baffle the truth', and death rays. He loved to play with model trench-diggers. He enjoyed watching demonstrations of experimental weapons, some of them, like the anti-aircraft rocket which fired wire cable, more of a danger to friends than foes. A lot of this was mere schoolboy relish for science fiction and it resulted in much wasted time and effort. On the other hand, Churchill's appointment of Admiral Pridham to the Ordnance Board was thoroughly beneficial and led to the production of valuable new armaments. Moreover his subsequent patronage of Millis Jefferis fostered such innovations as the limpet mine and the anti-tank gun. And his support for scientists fighting what he called 'the Wizard war' was of incalculable advantage to the nation.

However, as all this implies, Churchill had not lost his hussar's penchant for rushing in where angels fear to tread. This caused his most serious reverses at the Admiralty. His tenure of that office exactly coincided with the period of the 'phoney' or 'twilight' war, the 'Sitzkrieg' before the Blitzkrieg. But Churchill refused to be bound by a passive strategy, even though he assumed that the Second World War would resemble the First in being primarily defensive and he actually ordered a one-piece waterproof suit to wear in the trenches. The most damaging effect of his constant agitation for attack was that, although paying lip service to the importance of convoys, he weakened them in practice. He preferred warships to operate in 'hunting groups', scouring the oceans for U-boats. 'Nothing,' he asserted, 'can be more important in the anti-submarine war than to try to obtain an independent flotilla which could work like a cavalry division on the approaches.' Unhappily U-boats were difficult to find except when they congregated around convoys, which suffered because (until 1942) they were inadequately guarded.

As in the First World War Churchill was infuriated by the pusillanimity of neutral countries. He was cautious about the Americans, of course, for he always appreciated the need for their support, his most crucial strategic insight. But he had to be restrained from compelling Eire to let British warships use her harbours, from sowing mines in Norwegian territorial waters, and from sending an expeditionary force to Scandinavia. Sometimes his forceful, if illegal, actions paid dividends. In February 1940, for example, he ordered that the German ship *Altmark,* sheltering in a Norwegian fjord, should be boarded and he thus secured the release of 300 British prisoners. Often, though, Churchill's aggressive instincts led him astray. When Russia invaded Finland, for instance, Churchill conceived the crackpot notion of ordering two Polish submarines, on their way to join the British fleet, to sink a Soviet ice-breaker in the Baltic. This might have relieved naval pressure on the gallant Finns but it would probably have added another dictator to the list of Britain's enemies.

In the event the bear dispatched its prey before the lion leapt at its throat. However, Churchill's belligerent incentive was not to be denied. He pressed for the mining of Norwegian territorial waters, which was to be supported by an expeditionary force if the Germans retaliated by invading Scandinavia. This was just what Hitler had already planned to do. So in April the confused and disastrous Norwegian campaign began. The navy, though inflicting some damage, signally failed to bring the enemy fleet to action, and Hitler's forces seized all the key Norwegian ports. British attempts to dislodge them only served to reveal the devastating effects of German air superiority. The North Sea belonged to the Luftwaffe rather than to the Royal Navy and Churchill was unable to keep his promise that every German ship leaving the Baltic would be sunk.

By now Churchill was chairman of the Military Co-ordination Committee as well as First Lord of the Admiralty. So he bore considerable responsibility for the direction of the campaign. It was a complete muddle. Intelligence was poor. Plans were conceived and aborted from hour to hour. Everything was improvised. Grievous errors were made. Churchill himself had failed to issue written orders to Admiral Lord Cork and it was unclear whether he or General Mackesy was in command of the landings at Narvik. But having given Cork 'exceptional discretion' because (as contemporaries) they understood one another so well, Churchill could not resist interfering at a tactical level. Indeed on his private cypher line he told Admiral Cork that if General Mackesy 'appears to be spreading a bad spirit ... do not hesitate to relieve him or place him under arrest'. In fact Churchill was right in urging a swift, concentrated assault on Narvik instead of the piecemeal attack which actually took place. But though he often reduced members of the Co-ordination Committee to silent acquiescence, he could not always get his own way. He was to complain that at this Committee everything was 'settled for the greatest good of the greatest number by the common sense of most after the consultation of all'. Whereas war, he sagely remarked, was 'more like one ruffian bashing the other on the snout with a club'.

Because the public saw Churchill as the embodiment of the nation's fighting spirit he emerged without serious discredit from the Norwegian débâcle. Chamberlain was held to blame. Before the event Churchill had warned that the Nazis were saving up some new 'orgy of frightfulness' for the British and that 'an intensification of the struggle is to be expected'. By contrast Chamberlain had made his fatal remark that Hitler had 'missed the bus' – whereas Churchill tried to galvanise the French by warning, 'Nous allons perdre l'autobus.' Churchill had been active head of the most active service, while Chamberlain seemed to be conducting the phoney war as though it were an epilogue to Munich – his Secretary of State for Air initially turned down the idea of bombing Germany for fear of damaging private property. Churchill was (as Fisher had said) 'a war man' and he had irritated the Prime Minister by trying to take the entire conflict as his province. Chamberlain was a peacemaker, even in his dealings with Churchill, whom he found 'very responsive to a sympathetic handling' despite his 'violence and impulsiveness'.

Above all Churchill looked and acted the part of warlord. When crossing the channel with Chamberlain to meet the French high command early in 1940 Churchill suggested that a mine which had been spotted should be blown up by gunfire. The First Lord solicitously placed a tin hat on the Premier's head and was gleeful when the mine 'burst with a good bang' and a piece of debris narrowly missed the 'swells' on the bridge. The umbrella-bearing Chamberlain, abjectly ignorant about military matters, looked at home only in his black Homburg.

Churchill playing polo, 1921. As always his right arm is strapped up

Chartwell

Churchill and Lord Birkenhead

Churchill, bricklayer

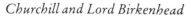

*Budget Day, 1929. From left to right: Robert Boothby (Churchill's PPS),
the Chancellor of the Exchequer, Clementine, Sarah, Randolph*

Churchill leaves the Admiralty for Buckingham Palace to accept the Premiership, May 1940

Churchill and Clementine on their way to take up residence at No. 10

Churchill and Clementine inspecting bomb damage, 1940

Churchill holding a tommy gun

Churchill feeding the lions

Churchill and General Smuts in Cairo, 1942

Churchill and Lord Beaverbrook on board the Prince of Wales, *August 1941* (left)

Churchill and General Montgomery, 1942

Churchill and Eisenhower in France

Churchill sails to France, June 1944

Churchill in liberated Caen

Churchill and Montgomery after D-Day

Churchill and General de Gaulle in liberated Paris

Churchill, Stalin and Roosevelt at Yalta, February 1945

Churchill climbing the Wesel Bridge, March 1945

Churchill and the Royal Family at Buckingham Palace, VE Day,
1945

*Churchill moved to tears by the ovation he received at the Council
of Europe, The Hague, 1948*

Churchill with Bernard Baruch

Churchill painting in his studio at Chartwell

*Coronation Day – Churchill and Clementine
leaving Buckingham Palace for the Abbey*

Churchill in his Coronation uniform

Churchill in his Garter robes

Churchill at his desk, November 1953

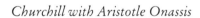

Churchill with Aristotle Onassis

Churchill on his 89th birthday

The State Funeral, January 1965

Churchill, snorting like a war-horse, was never happier than when decked out in the trappings of battle. He was, in the words of Sir Alexander Cadogan, Under-Secretary at the Foreign Office, 'theatrically bull-doggish'.

When on 8 May Churchill defended the government over the humiliating setbacks in Norway it was, willy-nilly, more of a tribute to his own loyalty than to Chamberlain's capacity. Not even Churchill's eloquence could save the Prime Minister. Chamberlain had been bitterly criticised by all sections of the Commons and on 9 May he determined to follow Leo Amery's advice: 'In the name of God, go!' That afternoon he held a meeting at No. 10 Downing Street with David Margesson (Tory Chief Whip), Lord Halifax (Foreign Secretary) and Churchill. Like most prominent men, including the King, Chamberlain wanted his successor to be Halifax. 'Holy Fox', as Churchill called him, was a conventional, godly aristocrat whose virtues, in his rival's opinion, had done much more harm than worse men's vices. Not long before, indeed, Churchill had rebuked Halifax for following the line of least resistance:

> That leads to perdition. Considering the discomfort and sacrifice imposed upon the nation, public men charged with the conduct of the war sh'd live in a continual stress of soul. Faithful discharge of duty is no excuse for Ministers; we have to contrive and compel victory.

When Margesson proposed that Halifax should succeed Chamberlain, Churchill, who had been primed by Brendan Bracken, for once restrained his volubility. There was a long, expressive pause in which the fate of the nation was decided.

Today it seems incredible that at this crisis there could have been any doubt about the choice between a genius with fire in his belly and a mediocrity who, at the prospect of the premiership, developed a 'bad stomach ache'. But doubt there was and it was not resolved until Halifax broke that silence. He murmured something about the impossibility of a peer being Prime Minister. Halifax later recorded that 'Winston, with suitable expressions of regard and humility, said that he could not but feel the force of what I had said, and the PM reluctantly, and Winston evidently with much less reluctance, finished by accepting my view.' Churchill did indeed think it by far the

141

most sensible view. In his moment of triumph he so far forgot himself as to go out into the garden with Lord Halifax and drink a cup of tea.

Before dawn the next day Hitler invaded France and the Low Countries. Chamberlain made a final, doomed attempt to reconstitute his ministry on national lines. But the Labour leaders refused to serve under him. So in the early evening of 10 May Chamberlain resigned and Churchill accepted King George VI's commission to form a government. That night he slept like a baby. He had no feeling of anxiety about the burden he had shouldered. Rather he was 'conscious of a profound sense of relief. I felt as if I were walking with destiny, and that all my past life had been but a preparation for this hour and this trial.'

Churchill's well-nigh miraculous achievement during the dire summer months of 1940 was to convert the nation to a mystical faith in its own providential destiny. It has often been said that Churchill himself was transformed on becoming Prime Minister. Stanley Baldwin, for instance, declared that all the base metal was smelted out of him in the furnace of war. Final responsibility was supposed to have made Churchill finally responsible. Overnight, apparently, the wild maverick turned into a sagacious statesman. Churchill himself gave some countenance to the myth by asserting that it was the British race which had the lion's heart; he only had the luck 'to be called upon to give the roar'. But this is to diminish and misrepresent his role. What really happened was that the nation changed and Churchill stayed the same. For a short spell, indeed, he created a new Britain in his own heroic image. With soul-stirring eloquence he banished the immediate past of attrition, depression and demoralisation. Instead he conjured up a more remote age of chivalry and romance. History came to meet him. With sonorous, archaic language he revived the dormant instincts of national grandeur and inspired a mood of patriotic self-reliance. The state was at bay and, as Isaiah Berlin wrote, Churchill dramatised the lives of its citizens. He made them 'seem to themselves and to each other clad in the fabulous garments appropriate to a great historic moment'. Of that moment Churchill could plausibly say: 'There was a white glow, overpowering, sublime, which ran through our Island from end to end.'

That Churchill himself had not changed is illustrated by his ministerial dispositions, which were made with an eye to his own predominance. He covered his flanks against Tory and Labour cross-fire by creating a true government of national unity, including in the war cabinet Chamberlain, Halifax, Attlee and Arthur Greenwood. But their functions were limited. Churchill appointed himself Minister of Defence so as to be supreme warlord. Apart from Ernest Bevin at the Ministry of Labour, Churchill promoted 'obedient mugwumps' to other key positions, men whom he could override and browbeat. For example, A. V. Alexander succeeded him at the Admiralty, so that in effect Churchill remained his own First Lord. As Robert Boothby wrote: 'If he sometimes enjoyed hauling up underdogs, he had no use for top-dogs other than himself.' With charming insouciance Churchill acknowledged his authoritarian bent: 'All I wanted was compliance with my wishes after reasonable discussion.' It turned out that by discussion he often meant Prime-Ministerial soliloquy.

Churchill set the tone for his administration in his first and perhaps his most famous speech as Premier, made on 13 May.

> I have nothing to offer but blood, toil, tears and sweat. . . . You ask, what is our policy? I can say: It is to wage war by sea, land and air, with all our might and with all the strength that God can give us; to wage war against a monstrous tyranny, never surpassed in the dark, lamentable catalogue of human crime. That is our policy. You ask, what is our aim? I can answer in one word: It is victory, victory at all costs, victory in spite of all terror, victory however long and hard the road may be.

The House of Commons responded with enthusiasm to this tocsin. Churchill was moved by the ovation and his eyes filled with tears. But on leaving the chamber he encountered his friend and aide Desmond Morton and the old ribald twinkle returned. Churchill observed smugly: 'That got the sods, didn't it?' It did. Courage is as contagious as cowardice and Churchill infected everyone with his own heedless fortitude.

Not that there was a widespread spirit of defeatism, though many were apprehensive and some still hoped for a negotiated peace. Those with most to lose seemed particularly prone to the jitters, apt to complain about the conscription of their servants, inclined to think that Hitler had the answers. It was perhaps with this in mind that the Prime Minister issued his message to all those in 'high places'. He urged them to 'set an example of steadiness' and 'check and rebuke expressions of loose and ill-digested opinions in their circles and by their subordinates'. This well reflects Churchill's out-dated view of Britain as a hierarchical, deferential society. Of course, he knew nothing of life as lived by the masses. He never rubbed shoulders with them on buses or tubes – indeed on the only occasion he had travelled by underground railway he had not known how to get off and had to be rescued. He had seldom bought anything in a shop and now, like royalty, never carried money on his person. He changed his shirts at least three times a day and found the toothpaste ready on his toothbrush. He was nannied by his valet and apparently assumed that his private secretary had a valet too. And his speeches were full of anachronistic assumptions. But none of this mattered. It was even, like Churchill's old-fashioned vocabulary ('men of valour' performed 'feats of arms'), an advantage. The people took this aristocrat to their hearts precisely because he was the personification of British history, a guarantor of continuity. He was their symbol of a glorious past, invoked to lay the spectre of a hideous future.

Churchill's greatest single contribution to the war was his oratory – the speeches he made while Germany was winning the battle of France and losing the battle of Britain. As President Kennedy remarked, he mobilised the resources of the English language, proving that the word was mightier than the sword. What Churchill said was compelling and so was the way he said it. For like the Earl of Chatham he was as great an actor as he was orator. The strange cadences, the gruff intimacy, the comic quirks of pronunciation (Narzies) – all made Churchill a spell-binding speaker, especially on the wireless, the household totem at that time of crisis. His vital phrases, with their antique reverberations, passed into common parlance. Never had a British leader so galvanised the nation by sheer force of rhetoric. As the writer Sir Evelyn Wrench said, 'It is hardly an exaggeration to say that during those anxious months we *lived* for Churchill's periodic surveys of the war.' These surveys provided, in the words of Ronald Tree MP, 'the mainspring of our existence'. Yet Churchill by no means relied only on magniloquence. The purple passages were lightened with flashes of ironic humour. Soaring flights of classical prose dipped all of a sudden into homely idiom. Churchill made skilful use of variety, harmonised pathos and bathos, varied climax with anti-climax. He wove arresting images and unexpected words into the texture of his discourse, giving it depth as well as clarity. The total effect was at once simple and sublime.

Still, it is the majestic summits of Churchill's eloquence which remain stamped on the memory. While the German panzers scythed their way through France he declared that it would be 'foolish to disguise the gravity of the hour', but 'still more foolish to lose heart and courage'. On 4 June, after the evacuation of the British army from Dunkirk he pronounced his celebrated litany of resistance:

> We shall fight in France, we shall fight on the seas and oceans, we shall fight with growing confidence and strength in the air, we shall defend our Island, whatever the cost may be, we shall fight on the beaches, we shall fight on the landing grounds, we shall fight in the fields and in the streets, we shall fight in the hills; we shall never surrender.

When France fell he announced that Britain would continue the struggle alone:

> Let us therefore brace ourselves to our duties, and so bear ourselves that, if the British Empire and its Commonwealth last for a thousand years, men will still say: 'This was their finest hour.'

When invasion threatened he told the nation that this was a 'war of peoples and of causes ... a war of the Unknown Warriors' and that 'we are prepared to proceed to all extremities'. As the RAF resisted the onslaught of the Luftwaffe in August Churchill paid his immortal tribute to the British fighter pilots: 'Never in the field of human conflict was so much owed by so many to so few.'

Churchill did not just rally Britain, he attempted to avert the collapse of France. Three times, at some personal risk, the Prime Minister crossed the channel and did his best to instil something of his own pugnacious spirit into the demoralised French government. In his diary for 16 May the French official Paul Baudouin penned a vivid account of Churchill, 'crowned like a volcano by the smoke of his cigars', conjuring up 'an apocalyptic vision of war' until one o'clock in the morning. 'We will starve Germany out. We will destroy her towns. We will burn her crops and her forests.' Even if England herself was razed to the ground Churchill vowed to carry on the war from Canada, bringing in the New World to redress the balance of the Old. Churchill's 'fire and fury' gave new heart to Reynaud, the French Premier. But Churchill would not, in the last resort, give Reynaud all the fighter squadrons he demanded. Spitfires and Hurricanes were Britain's Maginot Line, Churchill explained. His vital decision to support Air Marshal Dowding and preserve that line of defence intact enabled the RAF to prevent the establishment of German air superiority over Britain, a *sine qua non* of the invasion.

Churchill was often to recall this dramatic trip to Paris, where he saw distraught officials burning government archives on the Quai d'Orsay, and prophesied that the 'place will shortly become a charnel house'. He also heard General Gamelin make his admission that there was no strategic reserve. This was incredible but true. Flanking attacks to halt the German advance were therefore impossible, which did not stop Churchill clamouring for them. But his faith in the French army was shattered. For the first time he understood the gravity of the situation. That ardent apologist of the offensive began to realise that the Second World War would not, like its predecessor, be a defensive one. When trying to excuse his failure to appreciate the military revolution wrought by his own brain-child, the tank, Churchill somewhat speciously claimed that for ten years he had been deprived of official information. But he acknowledged that, like most of the soldiers, he had been preparing to fight the previous war.

Some of his colleagues apparently still hesitated to fight this one. Late in May, Halifax and Chamberlain tried to insist on a new diplomatic initiative. Britain should ask Italy to intercede with Germany on behalf of France. Churchill loathed the idea of sliding down this 'slippery slope' to appeasement. 'Nations which go down fighting rise again,' he declared, 'but those which surrender tamely are finished.' Churchill pointed out the humiliating absurdity of their requesting Mussolini to ask Hitler to 'treat us nicely'. His spirit was infectious. For when he said soon afterwards that whatever happened at Dunkirk Britain would never parley or surrender – 'If this long island story of ours is to end at last let it end only when each one of us lies choking in his own blood upon the ground' – his words were greeted with a spontaneous outburst of approval from the cabinet. Moreover he received full ministerial approval for the ruthless war measures he took.

At Dunkirk, for example, he ordered that wounded men should be rescued last. While the evacuation was actually in progress he was sending other British units to western France in a desperate bid to stop the rot. He laid plans to set fire to the sea and to spray British beaches with mustard gas if the Germans landed, though he explained his strategy to the French leaders at their second meeting in more prosaic terms. Being no military expert himself, said Churchill modestly, he was vague about the correct response to German invaders. But his technical advisers held the view that the best method of dealing with them was to drown as many as possible on the way over and to knock the others on the head ('frapper sur la tête') as they crawled ashore. Having proposed an indissoluble union between Britain and France in June, Churchill ordained the sinking of the French fleet at Oran in July. He was prepared to risk war with France in order to prevent her navy from falling into German hands. Actually had not Churchill been so precipitate he might have secured its surrender by negotiation, as happened at Alexandria. However this cold-blooded deed proved that Churchill would stop at nothing. For the first time he was cheered more enthusiastically than Chamberlain in the House of Commons. No one, at home or abroad, could any longer doubt Britain's inflexible determination to fight to the finish. The Prime Minister was the incarnation of that resolve. When asked if he wanted to reply to the Nazi peace overture in July Churchill answered, 'I do not propose to say anything in reply to Herr Hitler's speech, not being on speaking terms with him.'

The responsibility of his office did not alter Churchill's methods any more than they changed his nature. Some members of the staff at 10 Downing Street, initially fearful about his disruptive capacities, later said that they soon became reconciled to Churchill, who created a new mood of urgency. One aide represented him as a dynamo generating energy at the centre instead of humming away uncontrolled on the periphery. Others claimed that the new high command structure, with the good-natured 'eminence khaki' General 'Pug' Ismay mediating between the Prime Minister and his service chiefs, harnessed Churchill's drive and prevented him from going off the rails. There is some truth in all this. But it seems to imply that Churchill was more of a constitutional monarch than a benevolent despot. This was not the case, though there were, of course, real constraints on his power. Still age, experience, knowledge, temperament – everything conspired to make him an autocrat. As the historian A. J. P. Taylor pointed out, Churchill was the only Prime Minister, not excluding Wellington, to wear military uniform in office. And, as Sir Walter Scott once said of the Iron Duke, being a soldier 'was a bad education for a statesman in a free country'. The fact is that Churchill ruled a land which, like Germany, 'abandoned her liberties to augment her might'. The difference was that Britain did so voluntarily, bowing only to the inexorable pressure of war. Moreover her leader, though he shared a number of the Führer's characteristics – fascination with science, artistic aspirations, faith in the destiny of his race, 'a hypnotic dilation of the eye', capacity to soliloquise into the small hours – was neither mad nor bad.

Some of Churchill's antics, it must be said, did cause intimates to question his mental and moral health. The disillusioned Desmond Morton, for example, later asserted that without a curb on his actions 'Winston would have been a Caligula or worse, and quite properly had his throat cut'. In the first weeks of the new premiership Lord Trenchard was amazed to see Churchill playing the part of a local commander, discussing on the telephone whether 'a brigadier in charge of the defences at Boulogne nearly 100 miles away was doing the right thing in resisting the Germans at one end of a quay or another'. A month or so later Sir Alexander Cadogan compared No. 10 to 'behind the scenes at the circus; every crank in the world is getting hold of the Prime Minister', whose decisions were consequently 'half-baked'. Sir John Reith, who developed a pathological hatred for Churchill, considered him 'essentially rotten. He is the greatest menace we have ever had

– country and Empire sacrificed to his megalomania, to his monstrous obstinacy and wrong-headedness.' Lord Hankey called Churchill a 'rogue elephant'. Lloyd George thought he was 'entirely in the hands of sycophants who feed and fan his illusions' and said that 'Winston now feels he is God.'

In fact all the distressing symptoms of what Beaverbrook called 'Churchill up' were present during the fraught summer of 1940. The Prime Minister gave way to violent fits of irritation and petulance. Everyone who came into contact with him experienced these childish tantrums, often sparked off by quite trivial matters. The professional soldiers were his particular victims. Churchill wanted them to show vim and initiative in the face of defeat. He urged them to set up 'a Scarlet Pimpernel organisation', for example, in order to spirit anti-German French officers across the channel. Instead his generals were, in Churchill's opinion, hidebound and obstructive. Occasionally he suggested that one should be shot in order to encourage the others. And he once forced Pound to agree that the execution of Admiral Byng in 1757 had had a salutary effect on the navy. At the end of June, Churchill's outbursts of ill-temper provoked Clementine herself to make a rare and courageous intervention. With great reluctance she told him that 'there is a danger of your being generally disliked by your colleagues and subordinates because of your rough sarcastic & over-bearing manner'. She pleaded with him to combine 'urbanity, kindness and if possible Olympic calm'.

Nevertheless even Lord Halifax acknowledged that Churchill's virtues outweighed his vices. Few since have doubted that his achievements more than made up for his aberrations. Churchill's exasperating methods quickened the pace of work. His obsessive attention to detail increased general efficiency. His will to win was palpable – he even practised with bayonet and gun (a cigar did not seem to spoil his aim) so that he could resist German parachutists. All who surrounded him were inspired by his intensity of purpose. Those who met him only occasionally, like the scientist R. V. Jones, 'had the feeling of being recharged by contact with a source of living power'. Churchill set an example of dogged toil which it was impossible to ignore. He told a secretary who was flagging after hours of dictation, 'We must go on like gun-horses, till we drop.' When

Churchill became their taskmaster the staff at No. 10 found that weekends vanished, holidays were a thing of the past, sleep itself was a luxury. He made impossible demands on them. 'Gimme the moon', he bellowed on one occasion – he wanted the weather charts.

Yet most of his staff became completely devoted to Churchill. When he was ill, said one shorthand-typist, 'we longed for the old stamp and bark, the quick word of scorn, the snort of impatience and the final twinkle of forgiveness'. Churchill's scowling sulks made his moods of sunny cheerfulness all the brighter. His charm compensated for his rudeness; his loyalty redeemed his cruelty. His fundamental kindness of heart and generosity of spirit were never altogether obscured by perennial egotism and fleeting rages. In short, Churchill was admired not so much in spite of his faults as because of his merits. Sir George Mallaby, later Under-Secretary at the Cabinet Office, wrote:

> He was unusual, unpredictable, exciting, original, stimulating, provocative, outrageous, uniquely experienced, abundantly talented, humorous, entertaining . . . a great man.

Even those who had not been, in Lord Hankey's words, 'doped by Churchill's personality', found it hard to dislike him. Hankey himself, who had condemned his dictatorial habits, acknowledged, when exposed to the full glare of Churchill's fascination, that he 'has great points as a leader'. Churchill bore his responsibilities extraordinarily lightly. It is true that while the threat of invasion hung over Britain he was under terrific strain, which entitled him (in the view of his willing whipping-boy, General Ismay, and others) to blow off steam when he felt like it. Every morning that summer, despite his optimistic temperament, Churchill woke with dread in his heart. At odd moments he even gave way to despair. He confessed later that he had scarcely known what he said in his great speeches – he had just been overwhelmed by the conviction that it was better for Britain to be destroyed than for the Nazis to triumph. So, brooding and downcast, Churchill often indulged in what P. G. Wodehouse (who disliked him) called a 'silent grouch'. But he thawed out into conviviality, especially in male company when the brandy was flowing. He fought himself out of gloom by means of talk until, pacing the floor with the light of battle in his eyes and a ruined cigar between his lips, the old exhilaration with war returned.

When the mood took him he bubbled with good humour. He never stood on his dignity. He had once amazed guests by getting down on all fours under the Chartwell dining-room table and shaking swimming-pool water out of his ears like a dog. During an important conference he changed his socks and scratched his back like a bear by rubbing it up and down the edge of an open door, explaining that he must have 'picked 'em up in Egypt'. While the Blitz was raging he was delighted to find that his grandson's newly-bought electric train set had two transformers and two engines: 'Good! Let's have a crash!' Churchill also liked to deflate the dignity of others. He prodded old friends in the tummy with his forefinger. Making rumbustious sallies and chuckling at his own jokes, Churchill had, during his frequent trips of inspection and consultation, the air of being a schoolboy out on a jape. At home he could seem positively infantile. For example, he cherished a hot-water bottle cover embroidered with a panda. He adored lying in the bath kicking his legs in the air 'as at birth'. Sucking his cigar like a dummy and wearing his 'rompers' (as he called his siren suits), Churchill resembled nothing so much as a big baby. These comfortable and serviceable garments, sometimes made of striped and worsted material, were of course based on his bricklayer's dungarees. Dressed in them Churchill reminded Lady Diana Cooper of 'the good little pig building his house of bricks'. However his siren suit was not appreciated at the Kremlin: 'They thought I was pushing democracy too far.'

The army had been evacuated from France without its equipment and Britain was never so weak in the face of an aggressor as in the few months after Dunkirk. Yet Churchill would not sacrifice the initiative. As early as 5 June he was contemplating raids on enemy territory and planning a policy of 'butcher and bolt'. On 8 July he was discovering 'one sure path' to 'win the war' in 'an absolutely devastating, exterminating attack by very heavy bombers from this country upon the Nazi homeland'. At great risk he sent reinforcements to General Wavell in the Middle East, accompanied by detailed (and unwelcome) directives on how to use them. This gamble, which involved stripping

Britain of half its armour, paid off handsomely. Churchill also exploited his pen-friendship (begun at the Admiralty) with President Franklin D. Roosevelt in order to draw on the 'arsenal of democracy'. In particular he obtained, on stiff terms, some fifty old American destroyers, which were actually worth more as emblems of concord than as vessels of war. But Churchill's hawkishness was often ill-judged. He could not resist the lure of dramatic forays in irrelevant theatres of operations. Most of all he relished the prospect of amphibious descents on hostile shores. The trouble was that active preparations seldom lived up to imaginative conceptions. Churchill even admitted that he worried more about maintaining the offensive spirit than about the results it achieved. Anyway, he asserted, 'Safety first is ruin in war.' But taking risks could be more ruinous. The assault on the North African port of Dakar, which aimed to make General de Gaulle leader of the French colonial forces, was a bloody fiasco.

Yet even this did little harm to Churchill's monumental prestige. For by the early autumn of 1940 the RAF had successfully resisted the Luftwaffe and an immediate invasion seemed impracticable. In fact on 17 September Hitler postponed it indefinitely, as Churchill discovered some six weeks later thanks to the 'Ultra' code-breakers, whose work he supported and monitored ceaselessly – they were his 'geese who laid the golden eggs and never cackled'. Throughout the Battle of Britain Churchill's great achievement had been to stiffen national morale. Almost the only leisure exercise he ever took now was to potter out and feed his goldfish. But he was tireless in travelling round the country and keeping his finger on the pulse of war. He inspected invasion defences and was amused at Brighton to see Grenadier Guards making a machine-gun post in a kiosk on the pier where as a schoolboy he had admired the acrobatics of performing fleas. He watched 'dog-fights' from the roof of the steel and concrete Annexe to No. 10 at Storey's Gate. He visited fighter bases and witnessed the victorious climax to the Battle of Britain on 15 September at Fighter Group Headquarters Uxbridge, where red lights indicated that all the reserves were employed at once. He examined bomb damage and was everywhere greeted by cheering people who clustered round him wanting to touch or stroke his clothes as though he were a talisman. General Ismay left a record of a tour of London's east end:

> 'Good old Winnie', they cried. 'We thought you'd come and see us. We can take it. Give it 'em back.' Churchill broke down, and as I was struggling to get him through the crowd, I heard an old woman say, 'You see, he really cares; he's crying.' Having pulled himself together, he proceeded to march through dockland at breakneck speed.

At Ramsgate Churchill was much moved by the distress caused to the owner of a small tea-shop whose premises had been destroyed during an air-raid. Against Treasury advice he instituted a more liberal scheme of compensation. Encouraged by Clementine he also cut through bureaucratic objections to the use of underground railway stations as shelters during the Blitz.

When asked exactly what Churchill *did* to win the war Attlee would reply, 'Talk about it.' Churchill's tongue was certainly the principal weapon in Churchill's arsenal. He thought aloud about the conflict all the time. In this ceaseless discourse he did not necessarily require or relish the stimulus of a response. To the astonishment of a private secretary (the only other person present) Churchill once spent an entire luncheon addressing himself exclusively to the marmalade cat. Churchill dictated the war effort in both senses of the word, issuing a Niagara of minutes and insisting that his will should be done according to these alone. Above all he animated the nation by his speeches. These were endowed with added resonance by the fact that timeless sentiments were being delivered not just to his contemporaries but to posterity. For, to quote Attlee again, Churchill saw 'all events taking their place in the procession of past events as seen by the historian of the future'. But Churchill did not achieve victory by eloquence alone. He transmuted glittering phrases into glorious deeds by the terrific force of his personality. What he said was less important than what he was. During Churchill's finest hour the man spoke more loudly than his words.

CHAPTER X

WARLORD AT BAY

HAVING blocked Germany's invasion of Britain, Churchill yearned to take the war into the enemy's camp. But while the Blitz raged through the autumn of 1940 he had little save words to hurl at 'that bad man', as he called Hitler. In a series of speeches he flung defiance at 'this monstrous abortion of hatred and defeat'. The Führer had 'resolved to try to break our famous Island race by a process of indiscriminate slaughter and destruction'. But all he had done was 'to kindle a fire in British hearts, here and all over the world, which will glow long after all traces of the conflagration he has caused in London have been removed'. Churchill himself courted danger but he did take at least one sensible precaution against the nightly raids. He restricted sittings at the House of Commons to the day-time. With characteristic irony he told its members, 'We ought not to flatter ourselves by imagining that we are irreplaceable but it cannot be denied that two or three hundred by-elections would be a quite needless complication of our affairs at this particular juncture.' Churchill continued to woo Roosevelt and he encouraged the flow of vital supplies from the United States. He fostered what he took to be the fruitful rivalry between the bureaucratic Air Ministry and Lord Beaverbrook's piratical Ministry of Aircraft Production. In October, having succeeded the mortally ill Chamberlain as leader of the Conservative party, Churchill made a number of morale-raising tours of the country. But he itched for action. More and more Churchill focussed the bright spotlight of his attention on the Mediterranean – the one theatre of war in which there was a prospect of attack.

Italy, which had entered the war just in time to 'stab fallen France in the back', had altered the balance of power in that part of the world. Mussolini's fleet posed a serious threat to sea communications with the Middle East. His land forces menaced Wavell's army in Egypt. And at the end of October he attacked Greece. On 5 November Churchill told the House of Commons that Britain would carry on the struggle for supremacy in north Africa and the Balkans. It was a harshly determined speech. Rubbing the palms of his hands with fingers outstretched up and down the front of his coat – a characteristic gesture – Churchill explained the grim odds with clinical precision. Afterwards he slouched into the smoking room to scan the *Evening News* with furious attention, while MPs thanked God they had such a man to lead them. Actually Churchill, recurring to his theme of the soft underbelly of Europe, thought the Italians would be easy meat. His confidence was increased by the sinking of half Mussolini's battle-fleet in the harbour at Taranto by aircraft from the carrier *Illustrious* on 11 November.

True, Churchill was unsure of the cautious, taciturn Wavell, reckoning that he was better suited to be the chairman of a golf club or a Tory association than a general. But, often against military advice at home, Churchill gave Wavell all the reinforcements he could muster. He badgered him to smash the Italians in Libya, to defend Crete, to sustain the Greeks. He also pressed for the capture of the island of Pantelleria and for landing forces in the Dodecanese. Indeed, it required the War Office's entire 'apparatus of negation', as Churchill disgustedly called it, to persuade the Prime Minister that Britain lacked the resources to undertake these last two dubious ventures. However by the end of November Wavell was finally ready to mount an attack in the desert. Harold Nicolson saw the signals in the Prime Minister's eyes, which were 'glaucous, vigilant, angry, combative, visionary and tragic'. They were also preoccupied, 'the eyes of a man faced by an ordeal'. Churchill was profoundly relieved in the winter of 1940–41 when Wavell defeated the Italians at Sidi Barrani, capturing over 100,000 prisoners and much *matériel*. But in his message of congratulation the Prime Minister could not resist applying the goad. Now was the time to pursue the beaten foe, he urged. 'It is the moment when the victor is most exhausted that the greatest forfeit can be exacted from the vanquished.'

Churchill received further encouragement during the second winter of the war from the fact that the United States was becoming steadily more 'mixed up', as he delicately put it, in the affairs of Great Britain. In December 1940 Churchill sent a reluctant Lord Halifax to Washington as ambassador – his wife was even more reluctant and went on her knees to Churchill in an effort to persuade him to let her husband stay at his post. The Prime Minister was adamant, however, for he wanted to dispose of a 'man of Munich' and have Eden as Foreign Secretary. He was also anxious to flatter the Americans by sending an eminent politician, and Halifax, though an inveterate appeaser and an aloof aristocrat, proved a surprisingly successful choice. Roosevelt himself dispatched his shrewd friend Harry Hopkins to Britain. Hopkins was so frail that he resembled, according to one journalist, 'an animated piece of shredded wheat'. But he was an inspired emissary. Churchill greeted him with enthusiasm, though, as the US Secretary of the Interior Harold Ickes cynically remarked, the Prime Minister would have made much of the President's personal representative if he had been carrying bubonic plague.

Hopkins was overwhelmed by his 'rotund, smiling, red-faced' host with his 'clear eye', 'mushy voice' and 'amazing' personality. 'God, what a force that man has!' he kept exclaiming, 'Jesus Christ! What a man!' Everything about Churchill fascinated Hopkins – the extraordinary hours he kept, his mumbling rehearsal of sentences before dictation, his habit of taking snuff from a little silver box, his gargantuan appetite, his inflexible courage, the fact that the only warm place in his official country residence, Chequers, was the downstairs cloakroom, where Hopkins read his official papers. Churchill took Hopkins largely into his confidence. Thanks to his reports Roosevelt was confirmed in his belief that Britain's will would not falter and that America's aid would not be wasted. In February Churchill made his famous appeal, 'Give us the tools, and we will finish the job.' The following month the Lend-Lease bill became law in the United States, an earnest that the mightiest industrial power in the world was mobilising against Germany. At the same time the defeatist Joseph Kennedy was replaced as American ambassador by John G. Winant, a strong partisan of Britain. In practice American assistance remained meagre, despite Roosevelt's warm words. Churchill's own words were incandescent, but his wooing was coolly calculated. Gradually he inveigled the United States away from isolationism and into active sympathy for Britain – one of the greatest feats of his premiership.

Meanwhile the war had taken a turn for the worse. Shipping losses were growing at a fearful rate. The navy scored notable successes against surface vessels, destroying three Italian battle-cruisers at Matapan and sinking the German battleship *Bismarck* when it broke into the Atlantic. But it seemed to have no answer to the submarine. Churchill wrote, 'This mortal danger to our life-lines gnawed at my bowels.' He determined to lift the 'business to the highest plane' and in March 1941 proclaimed 'the Battle of the Atlantic'. This was a good instance of his assumption that a pronouncement was some-how equivalent to an achievement. In fact, obsessed as he always was with attack, Churchill refused to divert resources from the bombing of Germany to the long-range coastal com-mand aircraft which, when fitted with the new centimetric radar sets, were eventually to play such an important part in defeating the U-boats.

On land there were also serious reverses. The underbelly of Europe proved excessively hard when protected by German armour. At the end of March, General Erwin Rommel launched a raid against Wavell's weakened and extended forces, which led to the capture of all Cyrenaica apart from the enclave of Tobruk. Churchill peevishly remarked that Rommel had torn the newly-won laurels from Wavell's brow and thrown them in the sand. Actually the tanks which the Prime Minister had strained every nerve to send to the Middle East were no match for those of the Germans. In his eagerness to make up for lost time Churchill had not ensured proper testing.

Shortly after Rommel's victory Hitler went to Mussolini's aid in the Balkans, invading Yugoslavia and Greece. Mindful of British prestige, Churchill wanted to help the Greeks. But even he hesitated about embarking on 'a blank military adventure dictated by *noblesse oblige*'. Oddly enough Wavell came round and supported intervention. It weakened him disastrously in North Africa but he seemed determined to refute Churchillian slurs on his offensive spirit. In the event British troops had no sooner landed in Greece than they had to be withdrawn, with much loss of equipment. The Germans not only crushed their enemies in this Balkan *Blitzkrieg*, they realised Churchill's most thrillingly apocalyptic vision of war. In 1939, on a visit to see the giant panda at London Zoo, he had excitedly conjured up the prospect of wild beasts, blasted out of captivity by bombs, terrorizing the streets of the ruined capital. On 6 April 1941 the Luftwaffe bombed Belgrade and, as Churchill later wrote, 'Out of the nightmare of smoke and fire came the maddened animals released from their shattered cages in the Zoological Gardens.'

These spring setbacks caused the first serious grumbles at home about Churchill's administration. In Whitehall there were complaints about his awkward and unbusinesslike behaviour. Some officials genuinely feared that the spate of paperwork generated by the Prime Minister would swamp clear principles of policy. General Kennedy cited the typical military view: 'I don't see how we can win the war without Winston, but, on the other hand, I don't see how we can win it with him.' Cabinet ministers groused about Churchill's interminable monologues – he ignored set agendas in favour of magisterial surveys of the conflict, getting nowhere but turning each meeting into an historic occasion. Yet when Eden chided him for loquacity he was engagingly penitent: 'Yes, I'm afraid sometimes I do talk rather a lot. I'm quite ashamed of myself.' Unmollified bureaucrats insisted that it was easier to win the war against Hitler than the war against Churchill. Those invited to 'dine and sleep' at Chequers quipped that they had been invited to dine and stay awake. At Westminster, Lloyd George voiced another common criticism, that Churchill had surrounded himself with 'Yes-men'. The Prime Minister denied the charge, then somewhat inconsistently argued that he could not put positive impetus into the war-making machine if he were hemmed about by 'No-men'. But, having extracted a massive vote of confidence from the House of Commons, Churchill did make minor adjustments to his cabinet.

He also continued to nag Wavell and once again dispatched reinforcements to the Middle East. Moreover, in the face of strong opposition from his service chiefs, he insisted that the convoy should sail through the Mediterranean, the shortest route, but the most hazardous one. The convoy's success proved that if Churchill was erratic his military advisers were anything but infallible. However, Wavell's forces were still so thinly spread that he could only act effectively against soft targets, as in Abyssinia, Syria and Iraq. He was unable to resist the German airborne assault on Crete, in May 1941. Churchill told Wavell that victory in Crete was essential and urged him to 'keep hurling in all aid you can'. It was not enough. Another humiliating evacuation was followed in June by a further disaster in north Africa. Overriding Wavell's reluctance, Churchill had insisted on a new offensive against Rommel. But the grandly named 'Operation Battleaxe' was blunted after only two days. Churchill's response was to sack Wavell, making him swap jobs with General Sir Claude Auchinleck, Commander-in-Chief of India.

According to Desmond Morton, Churchill's motives for dismissing Wavell were those of a megalomaniac. He described how Churchill paced up and down the room, his chin sunk on his chest, glowering ferociously and muttering, 'I wanted to show my power.' Morton said that for the first time he 'deeply disliked Winston and realised the depths of selfish brutality to which he could sink'. Of course, Churchill was ill-disposed towards Wavell. He had never forgiven him for answering criticism of his relatively bloodless evacuation of British Somaliland in 1940 with the remark that 'a big butcher's bill was not necessarily evidence of good tactics'. Moreover Churchill was certainly capable of discharging men in a callous fashion. On occasions his behaviour was not so much pugnacious as downright savage. For example, in the same month as Wavell went, Churchill was enraged by the hostility of a former Secretary of War, Leslie Hore-Belisha. The Prime Minister propelled him into the smoking room of the House of Commons, sat him in an armchair and, scowling fiercely, threatened: 'If you fight me I shall fight you back. And remember this: You are using a 4.5 inch howitzer, and I am using a twelve inch gun.'

Nevertheless, Churchill did have reasons for replacing Wavell which had nothing to do with the crude assertion of his power. The Prime Minister had been made over-optimistic about the prospects of military success in North Africa by Rommel's over-pessimistic signals, which he read thanks to the 'Ultra' code-breakers. Consequently he was incensed by Wavell's 'worst case' plans, his proposals for abandoning Egypt if the worst came to the worst. These were only a prudent insurance policy but Churchill regarded them as pure defeatism. He talked about laying down the Premiership, and even renouncing cigars and alcohol, in order to take personal command of the desert army. He fulminated about 'cold feet', about the honour of Great Britain, about staff officers using their pistols to shoot Huns, about warriors in ancient times who cut the throats of their horses before going into battle so that they should have no means of retreat, about following Kitchener's example and using the 'peacock tail' of the army as an instrument of war instead of a decorative appendage. All this convinced soldiers like Wavell that Churchill had learnt nothing about warfare since Omdurman. Yet the intuitions of the invincible amateur were often worth more than the reasonings of the hardened professional. Churchill was right in attaching such importance to the Middle East and without his energy it might have fallen to the Axis powers.

On 22 June, the day after Wavell's dismissal, Germany attacked Russia. Churchill had long prophesied that when thwarted in the west Hitler would, like Napoleon, 'recoil eastwards'. The last big bomber raid on London had occurred in May – destroying the House of Commons: standing amidst the ruins Churchill had vowed tearfully that it would be rebuilt as before. Since then evidence of Hitler's design against the Soviet Union had been mounting. Churchill had even sent Stalin warning of the imminent attack. But for inscrutable reasons of his own the Russian dictator chose to ignore it. Now Churchill, his soul consumed by the single passion to win the war, declared his support for Russia. He did not disown his past statements but for the time being his hatred of Bolshevik tyranny was swallowed up by his will to triumph over a worse evil. Hitler still cherished delusions about uniting with Britain in a crusade against Communism but, as Ribbentrop shrewdly reckoned, Churchill would have signed a pact with Satan if he could thereby destroy Nazism. The Prime Minister himself remarked: 'If Hitler invaded Hell, I would at least make a favourable reference to the Devil in the House of Commons.'

It seems obvious today that by surrounding himself with unbeaten enemies Hitler was sealing his own fate. But at the time it was generally feared that the German panzers would slice their way into the Russian heartland in a matter of weeks. Churchill was more cheerful about Soviet prospects than his service experts. In July he reached agreement with Stalin that neither side would make a separate peace and that Britain would supply munitions to Russia. In return he received from Stalin grudging thanks, curt demands for the opening of a second front in Europe and a surly refusal to share military information. Churchill never realised that Stalin saw full-hearted co-operation with the democratic west as tantamount to laying the liberal axe to the root of his own totalitarian tree. When provoked, the British Prime Minister was quite capable of castigating the Russian dictator for churlishness. But, remembering the trials of his great ancestor, he attached supreme importance to achieving harmony between war-time allies. Romantic that he was, Churchill even seems to have cherished bizarre notions about forging a spirit of comradeship with Stalin. As a result he was over-conciliatory.

However, it was with Roosevelt, not Stalin, that Churchill dreamt of forming a 'holy alliance' such as had wedded Marlborough to Prince Eugene. He tried to lay its foundations in August 1941. Churchill crossed the Atlantic on board the battleship *Prince of Wales* (amusing himself with C. S. Forester's *Captain Hornblower R.N.* because the requirement of radio silence stopped him firing off his usual salvoes of memoranda) and met Roosevelt at Placentia Bay, Newfoundland. Harry Hopkins had expected a clash of 'prima donnas' but Prime Minister and President established an immediate rapport. According to Hopkins, Churchill behaved as though 'he was being carried up into the heavens to meet God'. He paid elaborate homage to Roosevelt as head of state, while the President confirmed in person the fond admiration he had expressed in his letters to the 'Former Naval Person'. Together the two men sang martial hymns at the Sunday service.

Together they discussed aid for Russia and extending the limits of America's 'constructive non-belligerency'. Together they drafted the formulae (Churchill added 'verbal flourishes') of the Atlantic Charter. This document was a vague affirmation of high-sounding principles. It was neither signed nor issued as anything but a press release. But it had a certain propaganda value and, to Churchill's disappointment, it was the main product of the Placentia Bay conference.

In its strength and its weakness the Atlantic Charter epitomised the historic relationship between Churchill and Roosevelt. They were united by bonds of sentiment and affection. But Churchill was not prepared to sacrifice Britain's empire or her other vital interests at Roosevelt's behest. And Roosevelt was unwilling to anticipate American public opinion by entering the war just to please Churchill. Each had different views about strategy – Roosevelt followed his advisers who likened the reinforcement of Egypt to throwing snowballs into hell. Neither could forget that his own national responsibilities were paramount. Moreover beneath the dulcet phrases there were personal strains. Roosevelt was exhausted by Churchill's animal vitality, his late nights and tireless harangues. Churchill was irritated by Roosevelt's assumption that he was a reactionary, the last of the Victorians. Roosevelt said that Churchill had a hundred ideas a day, only four of which were any good. When he heard of this remark Churchill angrily riposted that it came ill from a man who never had any ideas at all. Churchill was bored by Roosevelt's stamp collection.

However, despite tensions and difficulties which increased with time, their personal friendship was a crucial and a beneficial element in the developing relations between their two countries. It was cemented not only by big interests but by little civilities such as the exchange of birthday greetings and presents. In return for some gift Churchill sent Roosevelt his portrait, 'a tit for your tat'. Jokes and nicknames drew them together. Once when flying Churchill signed himself 'Present Aerial Person'. They were remarkably open with one another. It was a state of affairs symbolised by Hopkins' story, apocryphal or not, about Roosevelt's entering Churchill's room at the White House during their next meeting at the end of 1941 and discovering him naked after his bath. Roosevelt retreated in embarrassment but Churchill reassured him that 'The Prime Minister of Great Britain has nothing to hide from the President of the United States.' Each leader allowed himself to be fascinated by the other's charm, so much so that the Foreign Office sometimes cursed (though it sometimes blessed) the Prime Minister's 'private line' to the President, and Roosevelt's military advisers worried that he had been hypnotised by Churchill.

On its way home the *Prince of Wales* steamed through a convoy and as the ships recognised the portly figure on the bridge they sounded their hooters and foghorns, to Churchill's immense gratification. There was little else to gratify him in the autumn of 1941. The United States, as Roosevelt had told reporters after their conference, was 'no closer to war'. The German armies were advancing in Russia and Churchill believed that Moscow was 'a gone coon'. Grumbling and growling about six hundred thousand useless mouths to feed in Egypt, he tried to 'whip' (his word) Auchinleck into making a premature attack on Rommel, but without success. The bomber offensive was Britain's only direct method of hitting Germany but Churchill had growing doubts about its effectiveness. At the same time he could not convince the Chiefs of Staff that any amphibious assault on Europe was feasible. In his mind's eye he captured both Trondheim and Sicily with perfectly acceptable losses. Purple in the face he vociferated: 'Wars cannot be won by sitting still and doing nothing.' But he was forced to acknowledge the cogency of the professionals' arguments. Even so he exacted a terrible toll on chiefs of staff, declaring that they had no ideas themselves and frustrated all his offensive projects. Actually they directed the war machine with unprecedented efficiency, though Churchill himself would never admit it. He told Harold Macmillan:

> 'Why you may take the most gallant sailor, the most intrepid airman and the most audacious soldier, put them at a table together – what do you get? *The sum of their fears.*' (This with frightful sibilant emphasis).

Still, Churchill was reluctant to over rule them, though he was prepared to dismiss them. But when he replaced Dill by General Sir Alan Brooke (later Lord Alanbrooke) as Chief of the Imperial General Staff (CIGS) the latter proved almost as obstructive as the former.

Brooke had been subjected to a withering inquisition over the Trondheim plan and had evidently earned Churchill's respect by refusing to be browbeaten. Brooke's new post kept him up night after night – he reckoned himself lucky if he had six consecutive hours without seeing Churchill. Two months as CIGS, he said, felt like ten years. But though he criticised Churchill's impetuosity of spirit and narrowness of vision, Brooke admired his other 'marvellous qualities'. He wrote later:

> As I look back on those five years of close contact with the greatest war leader of modern times I carry away in my memory deeply engraved impressions of unbounded genius, unrelenting energy, dogged determination, a refusal to accept defeat in any shape or form, vast personal courage, a deep sense of humour, and an uncanny faculty for inspiring respect, admiration, loyalty and deep affection in the hearts of all those fortunate enough to work in close touch with him.

Reserved, abstemious and methodical, Brooke warmed to Churchill who was none of these things. The realistic general, though often driven to distraction, found abundant compensations in serving the fantastical Prime Minister. For example at nearly three o'clock one morning in late October, when he was aching for sleep, Brooke's spirits were uplifted by Churchill's lightheartedness. Instead of going to bed the Prime Minister, wearing a gorgeous multi-coloured dressing-gown over his siren suit, had the gramophone switched on. Holding a sandwich in one hand and water-cress in the other, he proceeded to trot round the room, giving occasional little skips in time with the music. On each lap he stopped near the fireplace: 'to release some priceless quotation or thought'.

Churchill's ebullience stemmed in part from complete physical well-being. The war had rejuvenated him. The puffy, pallid look had gone. Churchill glowed with health (which did not stop him from indulging in mild bouts of hypochondria). For someone of sixty-seven he was extraordinarily spry: his skin was pink, his eyes sparkled, his flesh was firm and plump. Care sometimes darkened his countenance but his mood was usually buoyant and at the slightest pretext his face lit up with good humour. When tired he went white and his speech became slow and slobbery. But in a way that astounded his colleagues he rose above fatigue. For Churchill's daily routine was perfectly geared to suit his curious metabolism.

He woke at about eight o'clock feeling (as he nearly always had, except when the threat of invasion hung over England) 'as if he had a bottle of champagne inside him and glad that another day had come'. His official red boxes were delivered with his breakfast. This meal was an unrationed, Edwardian feast which he consumed with visible and sometimes audible relish on the Johnsonian principle that a man who does not mind his belly will scarcely mind anything else. Churchill liked to begin the day with a main course of beef, cutlets, grouse or the like, sometimes washed down with white wine. He once refused to touch a magnificent salmon: 'No! No! I will have meat. Carnivores will win this war.' Churchill worked for most of the morning in bed. He read telegrams and memoranda, dictated messages or speeches of his own, interviewed key people. Sustained by weak whiskies and strong cigars (he chewed his way through some eight giants each day and used an ice-bucket from the Savoy Hotel as a bedside ashtray), he then got up and had his bath. He cleaned his teeth with meticulous care. His valet helped him dress and made sure that he was always beautifully groomed. The culmination of his toilette was to spray a handkerchief with scent and rub it on his head before brushing his sparse hair. Often during the late morning he would hold meetings of one kind or another. There followed a lavish luncheon, accompanied by champagne and brandy, at which Churchill discussed the war. He liked his guests to be witty but not frivolous, communicative but concise. Their task was to stimulate, not to hinder, his flow – Churchill once rebuked his son Randolph for interrupting while *he* was interrupting. After lunch the Prime Minister undressed and went to bed for his siesta, which might start at any time between three and six o'clock and usually lasted for about an hour and a half. Like a giant refreshed he rose to have iced whisky and soda for tea, continuing to wage his paper war until he took a second hot bath, followed by dinner.

This was the great meal of the day. Indulging his voracious appetite for food and talk, the Prime Minister occasionally finished with brandy *and* liqueurs. He was often accused of being an alcoholic (not least by Hitler) and Churchill himself was to boast that he could imbibe more than Stalin and Molotov put together. 'They only sip their liquor,' he remarked disparagingly. But he was seldom the worse for drink. Moreover he embarked on the serious business of the day, fortified by more whisky, after his dinner-time potations. Sometimes, it is true, he would play cards or watch a film. He particularly liked *Lady Hamilton*, starring Vivien Leigh, and saw it again and again. But usually he conferred with ministers, chiefs of staff and aides. They tried all sorts of stratagems to induce him to go to bed, from yawning pointedly to playing lullabies on the gramophone, but he was incorrigible. Early in the war a weary Lord Halifax requested him to postpone a cabinet meeting scheduled for ten p.m. and as a great concession Churchill put it off until 10.30. Late at night the Prime Minister liked to read the next morning's newspapers. When he finally retired to bed, between two and four o'clock, Churchill dropped off to sleep at once.

He had a marvellous faculty for taking cat-naps at odd moments in boats, trains or aeroplanes, shielding his eyes from the light with a black velvet bandage. Other gaps in his programme, the car journey from Chequers to Downing Street, for example, he used for giving dictation. No British statesman except Gladstone crammed more work into his life. Yet if Churchill saved time he also wasted it. Indeed, he treated time as a flunkey who would wait for him. He resisted all efforts to make him punctual and was compulsively late for everything, including his weekly luncheons at Buckingham Palace. He once explained that as a sporting man he liked to give trains and aeroplanes a 'fair chance of getting away'. The frantic struggles of his minions – speeding messengers, flapping secretaries, Whips at the telephone and chauffeurs at the wheel – to get him to the House of Commons on time were a regular Whitehall farce.

There was an element of farce, too, in the minutes which the Prime Minister churned out so remorselessly. He seemed to take a puckish pleasure in issuing vexatious memoranda about the most inconsequential matters. He demanded a new Admiralty flag in place of 'the present dingy object'. He agitated for the manufacture of more playing-cards. He laid down the law about the nation's jam ration. He ordained that the establishment of apes on Gibraltar should be twenty-four. He authorised the post-war wearing of dress caps instead of berets by the Fourth Hussars. Most irritating of all he fussed about the use of the English language. The establishment of 'Basic English', he asserted, would be 'a gain to us far more durable and fruitful than the annexation of great provinces'. Churchill complained about the BBC's reluctance to anglicise foreign names, attacked 'meaningless formulae expressed in official jargon', pleaded for brevity, clarity, cogency, urged senior officers to read Fowler's *Modern English Usage*, insisted that in matters of distance the word 'farther', not 'further', was correct (though Fowler disagrees). Linguistic precision was a lifelong obsession and as late as the 1950s Churchill was still dictating minutes to the effect that one says 'Bo', not 'Boo', to a goose, and that the American expression 'Top Secret' should not be adopted. 'Secrecy is not to be measured in altitude. If it were so, many might think that "Bottom Secret" would be more forceful and suggestive.'

Yet as George Orwell showed, in his famous wartime essay on the subject, a concern with language is by no means irrelevant to the business of politics. Many of the terms which Churchill coined with seeming pedantry had a rich propaganda value. Thus Eden's 'Local Defence Volunteers' he re-christened the 'Home Guard', a less bureaucratic and more evocative title. Similarly he barred the sinister designation 'Communal Feeding Centres' in favour of 'British Restaurants' on the ground that everybody 'associates the word "restaurant" with a good meal, and they may as well have the name if they cannot get anything else'. Of course, Churchill's more irksome minutes cannot be justified. They were the product of a hyper-active personality and they caused an immense amount of confusion, delay and annoyance, not to mention sheer hard work, much of which might have been better directed. On the other hand his paper darts, many of which were penetrating, galvanised officials in all sorts of burrows where the war effort was less than total. Lord Normanbrook likened his memoranda to the beam of a searchlight which might rest on anything and quickened everyone's activity. Churchill was no more afraid of being proved wrong or foolish than he was of causing trouble. Consequently he could make elementary points and ask simple questions, often fundamental ones, which might have escaped the notice of the experts. Moreover his perseverance in seeking the truth and his common sense in defining it, made it impossible for anyone to obscure matters with a fog of technical gobble-degook.

Victory seemed immensely remote towards the end of 1941. Everywhere the Germans were triumphant. Even when in November Auchinleck launched his long-awaited attack on Rommel, the Desert Fox withdrew in good order. Indeed, with Malta under siege and the British Mediterranean fleet taking a severe battering, Rommel was soon equipped to spring forward once again. Worse still, Japan seemed poised to strike and Churchill visualised having to abandon the Middle East in order to defend the Far East. He was quite prepared to do this if Britain's antipodean 'kith and kin' were threatened by invasion. But he had consciously neglected the 'yellow peril' on the assumption that Japanese aggression would suck the Americans into a true world war. This was a hope rather than a certainty and Churchill was to be bitterly censured for failing to protect Singapore. Yet in view of Britain's lack of resources and the immediate German danger his priorities must surely be judged correct. He could not sacrifice the present to the future. Like Kitchener, Churchill waged war not as he could but as he must. In the event he was as much blessed by instinct as he was by luck – the quality which Napoleon had so prized in his generals – and his oriental intuitions proved to be correct. On 7 December the Japanese bombed Pearl Harbor. When Churchill heard the news on the wireless at Chequers, he at once telephoned Roosevelt with the assurance that Britain would declare war on Japan. The Prime Minister was jubilant. For the outcome of the war, he believed, was now certain. 'So we had won after all!'

CHAPTER XI

CAMPAIGNS AND

CONFERENCES

O N 10 December 1941, three days after Pearl Harbor and two days before he departed for Washington to concert war measures with Roosevelt, Churchill received the most 'direct shock' of the war. Two of Britain's most powerful battleships, *Prince of Wales* and *Repulse*, which he had sent (against Admiralty advice) to act as a 'vague menace' against the Japanese, were sunk. It was an expensive way of driving home a lesson which Churchill should have learnt long since – that the battleship was vulnerable to air attack. All that he could do was, in the words of his oft-repeated motto, to KBO – 'Keep Buggering On' – and Churchill himself embarked on the battleship *Duke of York*. It sailed to the New World through submarine-infested seas with only minor mishap: the Prime Minister did not like the ship's water and he ran out of white wine.

As usual Churchill took a large staff, among whom for the first time was his doctor, Sir Charles Wilson, later Lord Moran. In his valuable (but unreliable) diary Wilson recorded that Churchill treated his trapped audience to particularly prolonged harangues, much to the boredom of Lord Beaverbrook. 'Winston feasts on the sound of his adjectives,' wrote Wilson, 'he likes to use four or five words all with the same meaning, as an old man shows you his orchids.' What Wilson's diary does not reveal is that Churchill made the good doctor one of his principal butts: 'Charles when ill refuses his own drugs with a sad air of inside knowledge.' Churchill put on a great show of looking after Wilson's health. When he got ill Churchill was delighted, hoped to pull him through, lectured him on medicines, and exclaimed: 'My God! I do have to work hard to teach that chap his job.'

More important, the diarist was excluded from the Premier's inner counsels so he missed the true importance of Churchill's voyage on the *Duke of York*. While on board the Prime Minister, aided by his chiefs of staff, mapped out the entire future strategy of the war. This was an astonishing feat which by itself makes up for Churchill's many aberrations in the strategic field. What Churchill proposed and predicted was that Germany should be defeated first. Meanwhile Japan was to be held at bay by air and naval forces. Victory in north Africa was Churchill's top priority, to be followed by the invasion of a Europe pulverised by bombing. Churchill persuaded Roosevelt to adopt his strategy, though not without much argument and some modification. On the main points Churchill was adamant, having rejected with a leer Brooke's advice to approach America cautiously: 'Oh! that is the way we talked to her while we were wooing her; now that she is in the harem, we talk to her quite differently.'

In the event Churchill addressed an enthusiastic joint session of Congress in a thoroughly caressing fashion. He harped on his American ancestry, complimented his hearers on their 'Olympian fortitude' and promised that their two peoples would 'walk together side by side in majesty, in justice and in peace'. It was a thrilling occasion. With eyes popping the Prime Minister exclaimed to Sir Charles Wilson, 'Do you realise that we are making history?' But the following night, when trying to open a stiff window in his bedroom, Churchill suffered his first heart attack. It was a very mild one and Wilson, anxious not to cause alarm, merely told the Prime Minister to avoid undue exertion. This was impossible. Churchill had to visit Canada, where he delivered to its parliament a speech partly in French and chiefly memorable for his comment on General Weygand's warning that within three weeks England would have her neck wrung like a chicken: 'Some chicken! Some neck!' Then he returned to Washington to sign the pact which produced the United Nations Organization and the treaty of Grand Alliance between twenty-six nations against the Axis powers. Only then could he take a short holiday before making the hazardous flight home from Bermuda, whose assembly he had also addressed.

Churchill returned to face six months of almost unmitigated disaster. At the end of January 1942 it was clear that startling gains were being made by the Germans in north Africa and the Atlantic, and by the Japanese in Malaya and the Pacific. Acknowledging the danger, Churchill demanded a vote of confidence in parliament. As Harold Nicolson wrote:

> When he feels that he has the whole House with him, he finds it difficult to conceal his enjoyment of his speech, and that, in fact, is part of his amazing charm. He thrusts both hands deep into his trouser pockets, and turns his tummy now to the right, now to the left, in evident enjoyment of the mastery of his position.

That mastery was shaken in February when Churchill had to announce both the escape back to Germany from Brest, via the English Channel, of the battle cruisers *Scharnhorst* and *Gneisenau*, and the taking of Singapore with its 60,000-strong garrison by the Japanese. The former was a humiliation. The latter was, Churchill acknowledged, 'the greatest military disaster in British history'. Now the House of Commons growled at the Prime Minister as Chips Channon had never heard it growl before.

Much to his fury Churchill was forced to make concessions. He would not, as his critics wanted, sacrifice the Ministry of Defence and thus the direction of the war. But he did effect some changes in the government, though the new war cabinet was not very different from the old. Indeed, it continued to submit to Churchill's brutal hectoring like – the comparison was frequently made – a parcel of schoolboys in front of a sadistic headmaster. Churchill's most conciliatory gesture was to appoint the strait-laced Socialist Sir Stafford Cripps to lead the House of Commons. At this time Cripps, formerly ambassador in Moscow, enjoyed the immense popularity reserved for everything and everybody associated with Russia. In fact Stalin had cordially loathed Cripps, who was always wanting to talk to him about Communism. Stalin preferred a convivial capitalist like Beaverbrook to this dour puritan who was said to be so humourless that he saw jokes by appointment only. Churchill agreed with Stalin, once remarking as Cripps left the Commons chamber, 'There but for the grace of God, goes God.' The Prime Minister relished destroying Cripps's unearned prestige. In March Churchill sent him to India on a fruitless mission to secure the war-time co-operation of nationalist leaders in return for independence afterwards. By then it looked as though Britain's empire was doomed anyway. Burma had fallen and a new navy dominated the Indian Ocean – the Japanese. Gandhi refused to accept 'a post-dated cheque on a crashing bank'.

British defeats abroad produced an outburst of criticism at home. Churchill resented it bitterly. He was particularly enraged by the *Daily Mirror*, which he wanted to suppress. Its raucous attacks on Munich muddlers sticking to public office and bone-headed brass-hats talking minced drivel he deemed seditious. In fact the *Mirror* was merely coming to terms with popular cynicism about the country's traditional rulers in order to mobilise the masses in a 'people's war'. Churchill preferred to exhort the masses rather than confide in them. Perhaps by now he was conscious that his rhetoric had a somewhat hollow ring. Certainly his wireless speeches, which had been heard with breathless attention and almost universal admiration in 1940, were widely regarded as pompous and overblown by 1942. Some greeted them with ribaldry while others simply switched off their sets. Churchill's bugle calls to glory were no longer in tune with the national mood, which was now moving in a radical direction.

The Prime Minister became correspondingly more suspicious of anything that might undermine what he took to be the simple patriotism of the common people. Already he had stopped J. B. Priestley's 'leftish' broadcasts. For some time, even after Russia had become an ally, he forbade the BBC to play the *Internationale* over the air. He actually tried to prevent the making of a comedy film called 'The Life and Death of Colonel Blimp' on the grounds that it would be 'detrimental to the morale of the Army'. He was convinced that the *Mirror*, in fact a brash and populist newspaper, was malignant and subversive. According to a journalist who knew him well, Churchill had an uncontrollable urge to exact vengeance on his Fleet Street critics. Hammering on the table, the Prime Minister vowed to 'flatten out' the *Mirror*'s staff. In the end the paper was let off with a warning. Churchill was to tell Stalin that he envied him his dictatorial powers over the press.

Churchill was as little intimidated by the unfriendliness of friends as by the enmity of enemies. It was one of his great strengths (though also sometimes a source of weakness) that he rose above opposition, whatever its origins, and pursued his own course undaunted. Thus in the spring of 1942 he effectively resisted intense pressure from America, Russia and from influential British figures like Lord Beaverbrook, to launch a premature second front in Europe (which did not stop him dreaming of, and scheming for, a number of impractical attacks on the continent). Against military advice he dispatched an expedition to capture Madagascar from the Vichy French, a gleam of success amid the surrounding gloom. Everywhere Britain was on the defensive yet he continued to send Auchinleck a stream of telegrams which were offensive in both senses of the word. Occasionally Churchill was worn down, even crushed, by the remorseless pressure of events. But he always bounced back and he never lost his capacity to enjoy himself, especially when going off on his travels.

In June, for example, he paid a flying visit to America. Dressed in his zip-shoes and carrying a gold-topped cane, Churchill walked towards the Boeing Clipper at Stranraer. Suddenly, General Brooke recorded, 'like Pooh Bear, he started humming, "We are here because we're here – we're here because we're here" '. Once on board Churchill informed the steward, 'My stomach is the clock and I eat every four hours!' All meals were washed down with champagne and brandy. Throughout the voyage Churchill was in tearing spirits and behaved just like a schoolboy on a joy-ride. Before landing he told the pilot that it would make a particularly bad impression on their allies if he crashed into the Washington Monument. Even when Roosevelt handed him a note containing the terrible news that Tobruk had fallen Churchill was only momentarily downcast. As Sir Charles Wilson wrote, 'With our military prestige at zero here, he has dominated discussions.' What Wilson – along with nearly everyone in the cabinet – did not know was that Churchill had a trump card. This was

Britain's vital secret contribution to what he and Roosevelt now agreed should be developed in America – the atomic bomb.

The President's immediate response to Rommel's spectacular push was to supply the Prime Minister with 300 Sherman tanks and 100 howitzers, torn from American forces. These were at last to give Britain qualitative superiority over German armour in the desert war. Meanwhile Churchill had to rely on exhortation. He reminded Auchinleck that he had 700,000 men on his ration strength. Every one of them should be 'made to fight and die for victory'. An 'intense, drastic spirit should reign' as if Britain herself were being invaded. Every post must be a winning-post and every ditch a last ditch. Auchinleck responded by taking personal command of his army at the front.

At home Churchill also had to wage war with words. For at the beginning of July a motion of censure expressing no confidence in the 'central direction of the war' was debated in parliament. Much of the criticism was apposite, if inconsistent. But when the motion's sponsor made the ludicrous suggestion that the Duke of Gloucester should become Minister of Defence it was at once apparent that there was no alternative to Churchill. The Prime Minister defended his record with his usual eloquence. He also rounded on his 'nagging and snarling' tormentors, accusing them of feeding the German propaganda machine. Churchill was sustained by 475 votes to 25. However he was stung by Nye Bevan's taunt that he won every debate but lost every battle. Churchill became frantic to see for himself how the Middle Eastern struggle was being conducted, only to be restrained by his advisers who feared another Antwerp. The chiefs of staff bore the brunt of his anxiety and frustration. He complained repeatedly that they met all his proposals with a negative but had no positive suggestions of their own. 'We'd better put an advertisement in the papers', he exclaimed bitterly, 'asking for ideas.' Still, when the Americans again tried to insist on a second front in 1942 Churchill supported his military men in their opposition. He felt duty bound to give the discouraging news to Stalin in person: it was, as he said, 'like carrying a large lump of ice to the North Pole'.

Churchill flew to Moscow in August, stopping at Cairo on

both the outward and the homeward journey. Auchinleck had just managed to stem the German tide. But Churchill never appreciated the significance of the first battle of El Alamein, for he thought a defensive victory was a contradiction in terms. Anyway he had long since lost confidence in Auchinleck. This was not restored by the shockingly low standard of smartness among the generals and the presence in Egypt of a large 'tail' of staff officers – 'gabardine swine'. So Churchill removed Auchinleck from his command (by letter) and replaced him with the victorious combination of Generals Alexander and Montgomery. The sympathetic intelligence of the former and the jaunty self-assurance of the latter appealed to Churchill though he looked askance at Montgomery's abstemiousness and his addiction to physical jerks. Actually Churchill himself, protected from the sunshine by a 'half-gallon' hat or solar topee, took a certain amount of exercise in Egypt. He inspected troops, visited Montgomery's prospective battlefield and bathed, rolling over in the waves and doing a V-sign with his legs. He also benefited much from talking, and sometimes listening, to his old South African friend General Smuts. Smuts considered Churchill small-minded in small matters but a great man where great concerns were at stake. Indeed he several times insisted that Churchill was 'a demigod'.

From the warmth of Smuts and Egypt Churchill progressed to the chill of Stalin and Russia. The Soviet leader, 'a hard-boiled egg of a man' in Churchill's immediate opinion, employed a familiar tactic against the British Prime Minister. He greeted Churchill and Churchill's news with studied iciness. He thawed somewhat when the Prime Minister explained plans for bombing Germany. The melting mood continued when Churchill, drawing a picture of the Axis crocodile, showed how Britain and the United States intended to rip open its soft underbelly. The next day the temperature dropped below zero again. Stalin bitingly reiterated all his old arguments in favour of a second front now, and all but stated that the British were cowards. Swallowing his anger, Churchill defended his strategy with a spirit that Stalin could only admire. However he determined to signify his displeasure by leaving Moscow ahead of schedule. Then Stalin invited him to dinner. Alone together in the small hours of the morning, while Stalin devoured the head of a sucking-pig, they established a high degree of cordiality. On the dictator's side it was surely just a calculated attempt to counterfeit human sympathy in the interests of Realpolitik. Responding with unaffected emotion, Churchill expected, as he told Roosevelt, to 'establish a solid and sincere relationship' with 'Uncle Joe'. He was too sanguine. Yet he always felt a peculiar ambivalence towards Stalin, being at once attracted by his brutal candour and repelled by his casual barbarity. There was a horrifying fascination about the Communist ruler, who once admitted to Churchill that his policy of collectivisation had surpassed, in the severity of its impact on the Russian people, the German invasion. But if Churchill periodically allowed himself to be seduced by Stalin's monstrous geniality, he knew that the only realities which the dictator recognised were facts and force. Moreover he never really trusted Stalin. An early lesson was the discovery that the walls of his luxurious State Villa No. 7 had ears. Churchill was naive enough to be outraged:

> 'We will soon deal with that. The Russians, I have been told, are not human beings at all. They are lower on the scale of nature than the orang-outang. Now then, let them take that down and translate it into Russian.'

The disastrous failure of the August raid on Dieppe, which Churchill translated into a 'not unfruitful reconnaissance in force', seemed to confirm the impossibility of launching a second front in 1942. Churchill became correspondingly more eager to press on in north Africa. Brooke, who endured many autumnal diatribes against timid generals, said that the Prime Minister's 'frightful impatience' to launch attacks was a 'regular disease'. Luckily the British commanders refused to be hurried or deflected. But Churchill's urgent pugnacity proved its worth with the American chiefs of staff, who now began to have doubts about the planned landings in French north Africa. With fiery words Churchill rekindled their faith in 'Operation Torch'.

So in November Montgomery triumphed over Rommel at the second battle of El Alamein. A few days later Anglo-American forces under the command of General Eisenhower landed in Morocco and Algeria, where they were surprised to meet stiff resistance. It was only overcome by inducing the Vichy French leaders to collaborate with the Allies, which led to much political friction. Churchill, who bore the heavy Cross of Lorraine with a typical blend of magnanimity and exasperation, thought the intractable Free French leader, General de Gaulle, quite capable of 'turning round and fighting with the Axis against us'. Still, El Alamein was an unaccustomed compensation and a major turning point in the war. It was not the beginning of the end, Churchill announced, but it was perhaps the end of the beginning. It was, in fact, the first and last victory over the Germans won by British troops alone. On the Prime Minister's instructions 'clashing, joyous peals' of bells were rung out in churches all over the country. The celebration was somewhat premature. Hitler reinforced Rommel, whose army had been defeated but not destroyed, and the struggle continued in Libya and Tunisia for another six months.

Nevertheless a further summit meeting had to take place in order to determine how the Allies should exploit their gains. So in January 1943 Churchill met Roosevelt at Casablanca for what was perhaps their most important conference. As always the Prime Minister liked to surround himself with a vast entourage, but on this occasion, far from confusing the issues, it proved its worth. After much heated debate with Churchill, the British delegation had hammered out a coherent set of proposals and it persuaded the Americans to accept most of them. They involved a continuation of the Mediterranean offensive in order to seize, as Churchill put it, the 'glorious opportunity' presented by their previous victories. Sicily was to be the next target and Churchill hoped to knock Italy out of the war. Other plans were made to prepare for a second front in France, to increase the bombing of Germany, to combat the growing submarine menace, to recapture Burma. Finally, Roosevelt announced that the Allies required Germany's 'unconditional surrender'.

This policy has been much criticised on the grounds that it stiffened Nazi resistance and lengthened the war. Churchill claimed that he was surprised when the President sprang the statement on him at a press conference and that he had to support it out of loyalty. But there seems little doubt that he had been consulted. Nor was there much chance that more generous terms would have altered Hitler's resolve to fight to the finish. Such grim considerations did nothing to mar Allied cordiality. De Gaulle, of course, struck his usual discordant note. He was so distrusted by the Americans that when he met the President the Secret Service kept him covered with concealed machine guns. As one diplomat noted, De Gaulle reduced Churchill to finger-wagging, denture-clicking, 'white fury'. 'Si vous m'obstaclerez,' growled the Prime Minister, 'je vous liquiderai.' On the whole, as Harold Macmillan wrote, Casablanca was 'a mixture between a cruise, a summer school and a conference'. Macmillan had never seen Churchill on better form. He spent most of the day in bed, most of the night in discussion and after dinner he sang songs with the President. Churchill 'ate and drank enormously all the time, settled huge problems, played bagatelle and bezique by the hour, and generally enjoyed himself'.

He concluded by showing Roosevelt a favourite haunt, Marrakesh. The 'Paris of the Sahara' was full of comforts including, Churchill added, 'the most elaborately organised brothels in the African continent'. At Marrakesh Churchill even took time off to paint a picture (a rare event during the war) which he presented to Roosevelt. But when the President departed Churchill wanted to continue his sunshine spree. In the face of stern opposition from the cabinet he flew to Turkey, where he vainly tried to induce President Inönü to enter the war. Then, after dramatic changes of destination, the last one decided on as his aeroplane was taking off, Churchill returned to north Africa via Cyprus. He inspected troops, conferred with Montgomery and deprived Eisenhower of his rest. The American even suspected that Churchill himself had given his aeroplane engine trouble because he wanted to stay for an extra day. At last, in February, the Prime Minister went back to London, only to develop a severe attack of pneumonia. Churchill once said that his life was 'a perpetual holiday', but this trip had been less of a vacation than it appeared. Moreover, Liberator bombers were scarcely designed for the comfort of eminent passengers aged sixty-eight. En route to Casablanca Churchill had been obliged to turn off the heating which threatened to set the aircraft on fire. He then began to wonder whether it was better to freeze than burn. Churchill wore nothing at night except a silk vest and, as Sir Charles Wilson recorded, the King's first minister 'cut a quaint figure with his big, bare, white bottom', crawling round the bomb bay trying to eliminate draughts.

In less than a fortnight Churchill recovered both his health and his appetite. Soon after his illness he dined off plover's eggs, chicken broth, chicken pie and chocolate soufflé, accompanied by champagne, port and brandy. He was also fortified by good news in the spring of 1943. The German army was smashed at Stalingrad. The Japanese navy, already weakened at the battle of Midway, suffered a defeat in the Coral Sea. New measures against U-boats, together with the breaking of their code, turned the tide in the Atlantic battle. The Allied armies were victorious in Tunisia and, as Churchill summed up this triumph of his personal strategy, one continent was now 'redeemed'. Only in Burma was there lack of progress, caused largely by lack of resources. But when more were demanded Churchill fired off a characteristic remonstrance:

> An operation of war cannot be thought out like building a bridge; certainty is not demanded, and genius, improvisation, and energy of mind must have their parts. I am far from satisfied with the way the Indian campaign is being conducted. The fatal lassitude of the Orient steals over all these commanders.

Typical also of his romantic approach to war was Churchill's incredible suggestion that Brigadier Orde Wingate should be promoted to command the Indian army. Wingate had fought behind the Japanese lines in the jungles of Burma – Churchill compared it to going into the water to fight a shark – and his exploits fired the Prime Minister's imagination. But, like T. E. Lawrence, Wingate was, in part at least, an eccentric charlatan and the proposed appointment could only have been disastrous. Churchill was too egotistical to be a sound judge of men. He was always inclined to mistake picturesqueness for originality, rashness for bravery, glibness for ability, restlessness for energy.

The United States too was preoccupied with the war against Japan. So, in May, Churchill crossed the Atlantic on the *Queen Mary* for the second of the four Allied conferences held in 1943. After much argument it was agreed that the invasion of

France would take place the following year and that meanwhile the Americans would suppress their renewed hankerings for a Pacific strategy in favour of a powerful effort in the Mediterranean. After another masterly address to Congress, Churchill flew to Algiers to conclude matters with Eisenhower. From the moment he arrived the Prime Minister subjected the general to a prolonged campaign of nagging and harassment. In order to persuade Eisenhower to knock Italy out of the war after capturing Sicily, Churchill brought all his weapons into play – charm, cajolery, humour, pathos, late-night harangues and quotations from sources as varied as the Greek classics and Donald Duck. Churchill was even willing to halve the short rations of the British people, thereby releasing the necessary supply ships, in order to eat his Christmas dinner with Ike in Rome. For he did not want to climb up the leg of Italy 'like a harvest bug', but to 'strike at the knee'. Eisenhower had been nurturing irrelevant designs against Sardinia but in the face of the Prime Minister's vociferations – 'I absolutely refuse to be fobbed off with a sardine' – he was willing to abandon them. So Churchill took time off from his crusade to interfere with the work of the British forces – Admiral Andrew Cunningham found him 'a perfect nuisance' but 'very amusing'. Churchill also went off to address British troops in a ruined Roman amphitheatre near Carthage. 'Yes,' he remarked afterwards, 'I was speaking from where the cries of Christian virgins rent the air whilst roaring lions devoured them – and yet – I am no lion and certainly not a virgin!'

In August Churchill was off on his travels again, this time to meet Roosevelt in Quebec. For it was imperative to decide how to exploit the fall of Mussolini, which followed immediately on the successful invasion of Sicily. Churchill, who was accompanied by a tense and exhausted Clementine and by his daughter Mary, together with an entourage of two hundred notabilities, sailed on the *Queen Mary*. He was in an exuberant mood or, as one diplomat put it, in 'a crazy state of exultation'. The humiliation of defeat concentrated Churchill's mind wonderfully but the euphoria of victory made it diffuse. At the Quebec Conference the Prime Minister darted from one project to another with more than his usual impetuosity. Now he urged the capture of Sumatra, now he pressed for a Balkan initiative, now he wanted a Norwegian offensive. His projects ranged from the bizarre to the inspired. He favoured the construction of aircraft carriers made out of shatter-proof ice and of the 'Mulberry' artificial harbours which were to be used on the shores of Normandy. Churchill's declamations became more rambling and less easy to interrupt. Harry Hopkins did manage to halt the late-night flow on one occasion. He informed the Prime Minister, whose buttons were bursting from his exertions, that he knew what was going to happen next. 'What?' asked Churchill. 'Your pants is coming down.'

Although the Americans found it difficult to silence Churchill they did manage to stress that there should be no more peripheral pinpricks against the enemy. With little regard for consistency they then went on to require that the D-Day invasion, fixed for May 1944, should coincide with landings in the south of France. What is more they endorsed not only an attack on Burma but the invasion of Italy in September 1943, which caused Marshal Badoglio's government to change sides and embrace the Allies. However Roosevelt would not support Churchill's efforts, that autumn, to seize various islands in the Aegean. Churchill's aim was to 'remind Turkey that Christmas was coming' and drag her into the war. Lacking the resources to sustain his commander General Maitland Wilson, the Prime Minister ordered him to 'improvise and dare'. But though, as Churchill said, Wilson 'improvose and dore', the result was a costly failure. For this Churchill was entirely responsible.

The truth was that, with the American war effort now well into its stride, Britain had become the junior partner. Churchill could propose common citizenship – a chimerical project – as though their two countries were equals. He could uphold Britain's status as a great power by his grand manner and his rhetorical afflatus. But he had to acknowledge Britain's weakness in practice. At Quebec he agreed that an American should be supreme commander of the Allied armies in Normandy, despite having earlier promised the job to Brooke, to whom he showed no sympathy and expressed no regret. From now on Churchill was, as he said, Roosevelt's 'lieutenant' and he had to pay court to the man in the White House.

At the Teheran Conference, in November 1943, where Roosevelt hurt Churchill by making overtures to Stalin at his expense, the Prime Minister became even more aware of being the smallest of the 'Big Three', a journalistic term he disliked for that reason. The 'poor little English donkey' was squeezed between the great Russian bear and the mighty American buffalo, yet only he knew the way home. Actually, it was clear that the way home led through northern France, as the Americans and Russians insisted. The Allies now had everything necessary to accomplish a cross-channel invasion. Churchill himself agreed to it in principle. He had for some time asserted that British loyalty to 'Operation Overlord' was the keystone of Anglo-American co-operation. But he still nursed fears of repeating in Flanders the slaughter of Passchendaele. And he still cherished hopes of righting in the Aegean the wrong which had occurred at Gallipoli. Churchill's implacable tenacity was alloyed with bewildering unsteadiness of purpose. He distrusted long-term plans because they hampered initiative. He took Beaverbrook's view that organisation is the enemy of improvisation. He once told Brooke that he did not want to know where he was going. Thus Churchill was at once too stubborn and too volatile to be a great strategist. But in the last resort he almost always capitulated to reality. He did so at Teheran and was soon agitating for stronger forces to be engaged in 'Overlord'. However, he finally managed to salvage the amphibious assault at Anzio from the wreck of his Mediterranean strategy.

Churchill was particularly inclined to stand back at Teheran and view the first meeting of the Allied leaders from the perspective of eternity. 'Stupendous issues are unfolding before our eyes,' he exclaimed, 'and we are only specks of dust, that have settled for a night on the map of the world.' Scarcely to be outdone by the American newspaper which described it as the 'Most Important Meal since the Last Supper', Churchill dilated on the memorable fashion in which he had celebrated his sixty-ninth birthday:

> On my right sat the President of the United States, on my left the Master of Russia. Together we controlled a large preponderance of the naval and three-quarters of all the air forces of the world, and could direct armies of nearly twenty millions of men engaged in the most terrible of wars that had yet occurred in human history.

Yet the momentous deliberations at Teheran were also influenced by tiny human quirks, not least those of Churchill himself.

During the festivities many toasts were proposed, in the Russian manner. 'I drink to the Proletarian masses,' said Churchill. 'I drink to the Conservative Party,' replied Stalin. With the good cheer flowing freely the Soviet leader indulged in much raillery at Churchill's expense. When the Prime Minister complained that Britain was becoming 'pink' Stalin responded that this was 'a sign of health'. But the dictator went too far when he spoke of weakening Germany after the war by killing fifty thousand of her top officers and technicians. Roosevelt countered chaffingly by suggesting a compromise figure of forty-nine thousand. But Churchill waxed indignant and stormed from the dinner table. Stalin, grinning broadly, brought him back, explaining that it had all been a joke. In view of his murderous propensities this remains an open question and Churchill himself was not convinced. However, the point is that Stalin could read Churchill, who had 'few reticences', like 'an open book'. The Prime Minister was as transparent as the dictator was enigmatic. Yet Churchill's vulnerability was a kind of strength. The Foreign Office tended to dismiss the Prime Minister's diplomatic activities as puerile and dangerous. Yet the Permanent Under-Secretary himself acknowledged that, thanks to Churchill, Britain's relations with Russia were based, for a time at least, on a degree of understanding and trust.

When the exhausting conference at Teheran was over, at the beginning of December, Churchill flew back to Cairo. There he had further talks with Roosevelt. They concluded their deliberations by visiting the Pyramids and the Sphinx. Churchill had been afflicted by a series of minor ailments and he evidently found it difficult to concentrate. During one lunch-time meeting he did nothing but swat flies, placing their corpses in a 'mortuary' and keeping a count of his bag. In the evenings he was so discursive that eminent guests had to keep prodding themselves into wakefulness. When Churchill arrived in Tunis, with the intention of going on to inspect the Italian front, he collapsed with another bout of pneumonia. It was so severe that on the night of 15 December Lord Moran despaired of his life. Churchill himself commented, 'I shuppose, it ish fitting that I should die beshide Carthage.' Specialists, nurses and medical supplies were rushed to his bedside. Clementine and Randolph converged on his villa. Bulletins were issued about his health. Slowly Churchill recovered. But he was a refractory patient and his condition was not improved by his refusal to give up whisky and cigars. Still, by 25 December he was able to confer with Eisenhower, just appointed Commander-in-Chief of Operation Overlord, and with other advisers. Wearing his quilted silk dressing-gown covered with blue, red and gold dragons, Churchill took his first meal outside his bedroom. He did full justice to a magnificent Christmas feast of soup, turkey, plum pudding . . . and champagne.

CHAPTER XII

VICTORY AND DEFEAT

CHURCHILL spent the first half of January 1944 convalescing in Marrakesh. Clementine described their villa as a 'mixture of Arabian Nights and Hollywood', a view shared by Lady Diana Cooper. 'The party is a circus,' she said, 'lodged in a millionairess's pleasure dome, all marble and orange trees, fountains and tiles in the richest Mahomedan style.' Churchill was irritated by the slowness of his recovery, by his inability to paint, by the incivility of de Gaulle, by being away from the hub of events. But in the mornings he still endeavoured to run the war. And during the afternoons he went on a series of elaborate picnics into the foothills of the Atlas Mountains. On one of them he alarmed his wife and his doctor by clambering down a rocky gorge and crawling to the top of a huge boulder. Two retainers dragged him up the hill using a tablecloth as a sling. Churchill, puffing like a grampus and stopping now and then for Lord Moran to take his pulse, had no thought of looking undignified.

Although not fully recovered and prone to bouts of lethargy, Churchill returned home just before the landings at Anzio on 22 January. He claimed to be unsteady on his 'pins', though he was quite happy to run upstairs two at a time and cock a snook at MPs below who had suggested he should use the lift. Moreover he seemed to have lots of energy to invest in the Anzio venture, which was a grievous disappointment to him, a lesser Gallipoli. He had hoped to throw a wild cat ashore but was left with a stranded whale. For the American commander failed to exploit the element of surprise and, much to Churchill's dismay, Alexander 'urged' him forward instead of ordering him. Soon the Anglo-American force was pinned down on its beach-head and Churchill was badgering Alexander about the size of its tail. With 70,000 men and 18,000 vehicles, he sneered, 'we must have a great superiority of chauffeurs'. After his illness, in fact, the Prime Minister returned to his 'old game of general-hunting' with renewed vigour. As General Pownall remarked disgustedly, 'like a pi-dog he goes looking for dirts in which to roll'. But, as Anzio demonstrated, the war was far from being won. Churchill told parliament that Germany still had 300 unbeaten divisions in the field and he called for 'preparation, effort and resolve'.

Churchill's own efforts, in the early part of 1944, were largely devoted to prosecuting his most bitter feud with the chiefs of staff. In order to placate American opinion and to restore Britain's prestige in the Far East, Churchill determined on the invasion of Burma and Sumatra. The military chiefs wanted only naval operations in the east in order not to weaken their western assault force. But Churchill pursued his goal with ferocious pertinacity. Brooke and his fellows were driven to the brink of resignation. In the end a Japanese offensive in Burma put paid to Churchill's schemes. Brooke was then invited to take a midnight cup of soup alone with Churchill. Having reduced the CIGS to despair for months on end, the Prime Minister suddenly became warm, confiding and conciliatory. He even admitted that he was not the man he had been. 'All that unrelenting tension was temporarily relaxed,' wrote Brooke, 'he ceased to work himself into one fury or another, and you left him with the feeling that you would do anything in your power to help him to carry the stupendous burden he had shouldered.' Oddly enough Churchill's other main campaign that spring, directed towards cancelling the proposed landings in southern France, was designed to strengthen 'Overlord'. He was not disturbed by the inconsistency. For in matters of war Churchill relied less on reason than on faith in his Marlborough blood.

Nothing stirred that blood like conflict, which was why Churchill evinced so little interest in the home front during the war. 'Can't we just confine ourselves to saying that agriculture is a very good thing and that there should be more of it?' he asked the cabinet testily. Still, there were moments when his combative instincts were roused by domestic issues. For example, feeling ill and depressed one day in the spring of 1944, he informed Beaverbrook, 'I'm through. I cannot carry the burdens any longer.' Just then his bedside telephone rang and Churchill learnt that the government had been defeated by one vote on the clause in R. A. Butler's Education Bill which denied equal pay to women. Churchill flung off the covers and leapt out of bed with the glint of battle in his eye. 'I need a life of action,' he told Beaverbrook. In fact he cared nothing about education – he himself had done very well without it. Indeed, he was unable to understand how Butler could be happy, at such a time, with a portfolio like education. Churchill even told Butler that he did less for the war effort than his black cat, Nelson, who saved fuel and power by acting as a Prime Ministerial hot-water bottle – and this despite the fact that Nelson skulked under the chest of drawers during air-raids and Churchill suspected him of semaphoring state secrets with his tail to the pelicans in the park. However, Churchill would not accept a defeat in the Commons and insisted on reversing it by a vote of confidence. 'I am not going to tumble round my cage like a wounded canary,' he told a group of MPs. 'You knocked me off my perch. You have now got to put me back on my perch. Otherwise I won't sing.'

He continued to sing, though on domestic matters he struck many discordant notes: for in the interests of the war effort Churchill had supported all sorts of socialistic measures. The authority of the state had been vastly increased. The economy was now ruthlessly planned. Many social reforms had been initiated. Rationing was imposed, the excess profits tax was set at 100%, free school meals for all were established, full employment prevailed, Keynesian budgets were introduced. On the other hand Churchill was clearly opposed to progressive policies for their own sake. Indeed, he was growing more reactionary all the time. He prevented the nationalisation of the coal industry, tried to shut down the Army Bureau of Current Affairs, accused the BBC of being 'a nest of Communists'.

Worst of all, from the public point of view, was his tepid

response to the Beveridge Report (1942) which advocated full social security after the war. Churchill claimed that he did not want to raise impossible hopes of building a land fit for heroes to live in, as Lloyd George had done. But despite his generous notions about the forward march of the common people, he obviously jibbed at a complete welfare state. 'Beveridge!' he exclaimed angrily, 'he puts his nose into too many things.' Churchill was increasingly out of touch with public opinion at home. He did not appreciate the spread of egalitarian feeling. Nor did he understand the desire of the masses to be rewarded in peace for their war-time sacrifices. These sentiments were well expressed by the Common Wealth party, founded in 1943, which scored several by-election victories. Churchill himself remained popular. But people wanted new houses not fine phrases. The old-fashioned political ideals which the Prime Minister personified were largely discredited.

Churchill's mood on the eve of D-day was peevish. He had done everything in the previous few months to push the operation ahead, probing, criticising, encouraging and harassing until his commanders and their planners ('uniformed, psalm-singing defeatists') were driven almost to distraction. Montgomery actually forbade the Prime Minister to question his staff about the length of his 'tail' and Churchill remained convinced that he was filling his transports not with bayonets but with dental chairs, spare bootlaces and YMCA institutions. In fact, the massive enterprise was prepared with the utmost care and skill. The bodyguard of lies surrounding the precious truth of where the landings were to take place was, thanks to Churchill's insistence, particularly efficient. But he was deprived of his reward. Churchill desperately wanted to sail with the invasion fleet. He justified his wish with a characteristic piece of special pleading: 'A man who has to play an effective part in taking with the highest responsibility, grave and terrible decisions of war may need the refreshment of adventure.' The high military powers were horrified by the prospect. But only one person was in a position to stop Churchill embarking on the hazardous voyage. This was King George VI, with whom the Prime Minister had established a devoted relationship. Protesting like a child deprived of a treat, Churchill eventually submitted to the royal arguments.

So he made a disconsolate tour of the Portsmouth area in a special train. Nor was his temper improved by the unmannerliness of General de Gaulle, who had not been let into the secret of D-day. Not until 12 June, six days after the first landings, was Churchill permitted to visit the bridgehead. He inspected everything and was delighted to find that Normandy remained as green in reality as it did in his memory. 'We are surrounded by fat cattle lying in luscious pastures with their paws crossed.' Churchill went home by destroyer. Never having seen naval guns fired in anger, he persuaded the admiral, who showed a proper 'sporting spirit', to shell the enemy-held coast. The Prime Minister was much disappointed that the Germans did not return their fire.

The main Allied army in Italy, having linked up with the Anzio force, occupied Rome just as Overlord was being launched. Churchill now hoped that Alexander would thrust a dagger into Germany's armpit while Eisenhower struck at her heart. So Montgomery received the ritual nagging to keep 'the front aflame' and Churchill renewed his campaign against the invasion of southern France. He tried every tactic, from advocating ill-judged alternative landing areas to threatening to 'lay down the mantle of my high office'. But the Americans were adamant. They did not share Churchill's reviving obsession about Russia, whose military steamroller was now gaining momentum, or his desire to shake hands with Soviet Communism as far to the east as possible. Eisenhower was content to advance on a broad, safe front. Churchill was made still more eager for a single drive forward by the beginning of the flying-bomb and (in September) rocket-bomb offensive.

This indiscriminate attack did not make a significant difference to the war. Moreover, thanks to good intelligence, the V1s were countered successfully. Still, this second 'blitz' was an ordeal for war-weary civilians, though it made Churchill, who after the frustrations of D-day could regard himself as being in the front line again, look ten years younger. But the 'doodlebugs' also strengthened his resolve to carry on with Britain's own bombing offensive. Churchill did not share the fanaticism of Sir Arthur 'Bomber' Harris. The Air Marshal seemed to think that his aeroplanes could win the war alone but for the handicap imposed by the other two services, and he disapproved of paratroops because they did not explode on landing. The Prime Minister had always been doubtful about the effectiveness of air-raids. Moreover he had periodic fits of revulsion against this form of warfare. While watching a film about bombing Germany he suddenly sat up and exclaimed, 'Are we beasts? Are we taking this too far?' Later he was obliged to withdraw a minute which seemed to deny his final responsibility for the shocking destruction of Dresden. Churchill's humanitarian scruples were genuine, but he over-rode them (as he was to do in the case of the atom bomb) in order to save Allied lives menaced by ruthless aggressors. Owing to more sophisticated planes, weapons and techniques, the air offensive was actually having a devastating effect by 1944. Albert Speer, Hitler's Minister of War Production, regarded it as 'the greatest lost battle on the German side'.

From the summer of 1944 until the end of the war Churchill was almost constantly on the move. Before the year was out he had visited Italy, North America, Russia, France and Greece, not to mention stops in between. He enjoyed these jaunts all the more when he could make them in the comfortable American Skymaster, a gift of President Roosevelt. Churchill's urge to see the conflict for himself, to stay with his generals in the field and to confront his fellow leaders in person, had not abated. Yet in a way all this travelling was a substitute for the effective direction of the war, which had largely slipped out of Churchill's grasp into the hands of his mighty allies. It was almost as if the Prime Minister was trying to persuade himself that by moving from place to place he was getting somewhere. Thus in August he went to Italy where he inspected the troops, met politicians and conferred with Alexander. 'I envy you the command of armies in the field,' Churchill told him. 'That's what I should have liked.' Alexander's progress was being impeded by the American insistence on diverting resources to the Riviera assault. To the last Churchill attempted to stop it, claiming that the southern French coast was too heavily fortified. His pleas were in vain. He himself observed from a destroyer that the landings were virtually unopposed.

By September, however, the massive Allied advance in northern France was being stemmed. Churchill, who had hoped that the German war might be over by Christmas, was sore and disappointed. As General Ismay said, when things were going well the Prime Minister was good; when they were going badly he was superb; but when they were going 'half-well' he was 'hell on earth'. Matters were made worse by another attack of pneumonia which Churchill suffered from on his return from Italy. It was a mild one and he insisted on continuing to work. Brendan Bracken tried to get him to rest, telling Churchill bluntly that if he went on 'playing the fool like this, you are certain to die'. But Churchill was incapable of relaxing even when he was ill. On 5 September he departed to Quebec in order to discuss the Pacific war with President Roosevelt. He sailed, with Clementine and an enormous retinue, on the *Queen Mary*. As always his moods were changeable. But for the most part he seemed ailing, depressed and bad-tempered. It was very hot and he complained that the sea had no business to be so torrid. The crossing was smooth but there were rough passages between the Prime Minister and his advisers.

As Churchill said, the second Quebec Conference was held in a 'blaze of friendship'. There were no serious strategic differences between the Allies. The Americans agreed that the British should play their full part in defeating Japan. Churchill and Roosevelt endorsed the Morgenthau plan for 'pastoralising' Germany, in other words for transforming her industrial economy into an agricultural one. Occasionally during the war Churchill had expressed deep feelings of hatred for the German people as a whole. He had toyed with the idea of punishing them as a nation, for example, by segregating large numbers of men from their womenfolk in order to reduce the birth-rate. During the Blitz he had even talked of castrating them. He had favoured the dismemberment of Germany as a state. But vengefulness remained foreign to his nature. He soon dropped the Morgenthau plan. And he became concerned with occupying as much of Germany as possible before the war ended in order to present a strong front to the Russians.

Churchill's attitude towards the Soviet Union continued to fluctuate wildly. In the summer of 1944 he had been outraged by Stalin's callous refusal to assist the uprising in Warsaw. But Roosevelt, always weak on the Polish question and prepared to make whatever sacrifices were necessary to end the war quickly, refused to support Churchill. Thus he was forced to make one of those 'terrible and even humbling submissions' to an ally in the interests of unity. However, on his return from America, Churchill determined to champion the cause of Polish freedom – after all Britain's *casus belli* – on his own. So in October he embarked on his second mission to Moscow. His reception was surprisingly cordial and Churchill warmed to 'Uncle Joe' more than ever before. The Russians entertained the British delegation to lavish ten-course banquets, with toasts every five minutes and long affectionate speeches. Stalin displayed Churchill in a box at the Bolshoi Theatre where the audience greeted him with enthusiasm. The Russian leader even broke precedent by dining at the British Embassy and seeing Churchill off at the airport, waving him good-bye with a pocket handkerchief. The Polish problem was not solved, though it seemed to disappear for a time in a haze of bonhomie and vodka. But Churchill and Stalin did agree, like two imperial potentates, to divide up Europe into their respective spheres of influence. For some time the question of how the victorious powers would police the world had been in the air. Now, in what he acknowledged to be a cynical and offhand manner, Churchill produced a precise list of European zones with percentages affixed. Russia was to exercise 75 per cent of the influence in Bulgaria. There were to be equal shares in Yugoslavia and Hungary. Russia was to have 90 per cent interest in Romania while Britain had the same percentage in Greece. Stalin inspected the figures carefully and appended a large blue tick.

Stalin's tick was his bond, at least where Greece was concerned. For both leaders liked stable, reactionary regimes and the Communist dictator was less committed to deposing kings than the Conservative Prime Minister was to enthroning them. In November, for example, Churchill restored to France an approximate monarch in the shape of General de Gaulle – on a freezing day they marched in triumph down the Champs Élysées, the tears turning to ice on the Prime Minister's cheeks as a rapturous crowd yelled, 'Churcheel! Churcheel!' In December Churchill became so obsessed with the need to return Greece to sovereign principles that he scarcely noticed

Hitler's last dangerous counter-offensive in the Ardennes. Stalin connived at Churchill's efforts to crush the Greek Communists who were struggling to seize power after the German withdrawal. Indeed Churchill's policy was less impeded by Russian Communists than by British liberals and American republicans. He was unmoved, asserting when censured in parliament that the Communist 'gangsters' were trying to impose 'mob law' on Greece. As one diplomat recorded, Churchill was in such a 'bloodthirsty mood' that he 'did not take kindly to suggestions that we should avoid bloodshed if possible'.

When civil war threatened between Communists and the official government, and clashes occurred with British forces, Churchill at once flew to Athens. Now a brisk seventy-year-old, he arrived on Christmas Day to face bitter cold, much discomfort and some danger. It was just the kind of jaunt – Harold Macmillan called it 'a sort of super Sidney Street' – Churchill enjoyed. He was, of course, sorry to have left Clementine in tears. But his pleasure was enhanced by Eden's evident reluctance to participate – Churchill had been equally pleased, when staying at the Quai d'Orsay in Paris, to discover that he had Goering's gold bath while the Foreign Secretary had to make do with one of silver. Carrying a pistol Churchill drove through strife-torn Athens by armoured car to confer with the various factions. It was finally agreed that Archbishop Damaskinos, 'a scheming medieval prelate' who quite caught Churchill's fancy, should head a Regency Council – a compromise that might well have been negotiated without his dramatic intervention. Churchill kept the Greek King George II up until 4.30 in the morning, finally persuading him to behave 'like a gentleman' and sanction a regency. So the Prime Minister was able to claim, with some justification, that he had made Greece safe from Communism.

Stalin evidently took this as his cue to make Poland safe from democracy. For at the beginning of 1945 the Soviet Union recognised its puppet 'Lublin Committee' as the provisional Polish government. This, together with hostility at home towards his Greek exploits and what he took to be Eisenhower's sloth on the western front, contributed towards Churchill's 'volcanic' mood in January. More irritating still was the disaffection among his own colleagues. Much of this was subterranean. Eden, for example, treated the Prime Minister with ingratiating joviality to his face while expostulating privately that his was 'the worst-run government I should say there has ever been'. But there were so many murmurings about Churchill's unbusinesslike behaviour, about cabinet meetings which took hours longer than necessary and accomplished nothing, about the incessant monologues, that Attlee took his courage in both hands and protested to the Prime Minister by letter. Churchill was furious. But he could find no one in his entourage who disagreed with Attlee. For almost a day Churchill stayed in bed, miserable and angry. Then he cast off his bed-clothes and his gloom. Beaming at his secretary he remarked, 'Let us think no more of Hitlee or of Attler; let us go and see a film.' Still in waggish vein Churchill cabled to President Roosevelt, 'No more let us falter! From Malta to Yalta! Let nobody alter!'

After preliminary Anglo-American discussions in Valetta, the Crimean Conference, designed to settle the future of Europe and the final strategy against Japan, met at the beginning of February. Once again Churchill failed to make any real progress over Poland. As if to disguise his intransigence here, Stalin lavished more than usually prodigious hospitality on his guests. Churchill was accommodated in a palatial villa overlooking the Black Sea. General Ismay was impressed by the efficiency with which the Russians had refurbished it after German depredations, though they had not managed to eradicate bugs or provide baths. He described it as 'a fantastic mixture of bogus Scottish castle and Moorish palace'. Churchill consumed buckets of Caucasian champagne and mountains of caviare – when his daughter Sarah remarked that the latter was improved by lemon juice the Russians planted a lemon tree in the garden. Stalin toasted Churchill as 'the man who is born once in a hundred years' and 'the bravest statesman in the world'. So great was the cordiality that the western leaders even let Stalin in on the secret of their nickname for him, 'Uncle Joe'.

Uncle Joe showed marvellous diplomatic skill at the conference. He was assisted by several factors: Roosevelt was ailing; Churchill had few bargaining counters; Russian forces were routing the Germans on the eastern front; there were serious differences between Britain and America. These Stalin exploited. For example, he egged Churchill on to make vehement speeches about the inviolability of the British empire. The President, described by Eden as 'vague and loose and ineffective', was unwilling to join the Prime Minister in standing up to the dictator. Nevertheless Roosevelt did not lose sight of his priorities. The President was determined to prevent what he regarded as minor issues from wrecking Soviet-American cooperation, which was vital not just to win the Second World War but to stop the outbreak of a third. So the best that Churchill could achieve was a vague declaration that Stalin would 'use his influence' to secure a free government in Poland. Stalin, who believed that 'sincere diplomacy is no more possible than dry water or iron wood', had no such intentions. He assumed that Churchill aimed to surround Russia with a democratic *cordon sanitaire*; so he proposed to protect her with a ring of totalitarian satellites.

The Polish issue apart, Yalta was notable for its spirit of conciliation and compromise. Russia did not insist on reparations or on the dismemberment of Germany. American views on the constitution of the United Nations were largely accepted and Russia confirmed her intention of declaring war on Japan after the victory in Europe. The British secured a French zone of occupation in Germany but – a deplorable concession – agreed to Russian demands about the compulsory repatriation of prisoners after the war. All might have been well, of course, if Stalin had been trustworthy. Churchill had no option but to 'assume the good faith of our ally'. During the euphoria of the conference that assumption seems to have been sincere. Churchill even said that the more he saw of Stalin the more he liked him. Indeed the Prime Minister's main source of hurt and irritation at Yalta was the President's uncooperativeness. But Churchill was not surprised by the eventual revelation of Stalin's perfidy, to which the tragic failure of Yalta must be chiefly ascribed.

The Allied delegations quitted the Crimea in a mood of 'supreme exultation'. Only Churchill, who spent the last day visiting the scene of the charge of the Light Brigade (in which his regiment, the Fourth Hussars, had participated), nursed gloomy

195

forebodings. Still, he was much relieved to get the 'bloody' joint communiqué agreed and, as Lord Moran recorded, 'he sang (very flat) snatches of old songs, "The Soldiers of the Queen" ' and so on. In 'tearing spirits' he then flew to Athens. The city was now peaceful and Churchill addressed a crowd of (he estimated) half a million people, packed into Constitution Square. It was one of the 'most vivid, impressive and agreeable' experiences of his life, for his speech, though a tired one full of uplifting platitudes, was rapturously received. Made wanton with delight, Churchill afterwards flatly contradicted Alexander's claim that the war was being fought to secure liberty and a decent existence for the peoples of Europe. 'Not a bit of it: we are fighting to secure the proper respect for the British people.'

From Greece Churchill flew to Egypt where he was keen to check Roosevelt's Middle Eastern machinations. He suspected that the President's hob-nobbing with various potentates in that area was part of a 'deep-laid plot to undermine the British empire'. In fact, as Hopkins surmised, Roosevelt was merely amusing himself with local colour tinged with royalty. After bidding his last farewell to the President – 'I felt that he had a slender contact with life' – Churchill himself met the Oriental despots. His encounter with King Ibn Saud of Arabia gave rise to two small contretemps. The first was over tobacco and alcohol, which were anathema to the Muslim monarch, who insisted that the Prime Minister should try water from Mecca. Churchill declared that smoking cigars and drinking hard liquor were part of his religion, sacred rites which he performed before, during and after meals. The second concerned the matter of mutual gifts; the extravagant Arab offerings (including some magnificent robes which Churchill could not resist dressing up in) put the meagre British presents to shame. The Prime Minister announced that they were merely tokens for his real present, to be delivered later, a Rolls-Royce. His quick thinking was to no avail. Having right-hand drive the car proved unacceptable, for etiquette forbade an Arab sovereign to sit on the left of any subject, even a chauffeur.

On his return home, Churchill had understandable difficulty in convincing the Commons that Stalin would honour his promises about Poland. The advent of victory made MPs more refractory. The Father of the House, Lord Winterton, was particularly troublesome and Churchill had to warn him that unless he showed more 'sagacity . . . he will run a very grave risk of falling into senility before he is overtaken by old age'. Still, Churchill himself grew increasingly perturbed about eastern Europe as the Russian grip on it tightened. But his pleas to Roosevelt were largely disregarded. The President even supported Eisenhower in his refusal to race for the German capital, much to the Prime Minister's annoyance. For, as Churchill guessed, Stalin's assertion that Berlin was not a significant Soviet objective meant that he attached supreme importance to its capture. Churchill assuaged his frustration by several visits to the western front. There he exposed himself in both senses of the word. With a beatific grin he mounted the remains of the Siegfried Line and relieved himself into the rubble. He told the photographers in his party: 'This is one of the operations connected with this great war which must not be reproduced graphically.' Having demanded a front seat in the stalls for the crossing of the Rhine he tried to occupy the stage. Churchill climbed onto the ruins of a bridge as enemy shells began to fall all around. The harassed generals begged him to leave but Churchill twined both his arms about a shattered girder and glowered at them with pouting mouth and angry eyes. Finally he came away, but Brooke was convinced that he longed to die there at the height of his fame, in the last battle. It would have been a fitting end to a fighting life.

In April Roosevelt's death struck Churchill like a physical blow. The Prime Minister's obituary speeches in parliament were always eloquent and he paid a particularly moving tribute to 'the greatest champion of freedom who has ever brought help and comfort from the new world to the old'. Churchill later felt that he made a grave mistake in not at once flying to the United States to establish relations with the new President. But in the short term this scarcely mattered, for German resistance was collapsing everywhere. By the end of the month the Axis leaders were no more. Mussolini was executed by Italian partisans – 'A bloody beast is dead,' Churchill declared. And Hitler committed suicide – 'He was perfectly right to die like that,' said Churchill. On 8 May the German surrender was accepted and Britain celebrated Victory in Europe Day.

Churchill announced to a huge crowd at Whitehall, 'This is your victory.' 'No, it is yours,' the people roared back and the Prime Minister conducted the singing of 'Land of Hope and Glory'.

Yet amid patriotic rejoicings Churchill's heart was aching and his mind was 'oppressed with forebodings'. For Stalin's baneful intransigence had become ever more apparent in the last weeks of the conflict. He had charged the western Allies with trying to make a separate peace. And he arrested Polish underground leaders, accusing them of terrorism, despite the fact that they were protected by safe-conducts. As hostilities with Germany ceased Churchill came to grips in his imagination with the resuscitated Bolshevik foe armed with new rocket weapons. He saw the cold war in the dying embers of the hot one. He forecast that Britain would become 'one vast bazooka aimed at aggressors who threaten Europe'. It was a fearful but also a thrilling prospect. Before long, even with Japan undefeated, Churchill was confiding to Moran, 'I feel very lonely without a war.'

In the early summer of 1945 he had to content himself with the political equivalent of war. The Labour party refused to continue the coalition and, as Churchill observed, it was time that the ten-year-old parliament refreshed itself by contact with the electorate. So on 23 May Churchill formed a 'Caretaker' government, based on the Conservative party, and prepared for a contest at the polls. He opened the campaign with one of the most vigorous and least judicious speeches of his career. In it he pronounced that 'no Socialist system can be established without a political police'. Such a 'Gestapo' might be 'humanely directed' at first but it would crush liberty in the long run. In a moment Churchill sacrificed his unique position as national leader and dived into the squalid mêlée of party politics. Such scaremongering was a shocking reminder of his controversial past. Yet he remained personally popular and his barnstorming tour of the country stirred up support as well as enthusiasm. But though he was universally acclaimed as a great war leader it was widely felt that, like Lloyd George, he would lose the peace. Despite Churchill's gestures in the direction of social reform people believed that the Labour party was better suited to build more houses, prevent unemployment and construct a welfare state. Churchill symbolised reaction and he was overwhelmed by a progressive tidal wave.

Owing to a three-week delay in counting the servicemen's votes the election results were not known until 26 July. Meanwhile Churchill took a painting holiday in south-west France. Then he visited Berlin and inspected Hitler's bunker before attending the final conference of the war at Potsdam. He established a strong rapport with President Truman and they agreed to employ the newly constructed atom bomb – 'the second coming' Churchill called it – on Japan. Worried about his fate at the polls Churchill was tetchy and unable to concentrate at Potsdam. He did little work but, according to Cadogan, 'butts in on every occasion and talks the most irrelevant rubbish, and risks giving away our case at every point'. Stalin handled Churchill with his usual skill, masking his designs behind extreme joviality. When Churchill introduced 'the Prof' (Lindemann was by now Lord Cherwell) as 'a member of my Gestapo', the Soviet leader replied that he thought only Attlee had a Gestapo. Churchill had taken Attlee with him and at one dinner he toasted 'the Leader of the Opposition . . . whoever he may be'.

Every omen seemed to point to Churchill's victory. But shortly before the vote was declared he experienced a sudden premonition of defeat – 'a sharp stab of almost physical pain'. Not only did Labour win nearly twice as many seats as the Tories but an unknown independent, Churchill's sole challenger in his own true-blue constituency, received over ten thousand 'protest' votes.

Churchill was dazed and dejected by his fall. He behaved with dignity, but, despite a deluge of sympathy from well-wishers, he could not repress feelings of bitterness at the base ingratitude, as he saw it, displayed by the British people. Clementine, on the other hand, hoped that the defeat would induce him to retire. 'It may well be a blessing in disguise,' she said. He replied, 'At the moment it seems quite effectively disguised.' Nevertheless defeat did improve his temper. For all the mellow characteristics of 'Churchill down' suddenly returned, having been for so long held in abeyance. What Beaverbrook called Churchill's 'extreme duality of mind' reasserted itself. Lord Moran, who accompanied him on a September painting trip to Lake Como, after the surrender of Japan, noted that in adversity Churchill became gentle, patient, brave and magnanimous. 'But when the sun shines his arrogance, intolerance and cocksureness assume alarming proportions.' Before his rejection Churchill had missed few occasions for indulging in 'some rather childish outburst of petulance, whereas nothing of the kind has marred the even serenity of these autumnal days'.

CHAPTER XII

INDIAN SUMMER

CHURCHILL did briefly consider retiring 'gracefully in an odour of civic freedoms'. But he seems to have had no serious intention of doing so. He did not relish the idea of being put out to grass or 'exhibited like a prize bull whose chief attraction is its past prowess'. Before long Brendan Bracken was telling Beaverbrook, 'Winston is in very good fettle and determined to lead the Tory party until he becomes Prime Minister on earth or Minister of Defence in Heaven!' Clementine, more exhausted by the war than her husband, desperately wanted him to resign and expressed her frustration in a series of domestic rows. She was not alone in resenting his continued involvement in politics. Anthony Eden was wont to exclaim: 'Oh God, I do wish the old man would go.' Churchill toyed with various impractical schemes of sharing the opposition leadership with Eden, whom he regarded as his heir apparent – 'my Princess Elizabeth'. But he was not pleased when Eden gave timid encouragement to intrigues against him among Conservative MPs. And when the Chief Whip told him that eight prominent Tories thought he should quit, Churchill 'reacted violently, banging the floor with his stick'.

There were many complaints about Churchill's leadership of the opposition, some of them justified, not all of them consistent. He was often accused of devoting too little time and energy to the House of Commons. It is true that he travelled widely during his six years out of office, receiving honours and attending functions all over Europe and North America. He also spent the worst of every winter in a warm climate as a precaution against his old enemy pneumonia. Moreover, when at home he neglected routine parliamentary chores – he did not even get to know young Tory MPs, whom he anyway thought 'pink pansies'. Instead he concentrated on his six-volume history of the Second World War, the sale of which made him a millionaire. He actually bought adjoining houses in Hyde Park Gate, one as a home, the other as an office. When it was suggested that his domestic base was too far from Westminster he took an expensive suite at the Savoy Hotel as his 'forward headquarters'. There he entertained members of the shadow cabinet to fortnightly lunches. They were astonished by his appetite. Sir David Maxwell Fyfe recorded that at one meal Churchill consumed a dozen oysters, two helpings of roast beef and vegetables and a large plate of apple pie and ice-cream, together with tomato juice, wine and brandy. It was no wonder that, as Woodrow Wyatt said, Churchill's 'face and body looked all of a piece, like some fabulous Humpty Dumpty'.

Churchill was criticised for doing too much as well as too little, for being a one-man band. Not only did he make truculent interventions in the Commons on his own responsibility, he also took important political initiatives without consulting his colleagues. It was said that Ernest Bevin dropped nothing of Eden's foreign policy except the aitches, but instead of being grateful Churchill embarrassed both supporters and opponents by embarking on a hazardous new course of his own. It was a course which to some extent anticipated and shaped the growing anti-Soviet mood in Britain and, more especially, in America. For, having disposed of the Nazi dictator, the Atlantic allies found that they were confronting a Communist one every bit as ruthless and much more powerful. Stalin's brutal activities in eastern Europe, combined with West Germany's willingness to embrace democracy, not to mention strong right-wing pressures inside the United States, were to bring about a diplomatic revolution. Churchill helped to precipitate it in his famous speech at Fulton, Missouri, in 1946, when he turned on his former friends behind 'the iron curtain'. Advocating 'a special relationship' between 'the English-speaking peoples', to be equipped with 'the sinews of peace', he fired the first major broadside of the cold war. Equally unpopular with the Tories was Churchill's plea for the formation of a 'United States of Europe' in which a restored and reconciled Germany should participate. Nor was Churchill in step with the majority of his party in condemning Britain's 'premature hurried scuttle' from India in 1947. There was nothing he could do about this retreat except forecast 'ruin and disaster' and deplore 'the clattering down of the British empire with all its glories'. But after independence he sternly rebuffed Lord Mountbatten, the last viceroy, when greeted by him: 'Dickie, stop. What you did in India is as though you had struck me across the face with a riding whip.' They were not reconciled until 1955.

Finally, the critics said that Churchill was losing his grip. Of course, some of his faculties were in decline. His deafness was obviously increasing and he sometimes found it hard to hear speakers in the hubbub of the Commons. He also experienced difficulty in adapting himself to the new mood of the House. His speeches had always been great set-pieces. As Aneurin Bevan said, because he was unable to manoeuvre easily Churchill 'had to wheel himself up to battle like an enormous gun'. But the polished phrases and rolling periods in which he had expressed the national temper during the war, were once more out of fashion. The heroic manner in which Churchill acted as 'the impresario of history' was unsuited to the drab conditions of the post-war world. Nor was Churchill's rumbustious blimpishness appropriate to the solemn socialist moment. To his bewildered dismay Churchill found himself being worsted in debate by the dry, colourless, almost monosyllabic Attlee. Of this modest, underrated man, whom he had been accustomed to bully and despise, Churchill remarked with unwonted malevolence: 'If you feed a grub on royal jelly you may turn it into a queen bee.'

Such a remark does not suggest that Churchill's powers were failing. Yet the charge had been made as early as the 1930s; it was widely echoed during his first premiership and would be repeated with mounting conviction until his retirement. In 1947, for example, Anthony Eden himself told a friend that Churchill had aged very much and 'is at times almost "gaga"'.

The truth is that he grew more volatile with the years not less, and his mental alertness fluctuated accordingly. He could seem 'tragically old' one minute and miraculously spry the next. Just as his body reflected his moods, his mind was the servant of his will. When he made the effort he was the most formidable politician at Westminster.

With a quip and a gesture – slowly flapping his arms as he condemned the 'gloomy state vultures of nationalisation' hovering over British industry – he could still convulse audiences. He remained master of the striking phrase: for example, he denounced deserters from radicalism who had 'lolloped into the slatternly trough of collectivism'. His energies were unimpaired: towards the end of the war he had sometimes been carried upstairs in a special chair by two strong Marines; after it he stumped up to bed unaided and as late as 1948 he went hunting. Churchill continued to intimidate opponents and cow colleagues, for his rages were as fierce as ever though, like summer storms, they quickly blew themselves out. When one tantrum provoked a similar outburst by his poodle Rufus, Churchill roared at his secretary: 'Take that dog away . . . we cannot both be barking at once.' He had lost nothing of his political craft. His ambition burned no less brightly. His ruthlessness had not abated; Beaverbrook described him as 'a hard-boiled politician with a dagger in his trouser leg'. He also noted that 'When Mr Churchill is in his seat, the opposition breathes fire. When he is not, the Tory front bench has the venom of a bunch of daffodils.'

Churchill's main difficulty in opposition was finding a positive theme. He could criticise the Labour government for 'apathy, paralysis and lack of good-housekeeping.' He could repeat the charge that Socialists were intent on establishing a dictatorship sustained by 'a police Gestapo'. Not only could he pour general scorn on panaceas like nationalisation, he could also ridicule particular proposals such as the half-hearted bid to restrict the power of the House of Lords. 'One year's suspensory veto by a hereditary assembly is the true blue of Socialist democracy; two years' is class tyranny.' But Churchill was hampered by the fact that his own administration had initiated many of Labour's domestic reforms as well as much of its foreign policy. Family allowances, national insurance, improved education, subsidized food, a national health service – all had been anticipated during the war. Admittedly Churchill had been lukewarm about these social advances, but it was difficult for him to disown them.

On the other hand he had no intention of trying to outbid Labour in the field of welfare legislation. He was not interested in R. A. Butler's Conservative Research Department, which was trying to formulate Tory policies to meet the needs of the second half of the twentieth century. But he had no imaginative ideas of his own and was to complain that 'today's problems are elusive and intangible'. To the annoyance of his colleagues he would give little attention to devising a new programme. Yet at the last moment he insisted on determining its style. This was not altogether advantageous for Churchill was fond of resounding anachronisms about the Tories' refusal to allow 'cottage homes' to be 'engulfed in penury'. For the most part, however, he contented himself with maintaining that it was the duty of an opposition to oppose. His only proposal was to demand at the election 'a doctor's mandate' to cure the body politic from the ills of Socialism.

Churchill's opposition was thus fractious and factious. He enjoyed parliamentary occasions where he could start a good row or make a big splash. Yet while he was publicly regaining his reputation as a party politician he was privately burnishing his fame as a national statesman. Churchill's massive account of *The Second World War* was really an elaborate justification of his political stewardship from 1930 to 1945. Like *The World Crisis* it was largely autobiographical and entirely subjective. Churchill had often advised people to wait for the verdict of history, adding with a chuckle, 'and I shall write the history'. Now he scarcely bothered to disguise the fact that his six volumes were personal apologia based on hindsight. During 'the late unpleasantness' he had deliberately refrained from keeping a diary on the grounds that it was foolish to record his fallible day-to-day opinions. Churchill much preferred to wait until the war was over, he once explained, so that if necessary he could correct and bury his mistakes.

This he did on a gigantic scale. Throughout the memoirs he minimised his failures and maximised his successes. He skated over some awkward facts, like the Morgenthau plan for pastoralising Germany and the bombing of Dresden. Others, such as his inconsistencies during the 1930s or his strategic *faux pas* during the war, he either omitted altogether or stood on their heads. He printed his own minutes, but gave no indication of the replies, though he was almost as benign towards others as he was towards himself. Everywhere he went in for special pleading. Although he employed a large team to help with the project he never allowed the product of their labours to interfere with his total design. As Churchill explained, 'I write a book the way they built the Canadian Pacific Railway. First I lay the track from coast to coast, and after that I put in all the stations.' The stations – the details which gave validity to the whole – were inserted with meticulous care, for, as is well known, Churchill revised interminably and treated his galley proofs as rough drafts. Yet he was probably unaware of the degree to which his interpretation of events was distorted. For, as Lord Moran said, his refusal to recognise his errors had grown on him insidiously. Churchill's assumption of infallibility was now so deeply engrained that history had become his story.

Yet Churchill's hypertrophied egotism was not altogether unjustified. For even more remarkable than the persistent bias running through his *Second World War* volumes was the innate clarity of vision. Churchill's view that the war was unnecessary, that it could have been avoided if the western powers had heeded his early warnings and resisted Hitler, has been widely challenged. Yet the disastrous failure of the appeasement policy is palpable and, flawed though it is in detail, Churchill's overall interpretation remains convincing. Furthermore, although Churchill presents his war leadership in the most favourable light, less flattering accounts cannot obscure the greatness of his achievement. As the head of a democracy engaged in a struggle for survival, he was without equal. His stature as a grand strategist is more questionable. But, if he lacked steadiness, he was right in essentials and successful in the end. Finally, Churchill's forecast of the threat posed to Europe by Communist Russia was tragically accurate. Churchill possessed a sublime understanding of the concrete. He had an unparalleled imaginative insight into the balance of great powers and the play of martial forces.

INDIAN SUMMER

Churchill luxuriated in his fame and fortune after the war. He collected countless honours, including the Order of Merit in 1946 and the Nobel Prize for Literature in 1953. Foreigners competed to give him decorations, freedoms, honorary degrees, illuminated addresses and awards of all sorts. Some of them he received in person and at the presentation ceremonies he often took the opportunity to spread his gospel about the need for a United Europe. Churchill rode in triumph through foreign cities like a king. In his cavalcade were cases of champagne supplied by Pol Roger and boxes of specially-made Cuban cigars with Churchill's name stamped on the bands. Immense efforts were made to welcome him and every creature comfort was put at his disposal. He flourished on the treatment. Apart from a hernia operation in 1947 and a few heavy colds, his health was good. His energy still caused astonishment. A fellow-guest at Beaverbrook's villa in the south of France reported in 1949 that Churchill 'was on the top of his form. He sang, swam, wrote and played cards.' But having stayed up, sustained by soup, cigars and excitement, until two o'clock in the morning on a gin rummy marathon, Churchill suffered another stroke. 'The dagger struck,' he said afterwards, 'but this time it was not plunged in to the hilt.'

The public was not informed and within a few days Churchill had returned to Strasbourg where the first session of the Council of Europe was taking place. Actually his attitude was more insular and imperialist than European. He favoured continental unity less for its own sake than as a counter against Russia. Nevertheless, at the assembly he was hailed as the 'first citizen of Europe'. This title was not much to the liking of Herbert Morrison, leader of Labour's delegation, who had always loathed Churchill, a sentiment which was warmly reciprocated. Morrison was even more furious when Churchill out-manoeuvred him and got his own candidate elected as Vice-President. The victory left Churchill exhausted but exultant. Lying on his bed fully clothed, Europe's first citizen declared repeatedly, 'This is the best fun I've had for years and years. This is splendid. This is really fun.' At another meeting Churchill and Morrison confronted each other before 'a crowd of astonished foreign delegates' and, as a witness recorded, 'exchanged not only rough words but rude gestures'. (Churchill well appreciated, and was quite unperturbed by, the fact that his Victory signs were open to an obscene interpretation.)

Churchill's domestic existence was scarcely more peaceful than his public life. Clementine was often harassed and her temper was not improved by the growing servant problem – few valets, for example, would endure her husband's imperious demands for long. Fond as he was of his family there were often furious quarrels. For a time Churchill banned Randolph from the house for striking his sister Sarah while in a drunken rage. He also despaired of Randolph's career which was marred by scenes, scandals, divorces and infirmity of purpose. As for Sarah, her acting suffered from drink and self-indulgence, and she went from man to man with little success and much unhappiness. Similarly Diana's marriage to the Conservative politician Duncan Sandys was beginning to founder as a result of her unstable temperament, much to her father's distress and her mother's anger. In fact, the only child who brought consistent comfort to her parents was the youngest, Mary. 'Wise and good', according to a friend, she married another Tory MP, Christopher Soames, in 1947.

They came to live in one of the Chartwell farm-houses. Soames established an immediate rapport with Churchill, gave him new contacts with younger Conservatives and supervised the estate. Chartwell was a continuing source of delight to Churchill, though he was now occupier not owner – to ease his financial position it had been bought in 1946 by friends who gave it to the National Trust with the proviso that Churchill should remain resident during his life-time. Churchill still liked to think of himself as a pastoral patriarch. In rationed Britain he also relished the farm fare. But one of his chief joys was to show visitors over the grounds. He would point out such landmarks as Chickenham Palace (full of hens supplied by Lord Beaverbrook) and its surrounding mud-patch, Chickenham Palace Gardens. By contrast, a quite new interest to which Soames introduced Churchill was horse-racing. Sporting chocolate and pink, which had been (approximately) Lord Randolph's colours, Churchill's grey colt Colonist II won several important events. He was particularly pleased because his winnings were free of income tax and he was now paying nineteen shillings and sixpence in the pound. Churchill never lost the urge to gamble but he was almost as exhilarated by little contests and small stakes as by large. In later years he became addicted to an American card game called Oklahoma. 'The degree of thrill that one gets from Oklahoma,' remarked Churchill, 'is in direct proportion to the effect on the nervous system of an attack of delirium tremens and a single whisky and soda.'

On 30 November 1949 Churchill celebrated his seventy-fifth birthday. He was sitting up in bed surrounded by telegrams, cards, presents and friends when a ladybird landed on his pyjama jacket. Churchill asked one of his entourage 'to remove this exquisite and charming creature from my sleeve and allow it carefully to fly out of the window'. He interpreted the ladybird as a lucky omen. The next election could not be long delayed and surely his ardent hopes of returning to Downing Street would be realised. If not, Churchill told Brendan Bracken, who was impressed by his good health and high spirits, he would retire and spend the rest of his life enjoying himself. After a family Christmas, celebrated with games such as Snapdragon in which competitors pulled as many raisins as possible out of a bowl of flaming brandy, Churchill went off to Madeira with Clementine on a painting holiday. There he heard the news that Attlee was indeed going to the country. Churchill flew home at once, announcing on his arrival that he intended to restore Britain to her 'true place in the world . . . at the head of an empire on which the sun never sets'. He conducted a campaign which was notable for its vigour. In fact he injected most of the life that there was into a surprisingly inanimate contest. He even replied to Labour's sniping about his age by issuing a formal denial that he was dead.

When polling took place, on 23 February 1950, Churchill was mortified to find that Labour had scraped home by a mere six seats. But the closeness of the result gave him the excuse he wanted to stay on as Tory leader. For a renewed electoral battle was inevitable. In fact it was postponed by the outbreak of the Korean War in the summer. Churchill had nothing to do with the inception of this conflict, for which (being anxious to live down his bellicose reputation) he was profoundly grateful to 'the old man', as he called God. But he behaved in a thoroughly aggressive manner towards the government over the next eighteen months. He claimed that it had only won the election by abolishing the special university franchise – 'What a cameo of gerrymandering and chicane!' He ridiculed its members as 'lion-hearted limpets' clinging to power with the help of 'a handful of invalids'. He harassed them with fiery speeches, constant interruptions, procedural ambushes and all-night sittings. Labour MPs, who were on average five years older than Tory ones, began to flag, whereas Churchill's zest for attrition seemed inexhaustible.

At the Conservative conference in the autumn of 1950, he brought down the house by the gesture – a long tugging motion of the arms – which accompanied his rallying call: 'We need just one more heave' to get the Socialists out. Churchill made no secret of the pleasure he derived from provoking crowds of 'green-eyed opponents, their jaws twitching with fury, shouting interruptions, holloaing, bellowing insults of every kind'. He displayed keen relish while baiting Bevin's inept successor at the Foreign Office, Herbert Morrison, 'a caucus boss . . . with a distorted, twisted and malevolent mind'. It was doubtless this incorrigible spirit of contention which encouraged the Socialists, in the general election of 1951, to brand Churchill as a 'warmonger'. Their slogan – 'A third Labour government or a Third World War?' – was extremely effective. It helped to keep down the Tory majority to only seventeen seats. And it made Churchill, whose tone was studiously moderate throughout the campaign, into a more determined peace-maker. The theme of his second ministry, which lasted from 26 October 1951 to 5 April 1955, was the search for a summit conference which would secure the peace of the world in a nuclear age. This, as Churchill remarked, 'is the last prize I seek to win'.

Churchill was elated by having gained an electoral victory in his own right at last. All that he now required to make his happiness complete was the return of the old familiar faces, or at any rate those that remained – Bracken had left politics and others were dead, including to his great sorrow, Churchill's brother Jack (in 1947). The Prime Minister brought back Ismay to supervise Commonwealth Affairs, Alexander to become Minister of Defence (after an abortive four months of trying to do the job himself), even John Colville to be his private secretary. Hardly knowing the names of junior Tories and hoping to sustain interest in the membership of his government, Churchill announced the names of senior cabinet ministers first – Eden at the Foreign Office, R. A. Butler at the Treasury and so on. But the delay in appointing the second tier of ministers, such as Harold Macmillan to the vital portfolio of Housing, was a mistake. It gave Churchill an appearance of indecisiveness. The charge that this was 'government by cronies' led by a dithering old man was hard to refute. It even became the orthodox historical verdict on Churchill's second ministry – though recent reappraisals have been more favourable.

Critics, however, rightly point out that Churchill's unbusinesslike habits had grown with the years. He was sometimes lazy, easily distracted from work by his tankfuls of gorgeous tropical fish or by the antics of his whisky-drinking budgerigar. He was inclined to put off decisions that were not urgent. His extraordinary memory began to fail and he found it difficult to relate one aspect of government to another. He enjoyed cabinet meetings because argument stimulated him and he had a captive audience for harangues that were more maundering than ever. (Churchill liked watching his colleagues squirm as he ate into their lunch-times.) He was bored by, and uncomprehending about, financial detail. But he had no distinctively Conservative solutions to Britain's parlous economic problems. Indeed, having such a relatively small majority, he was not anxious to implement any controversial domestic policies. He was quite prepared to build on Labour's achievements in the field of social services and he did not attempt to demolish the structure of nationalisation, except in the steel industry. To the surprise of his supporters Churchill even favoured making little concessions in parliament to avert the possibility of defeat. He told Harold Macmillan, 'It is never necessary to commit suicide, especially when you may live to regret it.' Churchill also took a conciliatory line towards the trades unions. The Prime Minister mischievously enjoyed undermining the efforts of his own Chancellor to hold down wage settlements. Butler remarked that Churchill was 'so brave in war but so cowardly in peace'. This was not altogether fair though the two men had, ironically enough, swapped attitudes towards appeasement. The fact was that Churchill, like Marlborough, saw himself as a national leader and in 1952 he actually canvassed the possibility of re-forming a coalition government. He also saw himself as a natural leader and his prime purpose was to stay in office.

If this was a negative ambition, his personal slogan – 'Houses, red meat and not getting scuppered' – suggests that he also had positive aims. Churchill had poured scorn on Labour's building programme – he gave a bizarre and far from melodious rendering of 'Home Sweet Home', substituting for the word 'Home' the Socialists' jargon term 'accommodation unit'. But he detested the bomb sites that still defaced London and he supported Harold Macmillan in his successful effort to construct three hundred thousand houses a year. Churchill also waged war on the whole apparatus of rationing and restric-tions (which Labour had already begun to dismantle). Unable to visualise from the measurements how much food each individual was permitted, he instructed the minister to bring him a model: a mound of sugar, a helping of meat, and so on. Churchill surveyed the result with approval. 'Not a bad meal. Not a bad meal.' But when it was explained to him that these were the rations for a week he exploded: 'A week! Then the people are starving. It must be remedied.' It was remedied, though not as quickly as he had hoped.

Churchill's powers had waned to some extent by 1951, though he could scarcely be said to have mellowed with age. His capacity for aggression was undiminished, but he exercised it less. His moods and his appearance varied more dramatically than ever. On good days he resembled a bouncing, pink baby ('all babies look like me'), full of genial animation. On bad days he appeared white, comatose, flabby and almost moribund. Early in 1952 he suffered from a fit of aphasia, a terrible afflic-tion to one for whom words were the breath of life, but it soon vanished. In general, however, office seemed to have rejuvenated him once more. Whatever his state he remained formidable, and he dominated both cabinet and Commons. A Labour opponent, Richard Crossman, marvelled at the 'astonishing power Churchill still has'.

As Sir George Mallaby wrote, Churchill 'could be patient, conciliatory, cunning, short-tempered, morose, procrastinat-ing, contradictory'. He proselytised for his ideas and saw to their implementation (reviving the Home Guard, for instance) with the same obsessive fervour as before. He still had great powers of concentration which he devoted to his speeches and to 'preparing improvisations' for Prime Minister's question time. His routine remained the same and though he fussed about details less he was quite happy to telephone ministers about small matters in the middle of the night. His fund of humour was by no means exhausted, and if his colleagues found cabinet meetings wearisome they looked forward to flashes of Churchillian wit. Referring to the disturbances in Bechuanaland, for example, the Prime Minister said: 'Indeed a terrible position. An angry mob, armed with staves and stones, inflamed by alcohol, and inspired by liberal principles!' Whatever the issue or event, Churchill had an original and often piquant contribution to make. He deplored, for instance, the fact that the number of letters sent to him by madmen had decreased, recalling that the same thing had happened during a particularly bad period of the war.

Churchill's first move towards earning the last honour which he really coveted, the Nobel Peace Prize, was predictably in the direction of the United States. In January 1952, only a few weeks after taking office, he embarked on the *Queen Mary* accompanied by an entourage of war-time proportions. During the voyage he refused to work on his papers, asserting that he was going to re-establish good relations not to transact business. In the event this was about all he did achieve. President Truman was friendly but he refused to be beguiled into making any significant commitments in an election year. Churchill's third address to Congress concluded with a familiar invocation: as their two countries spoke the same language so they must tread the same path. But his speech, received in a spirit of nostalgia, seemed more a salute to the past than a sign of things to come. A year later Eisenhower was little more responsive to Churchill's blandishments and the Prime Minister found his prissy Secretary of State, John Foster Dulles, positively 'obnoxious'. 'Dull, duller, Dulles,' he remarked. Sadly for Churchill neither the advent of a new President nor the death of Stalin in 1953 brought the prospect of a 'Big Three' summit meeting and another 'Locarno Treaty' any closer.

Churchill himself practised an American caution as far as

joining Europe was concerned. He paid lip service to the idea of a United Europe but dragged his feet about Britain's involvement, perhaps the greatest missed chance of his second ministry. At heart, no doubt, Churchill put his faith in Britain's power to save herself by her own exertions. By the end of 1952 the British atomic bomb had been successfully tested and Churchill sought to make the 'independent nuclear deterrent' a reality by ordering the manufacture of 'V' bombers. As ever he tried to achieve peace from a position of unassailable strength. He was to express this aspiration in his last great parliamentary speech: 'It may well be that we shall by a process of sublime irony have reached a stage in history where safety will be the sturdy child of terror, and survival the twin brother of annihilation.' Or in more homely idiom: 'When the advance of destructive weapons enables everyone to kill everybody else nobody will want to kill anybody at all.'

In February 1952 George VI died. Churchill, deeply moved, delivered an obituary oration on the wireless quite in his war-time vein:

> During these last months the King walked with death, as if death were a companion, an acquaintance whom he recognized and did not fear. In the end death came as a friend . . . I, whose youth was passed in the august, unchallenged and tranquil glories of the Victorian era, may well feel a thrill in invoking, once more, the prayer and Anthem, 'God Save the Queen!'

All Churchill's romantic devotion to the monarchy now focussed on the person of Elizabeth II. He idolised her and she revered him. He dispensed avuncular counsel; in 1953 she bestowed on him the Order of the Garter. Sir Winston, as he now became, compared their relationship to that which had existed between Marlborough and Queen Anne, but it actually resembled more Lord Melbourne's with Queen Victoria. Churchill sought to protect the vulnerable young sovereign and he even endorsed her wish that television cameras should be excluded from Westminster Abbey during the coronation. Public opinion would not tolerate this, but no close-up shots were permitted of the most solemn parts of the service.

Churchill threw himself into organising the ceremony with all the dedication of one who lamented the passing of ritual. He spent weeks discussing matters of protocol, precedence and pageantry, negotiating about who should ride with whom in what closed carriage, deciding on whether knee-breeches were the correct dress for cabinet ministers, ruling on which Commonwealth national anthems should be played – 'I will not have that Boer hymn!' The coronation itself triumphed over the bad weather, and further improved the morale of a nation which was already beginning to benefit from the revival of world trade. Accoutred in Garter robes worn over the bottle-green uniform of Lord Warden of the Cinque Ports, complete with plumed hat, decorations and an outsize Order of the Garter, Churchill was greeted by the crowds with acclaim. Depending on whether one accepts the saccharine opinion of *The Times* or the sour view of Noël Coward, the Prime Minister looked 'jovial and picturesque' or 'disagreeable and silly'. Certainly the strain of preparing for and attending the ceremony as well as presiding over innumerable subsidiary junketings such as the Commonwealth Prime Ministers' Conference, together with running the Foreign Office in the absence (through illness) of Eden, proved too much for him. On 23 June, only three weeks after the coronation, he suffered his third and most serious stroke.

CHAPTER XIV

ANCIENT MONUMENT

ACTUALLY it was more of a slow seizure than an abrupt stroke. Churchill was well enough, the following morning, to hold a cabinet meeting at which most ministers noticed nothing, though some observed that he spoke little and looked white. But during the next few days his condition deteriorated sharply. Churchill's jaw sagged, his speech became slurred, his left arm and leg were almost paralysed. Initially he bore the affliction, which was kept secret from the British people, though the foreign press published the news, with courage and humility. But it was not in his nature to be stoical for long. As the slow process of recovery began he gave way to fits of depression and self-pity, brooding continually about whether he should resign. He had originally planned to hold office for a year. But he had found excuses (like the King's death) to postpone his departure. And he had answers for those bold enough to question his intentions. He would stay until 'the pub closes'. He would 'certainly stand at the next election – probably as a Conservative'. He liked to tease his ageing and increasingly desperate Crown Prince, Anthony Eden, by recalling the splendid octogenarian achievements of Mr Gladstone. Now, he told Lord Moran ironically, 'circumstances may convince me of my indispensability'.

They did. Clementine nursed her husband devotedly through the summer, driving herself to the brink of nervous collapse in the process, and within a couple of months Churchill had

216

fought off the worst effects of his stroke. On 25 August he presided over another cabinet meeting. Macmillan recorded that the Prime Minister 'talked well and wittily, but not too much; handled the business well; had a kind word for everybody'. The effort left him exhausted and he went off to Lord Beaverbrook's French villa to recuperate. There he awoke one morning in tears and a temper because his arms were too weak to wield a paint-brush. But once again he struggled back to health. By the time of the Conservative party conference in October the only tell-tale signs were a slight unsteadiness of gait and a barely perceptible droop of the mouth. His oration was a magnificent success. Churchill concluded:

> If I stay on for the time being bearing the burden at my age it is not because of love for power or office. I have had an ample share of both. If I stay it is because I have a feeling that I may through things that have happened have an influence on what I care about above all else, the building of a sure and lasting peace.

The cheers confirmed his decision to remain, though in his peroration he sounded rather like a prelate explaining that it is his duty to accept the preferment to which God has called him. No doubt Churchill deceived himself. He was an old man in no hurry at all to relinquish power. On the other hand, there is no reason to doubt the sincerity of his quest for a final peace conference which would crown his political career.

Churchill's pacific endeavours were by no means fruitless. He cut defence costs and supported the Korean armistice. He discouraged the United States from precipitate involvement in Indo-China and refused to send British forces to help the French there. He sanctioned Germany's entry into NATO. Churchill even withdrew British troops from Egypt, quite against his natural inclinations. 'If I had my way,' he told backbenchers, 'I'd set the Israelites on them.' But over the crucial issue of negotiating a treaty between Russia and the west he made no progress. He discussed the matter with Eisenhower at Bermuda in December 1953 and again in Washington in June 1954. But although he tightened the bonds of Anglo-American co-operation, he could not persuade the President, or rather his Secretary of State Dulles ('a Methodist preacher'), that it was feasible to end the cold war. In his frustration Churchill toyed with the notion of blackmailing the Russian leaders into talking. He proposed to threaten them with the new hydrogen bomb, the destructive potential of which (to his delight) he recognised before any of his colleagues. In a more sober spirit Churchill made an independent overture, without consulting the cabinet, to Malenkov. But this too proved abortive. He continued to chase the will-o'-the-wisp of a peace pact until 1955. When it finally vanished, he resigned.

Churchill reasserted his authority in parliament with the first speech he made there after his stroke, in November 1953. Chips Channon recorded, 'Brilliant, full of cunning and charm, of wit and thrusts, he poured out his Macaulay-like phrases to a stilled and awed house.' Afterwards, the Prime Minister sat in the smoking room for two hours, 'flushed with pride, pleasure and triumph', sipping brandy, acknowledging compliments and beaming like a schoolboy. The occasion must have done much to restore Churchill's self-confidence, though even in bad times he found comfort in the conviviality of the smoking room. In return for their good cheer MPs received a generous measure of amusement. On one occasion Churchill announced that he had forgiven a persistent critic and was reserving such hatred as he had left for the future rather than the past: 'H'm. A judicious and thrifty disposal of bile.' A year before his retirement the Prime Minister told a 'highly flavoured' joke in the smoking room. He afterwards remarked, 'I'm not sure that it conformed altogether with the dignity of my office but,' with a gamin grin, 'they liked it very much.'

At his best, then, during the last months of his second ministry, Churchill radiated geniality. His dominance in the cabinet was scarcely impaired. Revelling in the parliamentary fray, he remained a dazzling performer at Question Time. He could still rise to the heights in his speeches, treading, as he said, the narrow path between 'platitude and indiscretion', skilfully avoiding 'what the French call "clichés" and what the English call "bloomers" '. He was capable of sudden bursts of energy and initiative. On the beach at Bermuda, to the consternation of his staff, he proceeded to crawl to the top of a twelve-foot rock. Harold Macmillan described an occasion when, shortly before his eightieth birthday, Churchill took him out to lunch at Buck's Club. The Prime Minister put on a sprightly performance for onlookers, bowing and smiling, manipulating his hat, stick and cigar and giving his 'V' signs like the 'superb showman' he was. He then proceeded to eat and drink his guest under the table. Churchill consumed a dozen oysters, cream soup, chicken pie, vanilla and strawberry ice cream, together with copious draughts of Moselle and brandy. As usual he also carried on a running commentary about the food and the service, and he interspersed this with confidential remarks uttered at full volume. As he departed, amidst cheering crowds, Churchill observed with a chuckle, 'I think I may still be not all on the debit side.'

He was not all on the credit side either. For though Churchill could still rise to the great occasion there were, indeed, 'bloomers' in some of his major speeches. In 1954, for example, he unwisely made a party issue out of a national concern about the hydrogen bomb. Moreover, he was increasingly succumbing to fatigue and lassitude, preferring to play cards than to work. 'A man in his eightieth year,' he told Lord Moran with a smile, 'does not want to do things.' By the autumn of 1954, when Churchill reshuffled his ministers, his failing powers were quite apparent. He was feeble, indecisive, and lacking in the qualities of leadership. Conscious of his debilitation, he was even more bad-tempered and difficult than in the past. At home he had fierce quarrels with Clementine, who was driven to a state of nervous prostration by his behaviour – though he was always quick to seek reconciliation. But he also made scenes in public. In July 1954, for instance, he gave vent to a childish fit of petulance on board the *Queen Elizabeth* because he found the restaurant too hot, much to the embarrassment of his staff and other diners.

Moran, who noticed that Churchill scoured the newspapers for flattering references to himself, put it down to an old man's vanity. Churchill *was* vain, though (to paraphrase his remark about Attlee's modesty) he had much to be vain about. But he was also, surely, searching for reassurance about his political prowess, which he must have known to be in decline. His disgust at Graham Sutherland's portrait which parliament gave him for his eightieth birthday on 30 November 1954, owed much to the fact that it represented him as unfit to hold office. Of course he expressed thanks for this 'remarkable example of modern art', which 'combines force and candour'. Privately he spluttered that the portrait was 'filthy' and 'malignant'; it made him look like 'a drinking sot'. In a furious access of partisanship Clementine was later to destroy this work of art. She had previously committed several similar acts of vandalism, censoring the pictures, so to speak, while her husband edited the text of history. Despite Churchill's own pictures (for which he had a strongly possessive affection) and his aspirations to be a great painter, there is no disguising his fundamental philistinism about art. In this, of course, he was at one with the Royal Academy. Its president, Sir Alfred Munnings, was delighted with Churchill's answer to his question, 'What would you do if you saw Picasso walking ahead of you down Piccadilly?' 'I would kick him up the arse, Alfred.'

Churchill struggled against the implications of the Sutherland portrait for a few months more. He kept flirting with the idea of retirement, putting off the consummation. At a meeting of seven cabinet ministers in December 1954 he vociferated: 'I know you are trying to get rid of me and it is up to me to go to the Queen and hand her my resignation and yours – but I won't do it.' However, there was no escaping the inevitable and early in 1955 a date was set. Churchill told Butler that he felt like 'an aeroplane at the end of its flight, in the dusk, with the petrol running out, in search of a safe landing'. But at the last moment the Prime Minister tried to delay the touch-down once again. He felt some bitterness towards impatient colleagues. But despite their private rows Churchill was genuinely fond of Eden who had married his niece Clarissa in 1952. Churchill finally acknowledged that Eden must serve a term at the helm before the next general election. So, after a large dinner party at Downing Street, Churchill resigned on 5 April. At his final audience, the Queen asked whether he would like a dukedom 'or anything like that'. He had considered becoming Duke of London but in deference to family wishes (Randolph had no wish for a title) Churchill refused. As the newspapers were on strike Churchill's public life ended without a journalistic fanfare. The final obsequies were postponed for another ten years.

Churchill left Downing Street, amidst the applause of his staff, with apparent cheerfulness. Comforted by his menagerie, busy with paints and books, awaiting extinction with fortitude, Churchill was even able to sustain, for the benefit of visitors to Chartwell, the impression that he was a resigned and happy man. But Clementine's sad summary was correct: her husband's retirement was his 'first death – for him a death in life'. Churchill expressed the same sentiment differently: 'I've got to kill time till time kills me.' Cards and painting, which chiefly occupied him during his spring holiday in Syracuse, helped to pass the days. But though for a while they kept lassitude and depression at bay such activities were no substitute for the excitement of power; nor was the new venture which he planned on his Sicilian holiday, the setting up in Britain of an equivalent of the Massachusetts Institute of Technology – which eventually led to the foundation of Churchill College, Cambridge. Ambition had been the dynamo of Churchill's career. Now that he had nothing more to achieve his terrific vitality began to flicker and dim. He kept losing his memory. He became slower and more somnolent. Though he abandoned his siesta he stayed in bed longer, assisted by sleeping pills and what Lord Beaverbrook delicately called 'an arrangement', presumably some sort of bedpan.

Yet even in the twilight there were gleams of the old fire. Churchill amused Macmillan with his sharp nickname for the Labour politician Sir Hartley Shawcross – Sir Shortly Floorcross. When Eden called a general election in May 1955 Churchill longed to put on his political armour once more. He received no call from Downing Street and had to content himself with conducting a local campaign and speaking in one or two constituencies other than his own. One reporter wrote that Churchill 'uttered nothing but clichés, but he spoke them better than any man alive'. Despite his disappointment, which was amplified by his son, Churchill was severe with Randolph for drunkenly inveighing against 'Jerk' Eden. Churchill attended parliament infrequently and made no further speeches. He occasionally let his feelings be known, over the death penalty, for example, which he favoured on the grounds that its abolition would hasten the British collapse into decadence. Churchill also supported Eden over the invasion of Suez and, despite the damage done to Anglo-American relations, thought him weak to withdraw. His last significant contribution to politics was to advise the Queen to appoint Macmillan and not Butler as Eden's successor, probably because the former had been staunch over Munich. He addressed Macmillan as 'my dear', and called Butler 'old cock'.

Otherwise Churchill had one task which he was determined to finish. This was his *History of the English-Speaking Peoples*, begun in the 1930s. Now, with the aid of research assistants and ghost-writers, Churchill set about the massive task of revising and completing the work. It was published between 1956 and 1958 in four volumes and is the least satisfactory of Churchill's books. Indeed, from the tale of Alfred's burning the cakes to the glorious flowering of the British empire, it is less history than myth, the kind of public-schoolboy myth that sees the past as a saga of kings and battles. Churchill complained that nothing happened between the Napoleonic Wars and the American Civil War. He also managed to dismiss in a paragraph what was perhaps the most momentous development since the birth of civilisation, namely the Industrial Revolution. There is almost equally little about important social, cultural, scientific and intellectual changes. Churchill's history is a succession, or more precisely a progression, of events whose unwritten climax and conclusion is his own career. His epic is told with dramatic force and sustained by rhetorical flourishes. That it tells the reader more about its author than about the past adds to its fascination. Full of spirit, majestic in scope, the book is a compound of prejudice, irony, pugnacity and heroism.

Soon after his retirement Churchill began to slide into a depression that was to become indistinguishable from senility. But the process, complicated by occasional arterial spasms (or small strokes) and bouts of pneumonia, was not a steady one. Until about 1959 he seemed able to throw off his gloom and climb back to full possession of his faculties. He was notably torpid in the mornings but, fuelled by food and drink and invigorated by congenial company, he could sparkle for a while. One American journalist who visited Chartwell in the summer of 1956 described the process vividly:

> It was like watching a very strong light bulb during an electrical crisis: first a faint reddening of the filament, then a flickering, then a glow, then a brilliant blaze of light. Finally, after being blinded by the sustained glare, again flickering, subsiding, just a red filament, then nothing.

Some activities also had the power to pull Churchill back from the brink of senescence. He drew satisfaction from being a member of parliament and took a small part in the election campaign of 1959. He enjoyed racing and gambling. The family Christmas at Chartwell was a high point of the year.

Churchill also attended many formal occasions, official banquets and state ceremonies, not to mention School Songs at Harrow. In 1958 he accepted France's highest honour, the Cross of the Liberation. De Gaulle kissed him on both cheeks and Churchill was much moved. He denied ever having likened the General to a female lama surprised in her bath, though Lord Moran did not believe him. In 1959 Churchill paid his last visit to the United States, where he met Eisenhower and was enthusiastically fêted. But he was too old to receive in person the honorary citizenship of the United States. Randolph accepted it from President Kennedy in 1963 and read his father's last message to the American people. It contained a characteristic statement rejecting the view, expressed by Dean Acheson and others, 'that Britain and the Commonwealth should be relegated to a tame and minor role in the world'.

For the most part Churchill lacked stimulus during his sad declining years. He enjoyed basking in the sun at Marrakesh or, more often, in the south of France, where he seriously considered buying a villa. In the event it proved easier to stay, as he did many times, with Lord Beaverbrook or with the agent for his foreign literary rights, Emery Reves. According to Malcolm Muggeridge, Churchill possessed 'the characteristic 18th Century nobleman's attitude that he should have a Jew to look after his financial affairs'; whatever the truth of this Reves did so with spectacular success, making himself a fortune in the process. In return he surrounded Churchill with every luxury at his beautiful house on the Riviera. Reves's American consort, the former model Wendy Russell, was also very beautiful. Writing in June 1956, Noël Coward gave a spiteful account of Churchill's 'impotent' infatuation with her, which is worth quoting for such light as it may cast on his state:

> There was this great man, historically one of the greatest our country has produced, domestically one of the silliest, absolutely obsessed with a senile passion for Wendy Russell. He followed her about the room with brimming eyes and wobbled after her across the terrace, staggering like a vast baby who is just learning to walk. . . . [Later]

he pointed to a Toulouse-Lautrec painting of a shabby prostitute exposing a cruelly and cynically naked bottom, flaccid and creased, and said in a voice dripping with senile prurience, 'Very appetising!'

Reves introduced Churchill to the Greek shipping millionaire Aristotle Onassis, who cosseted him even more lavishly during several cruises on board his palatial yacht. The *Christina* was a converted British frigate fitted with every convenience from gold ashtrays to air-conditioning and a hospital. Onassis was evidently intent on buying his way into global society but he also seems to have been genuinely kind to Churchill, talking to him for hours in the hope of arousing some flicker of response. Back in England the same office was performed by Viscount Montgomery, who sometimes stimulated gleams of animation in Churchill as he re-fought the old battles. But at last apathy prevailed. By the 1960s Churchill's mind was largely dormant and his memory was virtually extinct. He did not recognise his friends. During his last years he could not read and his talk, when he uttered at all, was inarticulate. The news sometimes stirred him: he apparently commented about the Cuban missile crisis, 'We are all going to be blown up.' He could flare up about little things, like the noise of a lift or an object out of place. But for the most part he was silent. He lay in bed doing nothing, his great head sunk on his chest. He stared at his plate or into the fireplace for hours on end. A huddled, shapeless figure, he gazed with blank eyes into the middle distance.

A large staff, the nurses being kept as inconspicuous as possible, coped with all Churchill's needs, for Clementine too had ailments. The strain of caring for him in extreme old age took its toll and she often went off on her own. Churchill had to be almost carried to the few functions he still attended and at them he remained rheumy-eyed, expressionless and immobile. Moving by himself was dangerous. He fell twice, breaking a bone in his neck in 1960 and his thigh in 1962. One who saw him in that year at the Royal Academy dinner received 'the impression of death in life'. Churchill had long ceased to contribute to debates in the House of Commons, though he made occasional appearances in the chamber. He formally retired from Parliament in 1964.

Most of Churchill's friends pre-deceased him – Lord Camrose

died in 1954, Lord Cherwell ('the Prof') in 1957, Bracken in 1958, Beaverbrook in 1964. In that year Churchill's daughter Diana committed suicide. But age seems to have largely anaesthetised her father from grief. In such lucid moments as were left to him Churchill too longed to die. 'I look forward to dying,' he had earlier said, 'sleep, endless, wonderful sleep – on a purple, velvety cushion. Every so often I will wake up, turn over and go back to sleep again.' Churchill had often been haunted by the prospect of a degrading second childhood, and death was certainly preferable to this tragic parody of life. He always harked back to the great Duke of Marlborough who had 'lingered on in surly decrepitude. How much better would it have been, had he been cut off in his brilliant prime.' Though Churchill had misty notions about providence, especially where his own destiny was concerned, he had no real belief in the Christian dispensation, no faith in God, no hope of heaven. Death was the end and he did not fear it. All the rest was the subject for mild ribaldry. Sometimes he had visualized paradise as a desegregated, egalitarian welfare state and therefore 'no place for me'. 'I'm ready to meet my Maker,' he had said on his seventy-fifth birthday, 'whether my Maker is prepared for the great ordeal of meeting me is another matter.' The matter was put to the test after Churchill suffered his final stroke early in 1965. For many days he lay in a coma without moving. Then, shortly after 8 o'clock in the morning of Sunday 24 January, Churchill died – exactly seventy years after his father. Clementine was to outlive him by almost thirteen years.

Flags flew at half mast all over the country. Obituaries extolled Churchill as the greatest Englishman of his time, perhaps of all time, the saviour of his country. More than 320,000 people filed past his coffin as it lay on a great catafalque at Westminster Hall. His state funeral, the first given to a subject since the death of the Duke of Wellington, was not just a national spectacle. The procession to and from Westminster Abbey and the service itself were witnessed on television throughout the world – it cost the American networks millions of dollars in lost advertising revenue. Churchill had not planned the ceremony in detail himself, though he had expressed the wish that there should be several brass bands at his funeral. Certainly the music would have pleased him, including as it did *The Battle Hymn of the Republic*. So would the royal participation. So would the strong military element, the multi-gun salutes, the RAF fly-past, and the playing of *Rule Britannia*. So would the elaborate pomp and pageantry, something at which the British still excel – even General de Gaulle expressed admiration for the efficiency with which the arrangements were carried out. Churchill did not want to be interred at Westminster Abbey, perhaps because it was full of people he disliked. Instead he was taken up the Thames and then by train to Oxfordshire, to be buried in Bladon churchyard beside his parents and within sight of his birthplace, Blenheim Palace.

In the Abbey itself there is a marble tablet inscribed with the words, 'Remember Winston Churchill'. Though Ozymandian memorials crumble he will not be forgotten. Not only did he carve out a famous political career (further promoted by his books) in a nation whose empire occupied a quarter of the earth. He also played the last great global role vouchsafed to a British statesman. He led and inspired his country as it fought alone against an enemy which threatened to conquer the world. But though Churchill's achievements will last as long as humanity itself, there is a danger that the man will be lost behind the monument. Even during his lifetime Churchill was treated as a symbol. He was invested with magical attributes and imbued with seraphic or demonic capacities. Since his death, over-abundance of fact as well as deposits of myth have begun to obscure Churchill's personality like soot on a statue.

Yet the essence of Churchill, which this book has attempted to explore and to celebrate, was his heightened vitality, the terrific immediacy of his existence. Life as it was ordinarily lived was too tame for him: he needed the stimulus of constant adventure. Sometimes he generated his own excitement; sometimes thrilling challenges presented themselves spontaneously. Whatever happened Churchill, to use his own favourite criterion, rose to the level of events. He paraded his qualities and defects in exaggerated form, like a great actor playing to the gallery of posterity. Yet this was his natural part. For if Churchill cast himself in an heroic role no one has a better title to be considered an authentic hero.

FURTHER READING

THE fullest and most authoritative biography of Churchill is the official one, entitled *Winston S. Churchill*, begun by his son Randolph in 1966 and continued by Martin Gilbert. So far it has taken its subject to the end of 1941 in six large volumes, each one accompanied by several 'companions' full of original documents. Altogether it is a magnificent work to which every writer about Churchill is indebted. But the authorised life is so packed with historical detail that it is often hard to see the wood for the trees. A more manageable biography is Henry Pelling's scholarly *Winston Churchill* (1974), though even this is nearly 700 pages long. Pelling provides a substantial bibliography.

Churchill emerges vividly in his own writings which have been edited in 34 volumes by Frederick Woods – *The Collected Works of Sir Winston Churchill* (1973–6). Mr Woods has also compiled a *Bibliography of the Works of Sir Winston Churchill* (revised edition, 1975). Robert Rhodes James has edited Churchill's *Complete Speeches* (1974).

A brief selection of further books about Churchill follows. The place of publication is London unless otherwise stated.

M. Ashley, *Churchill as Historian* (1968)
D. Bardens, *Churchill in Parliament* (1967)
D. Barker, *Churchill and Eden at War* (1978)
I. Berlin, *Winston Churchill in 1940* (1964)

WINSTON CHURCHILL

V. Bonham Carter, *Winston Churchill as I Knew Him* (1965)

L. Broad, *Winston Churchill* (2 vols., 1963–4)

Captain X (A. D. Gibb), *With Winston Churchill at the Front* (Glasgow, 1924)

P. Cosgrave, *Churchill at War* (1974)

V. Cowles, *Winston Churchill: the Era and the Man* (1953)

C. Eade (ed.), *Churchill by His Contemporaries* (1953)

B. Gardner, *Churchill in His Time 1939–1945* (1968)

W. Graebner, *My Dear Mister Churchill* (1965)

P. Gretton, *Former Naval Person* (1968)

R. Howells, *Simply Churchill* (1965)

R. Hyam, *Elgin and Churchill at the Colonial Office* (1968)

R. Rhodes James, *Churchill: A Study in Failure, 1900–1939* (1970)

F. Kersaudy, *Churchill and De Gaulle* (1981)

J. P. Lash, *Roosevelt and Churchill 1939–41* (1977)

R. Lewin, *Churchill as Warlord* (1973)

N. McGowan, *My Years with Churchill* (1958)

W. Manchester, *The Last Lion: Winston Spencer Churchill* (Vol. 1, 1983)

A. J. Marder, *Winston is Back: Churchill at the Admiralty, 1939–1940* (1972)

P. de Mendelssohn, *The Age of Churchill* (1961)

Lord Moran, *Churchill: The Struggle for Survival, 1940–1965* (1966)

T. Morgan, *Churchill 1874–1915* (1983)

E. Nel, *Mr Churchill's Secretary* (1958)

Observer (ed.), *Churchill by His Contemporaries: An Appreciation* (1965)

G. Pawle, *The War and Colonel Warden* (1963)

S. Roskill, *Churchill and the Admirals* (1977)

A. Seldon, *Churchill's Indian Summer* (1981)

M. Soames, *Clementine Churchill* (1979)

P. Stansky (ed.), *Churchill: A Profile* (1973)

A. J. P. Taylor *et al*, *Churchill: Four Faces and the Man* (1969)

R. W. Thompson, *Churchill and Morton* (1976)

W. H. Thompson, *I Was Churchill's Shadow* (1951)

J. W. Wheeler-Bennett (ed.), *Action This Day* (1968)

K. Young, *Churchill and Beaverbrook* (1966)

INDEX

INDEX

INDEX

177–86; and the home front, 187–8; and the invasion of Europe, 188–91; and Greece, 192–3, 196; at Yalta, 194–5; and the end of the war, 197–8; forms the 'Caretaker' government and is defeated, 198–200; opposes Labour, 201–5, 209–10; and the cold war, 202–3; and Europe, 207–8, 214; seeks world peace, 213–14, 217–18; his retirement, 221–5; his death and state funeral, 225–6

INDEX

INDEX

INDEX